AFTER EXILE

Also by Amy K. Kaminsky

READING THE BODY POLITIC
Feminist Criticism and Latin American Women Writers

WATER LILIES / FLORES DEL AGUA
An Anthology of Spanish Women Writers
from the Fifteenth through the Nineteenth Century

AFTER EXILE

Writing the Latin American Diaspora

AMY K. KAMINSKY

University of Minnesota Press

Minneapolis

London

Every effort was made to obtain permission to reprint poetry that appears in this book. If any proper acknowledgment has not been made, we encourage copyright holders to notify us.

The University of Minnesota Press gratefully notes permission to reprint the following in this book. Lines from "Hymn and Return," by Pablo Neruda, in *Neruda and Vallejo: Selected Poems*, edited by Robert Bly (Boston: Beacon Press, 1971), pp. 96–97, reprinted by permission of Beacon Press and Robert Bly. Lines from "Land of Absence," by Gabriela Mistral, in *Selected Poems of Gabriela Mistral: A Bilingual Edition*, edited and translated by Doris Dana (Baltimore: Johns Hopkins University Press, 1971), pp. 82–85, copyright 1971, reprinted by permission of Johns Hopkins University Press. Lines from "Diving into the Wreck," in *The Fact of a Doorframe: Poems Selected and New, 1950–1984*, by Adrienne Rich, copyright 1981, 1984 by Adrienne Rich and copyright 1975, 1978 by W. W. Norton & Company, Inc.; reprinted by permission of the author and W. W. Norton & Company, Inc. Poetry from *Descripción de un naufragio*, by Cristina Peri Rossi (Barcelona: Editorial Lumen S.A., 1975), pp. 82–83, 87–88, reprinted by permission of Editorial Lumen S.A.

Published by the University of Minnesota Press
111 Third Avenue South, Suite 290
Minneapolis, MN 55401-2520
http://www.upress.umn.edu

Printed in the United States of America on acid-free paper

The University of Minnesota is an equal-opportunity educator and employer.

Library of Congress Cataloging-in-Publication Data

Kaminsky, Amy K.
    After exile : writing the Latin American diaspora / Amy K.
Kaminsky.
        p.   cm.
    Includes bibliographical references and index.
    ISBN 0-8166-3147-6 (hc). – ISBN 0-8166-3148-4 (pb)
    1. Spanish American literature – Southern Cone of South America –
History and criticism.   2. Spanish American literature – 20th
century – History and criticism.   3. Exiles' writings, Spanish
American – History and criticism.   4. Exile (Punishment) in
literature.   5. Political refugees in literature.   I. Title.
PQ7551.K36   1999
860.9′.98 – dc21   98–52054

10 09 08 07 06 05 04 03 02 01 00 99   10 9 8 7 6 5 4 3 2 1

for David and Jonathan

Contents

ACKNOWLEDGMENTS

I believe I could never have undertaken this project without the assurance of friends and colleagues that it was permissible for me to trespass on the painful territory of exile. Sylvia Molloy and Saúl Sosnowski gave me that assurance early on, and I am grateful to them. Once the writing was under way, careful readings of individual chapters by Ruth Ellen Joeres, Connie Sullivan, Joanna O'Connell, Eric Sheppard, Nathan Stormer, Naomi Scheman, David Kaminsky, and Cheri Register helped keep me on track. I also owe thanks for the encouragement and feedback I received when I read early versions of various chapters of the book at the Alumni Symposium at Penn State, the annual meeting of the Midwest Modern Language Association, the "Seminar on Body and Culture" in the Department of Sociology at Gothenburg University, as well as at the Research Seminar in the Department of Spanish and at the Ibero-American Institute at that institution, the Goytisolo project at Lund University, and the MacArthur program at the University of Minnesota. Conversations with Leonardo Rossiello and Edmé Domínguez taught me much I did not know about life for Latin Americans in Sweden.

William Murphy, the editor with whom I worked at the University of Minnesota Press, has been unfailing in his support and good cheer. The Press's readers, Debra Castillo and Rosemary Geisdorfer Feal, read the manuscript with characteristic care and generosity. I am grateful for their suggestions, and to the extent to which I carried them out the manuscript is much the better. To Román Soto, who patiently read the entire manuscript when it was still very rough, who plied me with books, articles, and wonderful suggestions, and who showed me the very spot on Chiloé where Mañungo Vera was born, I owe a debt I cannot begin to repay.

Much of After Exile was written while I was on sabbatical from the University of Minnesota. I am grateful to that institution and to Kenneth Kaminsky, who continued to teach so I could have the time to write. His unwavering and matter-of-fact confidence in me is a gift always.

PROLOGUE

In 1985, one year after dictatorship ended in his country, Álvaro Barros-Lémez published an anthology of writing from the Uruguayan diaspora. The collection contains a line of poetry that continues to resonate for me: "Let everyone know, once and for all: / Exile cannot be just rhetoric anymore."[1] Cristina Peri Rossi wrote those words as some U.S. feminists were invoking exile to describe the situation of even privileged women whose unquestionably painful cultural disenfranchisement may have, ironically, included a prohibition against leaving the home. The evacuation of meaning of the term "exile" in this usage seemed to me when I first encountered it, as it still does, an ethical breach. It suggested a no doubt unintentional indifference to, if not an ignorance of, the suffering caused by the literal displacement imposed by the brutal and deadly military regimes of Latin America in the 1970s. The colors, shape, and weight of the word "exile" were being eroded by the carelessness of those who picked it up and made use of it in their desire to name something else. Exile and all the processes related to it have a material component, and that component is felt, experienced, and known through the body. This is not to say that it is not theorized, interpreted, and/or represented through language; but that without the emplaced human body, there is nothing to know or represent about exile and its aftermath.

My encounter with exile as metaphor has made me anxious about metaphor in general. I wanted to get beyond it. I have, of course, had to come to terms with the contradiction between this desire and my conviction that in language there is no "beyond metaphor," that metaphor not only is the inevitable condition of language but is, at times, a gift of beauty and wisdom. Still, I remain uneasy. I am troubled as well by another metaphor I invoke implicitly in the work of this book. It is the metaphor of the world as text that allows those of us who spin webs of literary analysis, and are trained to read novels and poems, to draw the world into our parlor of textual analysis. What does it mean, I wonder, to think of the world as text, both for our subsequent behavior toward and in the world and for the way it diminishes the real texts that are the grounding term of the metaphor?

The pleasures and dangers of metaphor are where I begin, but language, more broadly speaking, is an object of this study. In contemporary scholarship in the social sciences as well as the humanities, language gets evoked over and over again as a structuring device. It is taken as given that language determines our knowledge and understanding of the world, ourselves, each other. Theory enshrines language as the constructor of what we think of as reality. That elevation of its place alone suggests that language needs to be interrogated. One question evaded by the reification of an abstract notion of language is precisely that of its specificity — of language as an instrument of communication within and between cultures, of the politics of language, of the relationship between linguistic competence and citizenship, of the physiological experience of learning, hearing, and speaking language.

The simple act of communication is interrupted under dictatorship, reminding us sharply that language is in the first instance fundamental to a sense of community. As Rodrigo Cánovas points out, "Authoritarian societies are characterized by their prohibition against dialogue within a community."[2] Cánovas goes on to argue that this censorship induces the individual to forget any sense of the self as part of a collectivity. He characterizes this process in the first years of the Chilean dictatorship in the appropriately extreme terms of aphasia and lack of meaning:

> In the first years of the dictatorship in Chile, the interruption of the dialogue generates a collective aphasia. At the level of culture, aphasia implies speech that says nothing, an amorphous weave of signifiers that is the equivalent of what linguists call, simply, "noise." Besides constituting a symptom of the loss of a community's cultural referents (having to do with ideological discourses that are absolutely ineffective in explaining a new historical situation), this dislocated language is the effect of a disruptive censorship, which the community has internalized.[3]

Cánovas reminds us that language is absolutely fundamental to the healthy functioning of a community, and that repression and exile have a pernicious effect on language as a daily thing, ripping at the fabric of communal life. His metaphors of discontinuity and rupture (dislocated language and disruptive censorship) tie language to space as well as to history (the lost memory of aphasia) and the body ("internalized" censorship).

In current theory, language is linked to sexual difference, making it a prime site for feminist analysis, one of whose central tasks is to look at the gendered, as well as the sexed, female body as it is brought into contact with social, economic, and political exigencies. One theory holds that language develops in relation to the separation from the mother and entry into the law of the father; another contains the insight that a language constituted and evolved in an androcentric culture is inadequate for, and even detrimental to, women, who are necessarily caught up and reinscribed in it even as they use it. Both demonstrate a concern with language as a bearer of sexual difference, a concern that has quite rightly been a focus of various strains of feminist scholarship. My approach is somewhat different. I try to understand language materially, with attention to the specific historical conditions in which it occurs, looking at the relationship of language to body in a way that broadens our understanding of both terms.

Feminist theorists have demonstrated that the body, derogated in Western thought since Descartes at least, has been identified with the feminine.[4] But the reproductive system has become, far too much, a metonym for the female body, making sexual difference a primary locus for theorizing in academic feminism. This emphasis on what most spectacularly differentiates women from men not only replicates the grounds on which women's oppression has been constructed but also threatens to occlude the very real differences among women and to preclude discussions of social justice, the struggle for which is the taproot of feminist scholarly and political work.

Gender defines a difference that has, historically, rested on notions of (feminine) lack and justified (masculine) possession. What the masculine (norm) is, has, or does contrasts with what the feminine (deviant) is not, has not, or does not. This is the case even if the norm lacks what the deviant has, in a kind of double negative. So to be, as women are, the bearers of the body in a culture in which the norm is to subordinate or deny the body, is to be shamefully not not bearing the body. Feminist scholars have understood that this projection of disgraceful carnality onto woman does not mean that we should retreat from the body but rather that we need to look at its meanings more closely. We have had to learn that the healthy, white, male, heterosexual body, whose gender, race, and so on are unmarked, is still a body after all.[5] We have had to learn as well how to revalue and reclaim the female body — which is really many bodies marked multiply — and rescue it from sexist, and therefore heterosexist, thrall. Empirical and theoretical work by lesbian scholars has been a central part of this effort, showing how gender difference is tied to sexual difference. Both are linked to the ideology of heterosexuality.[6] The connection of language to both sex and gender, and of all these to body (which itself is now reductively understood in terms of the site of morphological difference, that is, the organs and processes of reproduction), has meant that feminist thinkers have been able to look at language in relation to sex/gender difference and ignore its other bodily aspects. Lesbian scholarship derives from the sexual, but because it challenges conventional meanings of what constitutes the properly sexual, it cannot for long stay in the realm of the purely sexual. The sexed body is what most catches our attention when we talk of gender, but it is merely where we need to start. The body is more than its sexual parts, as charming and delightful as we may find them. However much the sex organs have become a functioning metonym for the body, particularly as it is coded feminine, awareness of the way tropes function can let us know a metonym when we see one — as well as recognize to what extent rhetoric can make reality.

Gender is, of course, a category of difference (of women in relation to men), but it is also a category of apparent sameness (of women in relation to each other). And as a bottom-line concept for feminist scholarship, gender, like the sexual difference to which it is connected, is just a place to start from. When feminist work turns its attention to differences within the category "woman," to what produces those differences, the rest of the body comes into focus: how it is racialized, its relation to production, how it is positioned or moved in space, how it is marked for health, beauty, ability, age. If, as well, we consider language as it is produced and received in a body that is more than its reproductive organs, we can begin to see the not-sexual (or not overtly sexual), but still perhaps gendered, elements of both body and language.

Exile is, as much as anything, a spatial phenomenon, and space is a condition of, and a precondition for, the body. However, in this study I am deliberately uncoupling body from its recent identification with space. Imagining body as space has drawn scholars to the maternal body as a primary instance — any human being's first experience — of space. This insight has occasioned some very exciting feminist scholarship, both in the new feminist geography and in cultural and literary analysis.[7] Nevertheless, I am bracketing the notion of body as space in order to attend to the problematic of the sentient body in space.[8] I do this in part to maintain a critical attitude toward the reduction of woman to mother and of mother to womb. Space is still ground, not noted for its consciousness of itself, or of anything else.

Feminist theorists have made considerable use of spatial metaphors to describe the gendered relations of power and resistance. Myra Jehlen's "Archimedes and the Paradox of Feminist Criticism" rehearses the conundrum of trying to create change from without when one is situated within, of "the improbable feat" of "being at once on and off a world."[9] Bell hooks's *Feminist Theory from Margin to Center* describes Black feminism's claim to centrality within a theory and practice of feminism.[10] The standpoint theory of Nancy Hartsock, adapted and modified by Patricia Hill Collins and others, and Adrienne Rich's politics of location suggest the richness of the geographical metaphor for feminist theorists at all points on the theoretical spectra.[11] Exile itself, as I noted earlier, has been used as a metaphor for women's relation to dominant culture.[12] Recently we have seen a shift from the stasis of these positionings to a new focus on movement in and through space. Rosi Braidotti, for example, promotes the idea of nomadic consciousness as metaphor for liberatory thought. As such, this consciousness has no center from which to name a periphery, yet it is not random either:

The nomad does not stand for homelessness, or compulsive displacement; it is rather a figuration for the kind of subject who has
relinquished all idea, desire, or nostalgia for fixity. This figuration
expresses the desire for an identity made of transitions, successive
shifts, and coordinated changes, without and against an essential
unity. The nomadic subject, however, is not altogether devoid of
unity; his/her essential mode is one of definite, seasonal patterns of
movement through rather fixed routes. It is a cohesion engendered
by repetitions, cyclical moves, rhythmic displacement.[13]

Taking a somewhat different tack, Panivong Norindr posits the seman-
tically rich term "errance," which means wandering, but also error and
transgression:

> ...a process I call "errance," to play on the meaning of both swerv-
> ing from the path of truth — as deviation or perversion — and
> wandering from one place to another, an accidental journey more
> than a process of forced displacement. I argue that it is precisely
> in the erotogenic zones — dramatized in "la traversée de la fleuve"
> or urban peregrination — that the Western female subject comes
> to an "imaginary" understanding of the colonial situation. Wan-
> dering creates a different type of spatial relation and circumscribes
> another space where the subject both inscribes herself and is being
> reinscribed. Placed in this "new" space, she encounters the other,
> the native, the subject of desire, and derives pleasure. The dis-
> covery of the colonial city is not linked only to sexual knowledge,
> but...to the liminal site of a journey into..."a different zone of
> the journey,"...what Michel de Certeau calls "another spatiality
> (an 'anthropological,' poetic and mythic experience of space)."[14]

Both Braidotti and Norindr take care to distinguish their roamings from
exile. Norindr's errance is "an accidental journey more than a process of
forced displacement" (54). Nor is Braidotti's nomadism coerced. These are
privileged movements in space and depend on a certain amount of economic independence. Norindr's wandering subject is the colonial woman,
not the colonized, and Braidotti's nomad is a member of the intellectual elite. This privilege of movement in Braidotti is something everyone,
ideally, should be able to enjoy; she evokes "a massive abandonment of
the logocentric polis" (32). For Norindr the privilege is more troubled, at
the expense of the colonized other.

Somewhat different is Gloria Anzaldúa's attention to space and movement in the borderlands.[15] Unlike Braidotti, a philosopher, and Norindr,
a literary theorist, Anzaldúa is primarily a poet, with roots in the Chicano working class. Whereas for Braidotti and Norindr the space in which
wandering is to occur is a given, for Anzaldúa it must be claimed and

won. The territory she charts is a lived space that had not before been
so overtly acknowledged in language or on the political map. It had been
masked by a one-dimensional border, established to contain all of Mexico and all of what is Mexican south of the Río Bravo in confirmation of
the self-declared manifest destiny of the United States. Anzaldúa's book
Borderlands/La frontera was a kind of guerrilla action, blowing the cover
story of the border — in fact blowing the border itself open to reveal
the borderlands, a three-dimensional, fluid space that spans parts of the
U.S. Southwest and northern Mexico. Once opened, this *frontera* territory, identifiable in part by its languages (Spanish, English, and a number
of local variations, themselves tied to particular class positions, which Anzaldúa goes to some pains to enumerate and claim), could then be mined
for its metaphoric value. Anzaldúa herself began this process, exploring
the borderland quality of ethnicity and sexuality; and other thinkers have
followed suit. It is no exaggeration to say that Gloria Anzaldúa's territorial metaphor, creating space for movement and interaction in the spaces
where differences meet, has provided new paths, new ground, and new
directions for feminist thought.

Braidotti's and Norindr's spatial metaphors celebrate movement
through space, language, and sex. Anzaldúa names the space itself, creating a discursive territory and giving cultural and political currency both
to those wandering through that land and to its permanent residents. The
end of exile that expresses itself as diaspora finds a home in a similar
paradoxical space — permanent residence in the state of flux. Yet Anzaldúa's reclamation of borderland space by necessity also challenges the
complacency of stable territoriality.

Exile as I am using it here is, like nomadism, errance, or Anzaldúan
border-crossing, a process of movement and change, not solely a displacement beyond a border (although it is also that). The relation of exile
to space, a relation that is mediated by language, is a central concern
of this book. For philosopher María Lugones, the shift in perception,
behavior, and being that she calls travel, and that is therefore linked
to, though far from coextensive with, exile, nomadic movement, border-
crossing, and errance, causes profound linguistic and spatial alteration:
"The shift from being one person to being a different person is what I call
'travel.'... Even though the shift can be done willfully, it is not a matter
of acting.... Rather, one is someone who has that personality or character
or *uses space and language in that particular way*."[16]

In looking at language and space, I am trying to hold on to the material: exile as a lived reality; language as produced in, and received by,
the body; space as located matter, with measurable distances, and occupied. This book, then, is not an exhaustive study of the literature of exile
and return in Latin America's Southern Cone, but rather a meditation
on exile and its aftermath.[17] It addresses the process of deterritorialization

(*destierro*), alienation, acculturation, and, in some instances of after exile, reterritorialization. It considers such questions as the instability of exile itself (exile viewed as a process rather than a singular state); the mutual constitution of language and space in texts; the notion of national iden-tity as a condition of an exile sensibility; and memory and forgetting. It pauses to consider representations of exile and return, and their relation to body and language, in the work of a number of Southern Cone writers, including well-known, widely translated figures such as Luisa Valenzuela, José Donoso, Cristina Peri Rossi, and Mario Benedetti, as well as (to date) less-known writers such as José Leandro Urbina, Leonardo Rossiello, and Vlady Kociancich.

My argument concerning the importance of the geography of writing indicates that I ought to mention the spatial coordinates of this study. The act of writing this book about exiles from Chile, Uruguay, and Ar-gentina has taken place in the United States and Sweden. The writers whose work I look at have written in all those places, as well as in Spain, Mexico, and France. The outlying geographical term here would seem to be Sweden, a place that elicits variations on the question, What's a nice Latin Americanist like you doing in a place like this? Beyond my practical need to negotiate life in a family, there is the important part that Scan-dinavia, but especially Sweden, played in the international community that received exiles in the aftermath of the military coups of the 1970s in Latin America's Southern Cone. Sweden's Social Democrat govern-ment maintained a generous and lenient policy toward political refugees throughout the 1970s. Not only did Sweden accept a larger proportion of political refugees (measured against the size of its own population) than any other country; it also fostered cultural production — in the form of writing workshops, theater groups, publication venues, and the like — among its asylum-seekers. While high-profile and more highly educated exiles tended to gain entry to countries like Mexico, the United States, France, and Spain, Sweden took in many more workers and individuals without previous international connections. This has meant that although a large number of Southern Cone writers have emerged in Sweden, some of whom are very good indeed, few have gained international recognition.

The texts I look at in relation to exile and its aftermath are primar-ily literary. But it is instructive to remember that writing about literature has itself been an exilic practice.[18] Although critics of national/regional literatures may be less likely to problematize their exilic connections than are scholars of comparative literature, it should be noted that the shift in the canon of North American Hispanic studies — a shift from a virtual monopoly of peninsular Spanish texts in the 1940s to an increasing em-phasis on Latin American literature — was generated in large part by the replacement in U.S. universities of a generation of exiles of the Spanish Civil War by a generation of exiled and brain-drained intellectuals from

Latin America, beginning with the Cuban diaspora of the 1960s. I, however, enter this discussion not as an exile but as an outsider, writing in safe places, far from Argentina, Uruguay, and Chile, about a part of people's lives that is both private and painful. My own belief is that the stories of exile, which include within them the terrible stories of torture, disappearance, prison, and loss, need to be told and remembered. I know myself to be linked to these stories, however tenuously, beyond being a reader of them: I am, after all, a citizen of the United States, and my country's policies and resources helped to produce and then support two decades and more of state terror. I am also a friend and colleague of individuals who themselves survived that terror. For both these reasons I am on the side of those, like Mabel Moraña, who want these stories told, who will tend their memory, however complicated by our understanding of the partiality of knowledge and of situated meaning.[19] I understand the validity of the fear that too much remembering might mean provoking the still-armed forces into staging new coups, might destabilize fragile democracies. For this very reason, it is useful for outsiders like me to speak, since our words add to the already existing ballast of those who insist on remembering. We add our voices from outside, to bear these stories to readers in our own countries. Those of us speaking from the United States act as part of the effort to keep our own government from repeating its past practices. If memory is dangerous from within, it is far less so from without. If in Chile, Uruguay, and Argentina it reminds the military that there is still opposition, in the United States it serves to remind us of our shameful part in what the military in those countries perpetrated. If voicing the memory of state violence too loudly and insistently in the Southern Cone might elicit dictatorship anew, then those of us outside must speak resoundingly to make sure the United States does not support any such resurgence. But I also speak as a Jew, writing, at the moment, in northern Europe, where, as in the United States, neo-Nazi movements are growing and the denial of the Holocaust is increasing. "Never again," say Jews of the mass extermination of our people; "Nunca más," echo the reports issued by the official Argentine and Uruguayan commissions on the torture, disappearance, and state-sanctioned murder of political dissidents, workers, and students. "Never again," "nunca más": we are enjoined to remember what we cannot allow to be repeated.

Chapter One

AFTER EXILE

Perhaps the worst condemnation of all is to watch our country
recede from our reach like a foreign, distant, indecipherable
tide and to witness how indecisively our bodies begin to seek
stability after many precarious years; our bodies, unconsenting
and perhaps irremediably, grow accustomed to a country which
they did not choose of their own free will.
                                    — UNNAMED EXILED JOURNALIST

In the early months of 1994 a new restaurant opened in Manhattan. It
was called Patria; its chef's name was Douglas Rodriguez; and the food
was described in the *New York Times* as "cuisine nuevo Latino," which, as
anyone who has ever taught — or taken — Spanish 101 knows, ought
to be "cocina nueva latina," small *l* and inflected feminine.[1] But then
again, all things considered, the *Times's* phrase is apt. After all, the whole
postmodern point of an upscale restaurant on Park Avenue whose name
means "homeland" in a language that is both foreign and widely spoken
locally, using a lexical item that refers to something quite adamantly but
imprecisely elsewhere, is dispersal and instability. "Cuisine nuevo Latino"
and "Douglas Rodriguez" (no accent mark) are audibly macaronic, and
the food is similarly hybrid. According to the reviewer, it is often deli-
cious, but it sometimes goes too far in its audacious reinterpretation of
traditional dishes. In the not-so-simple gesture of making a ceviche out of
duck and fancy mushrooms and putting it into an empanada, Patria's food
is simultaneously deterritorialized and made familiar to the palates of Park
Avenue (a street, by the way, that not many months before the opening of
the restaurant was the site of a several-mile-long exhibit of monumental
Fernando Botero sculptures).

Patria is a different sort of place from the Colombian, Dominican,
and Argentine restaurants that serve the expatriate residents of Jackson
Heights and Corona in Queens. These restaurants do not line the wide
green boulevard east of Central Park; they sit in the shadow of the ele-
vated train that rises out of the ground after crossing the East River on
its way from Times Square and Grand Central Station to Main Street,
Flushing. These neighborhood restaurants have been around for approximately twenty years, and they serve the communities they inhabit. There

is nothing self-consciously chic about these places; they simply re-create the familiar food of home — empanadas de choclo, with nary a trace of duck. When the *Times* writes about these restaurants, it suggests their slightly exotic nature (and flavors): "Along Roosevelt and 37th Avenues from 74th to 102nd Streets, in the Jackson Heights, Elmhurst, and Corona sections of Queens, there is a little Latin America, where Spanish is the language of currency, and the sign 'Cuy ahora' ('Guinea pigs today') makes the heart of an Ecuadoran or Peruvian beat a little faster."[2] A trip to Queens and to "authentic" Latin American dining requires subway directions, a map, and an interpreter; they are an anthropological experience for the Manhattan paper. But in Elmhurst, Jackson Heights, and Corona, Latin American neighborhood restaurants are part of a familiar landscape. Between the imaginative gastronomy of Patria and the home cooking of La Porteña lies the territory of "after exile."

The postexilic Latin America I will be discussing in this book is more specifically a region — the Southern Cone, and more particularly, Chile, Argentina, and Uruguay.[3] In the 1970s and 80s, these three countries suffered overlapping coups and dictatorships; and now all three are in the difficult process of redemocratization, each (at this writing) having survived two elections since the end of dictatorship. As of now, Argentina is on its second democratically elected president, Carlos Menem, since voting the generals out of office in 1983. Uruguay's first postdictatorship election was in November 1984; the winning candidate, Julio María Sanguinetti, lost the 1989 election but was returned to office in 1995. Chile was restored to democracy in March 1990 with the election of Patricio Aylwin to the presidency, followed by Eduardo Frei in 1994.[4]

Compulsory political exile is over. Countless exiles have returned, but others have not. Some manage a life between two countries or establish a routine of travel.[5] Clearly, the notion of "after exile" presents its own complexities. Perhaps because we are reaching the end not only of the century but of the millennium, we are consumed by the notion that everything is past — or "post," a prefix that has been attached to the whole range of the modern world's organizational structures: political movements, intellectual currents, economic systems, and even whole countries.[6] Some such designations are wishful thinking. Postfeminism, as more than one observant woman has pointed out, will be an option when we get to postpatriarchy. "Postcolonial" is often an optimistic label of denial: colonialism and its fallout are still very much with us.[7] And in this postmodern era, most folks cling desperately to the modern: coherence, progress, and the stable self are still important values. In this deracinated apocalyptic vision of the intelligentsia, every "post" contains what it purports to supersede, marked always by the term whose decadence it reports. The more colloquial "after," as in "after exile," also registers perpetuation in change, strangely denoting the pursuit of the original term. After exile, then, presumes something definable called "exile," a term that requires some interrogation. For exile itself, in what is beginning to look like an infinite regression, is marked by notions of home.

Although I thought I was being utterly original when it dawned on me that you cannot quite say "home" in Spanish, that Romance languages lack a single term that denotes both "dwelling place" and the affective meaning connected to it that "home" does in English and *heim* and *hem* do in other Germanic languages, it turns out that virtually everybody working cross-culturally who has paid the slightest bit of attention to the issue has had that insight. Still, new discovery or not, this semantic oddity deserves some elaboration. If one cannot get the full flavor of "home" with the Spanish *casa*, or even *hogar*, it is also the case that the full meaning of *patria* is unavailable in a single English word. Place and affect come together differently in English and Spanish, and the associations crisscross. Home is to house as *x* is to country, just as *patria* is to *país* as *x* is to *casa*. That is, the affective components of *patria* and home are analogous. One is in reference to a contained private space; the other refers to a public one. An intermediate term, nation/*nación*, is somewhere between *país* and *patria* and points toward the *x* in "the country is to *x*" formulation.[8] Of course, there are ways to begin to render *patria* in English: compound words that invoke the domestic space of home — "hometown," "homeland," or the familial "fatherland" or "motherland," just as certain idiomatic expressions in Spanish (*en casa, a casa*) approximate the affective resonance of "home" in all its domestic immediacy. José Donoso's exiled protagonist in *El jardín de al lado* (*The Garden Next Door*), who rails against the selling of the house he grew up in, certainly expresses this affective melding of house and home. Once *casa* is lost, there is no term, no place, that is home. There is only the locution of "a closed and limited space" (*un lugar cerrado y limitado*), rendered by the translator as "a house, a limited space" that resonates with its own absence: "Where does he want me to go back to, if he sells the house? You don't go back to a country, a people, an idea, a city: you — I mean me — go back to a house, a limited space where your heart feels safe."[9]

Whereas people fairly easily refer to their hometown (usually when they are away from it), when they talk about their country in this affective way, they are more likely to say "home" than "homeland," for "homeland" is a formal word, most often reserved for writing down. "Fatherland" and "motherland" are even less likely to be part of the spoken lexicon. The Spanish equivalent of the smaller geographical area, "hometown," is *pueblo*, which collapses place into inhabitants — people (*pueblo*); *patria chica*, not used much in Latin America anyway, refers to the smaller space of region or province, still covering a substantial area. The point here is that the term that gets used for the affective is the enclosed, domestic "home" in English and the unbounded (farther than the eye can see) *patria* in Spanish, one needing expansion to represent what is beyond what the house contains, and the other needing contraction to make it about some more manageable place. Yet these modifications (homeland, *patria chica*) are not, as we have seen, wholly satisfactory.

The ideological divisions that align woman with private space (house/home) and man with public space (*país/patria*) play out in interesting ways around these linguistic and affective divides. Surely both men and women partake of the benefits of both home and *patria*. Surely, too, they have differential access to those benefits. But the gender divide cuts across these terms in another way: the affective (home/*patria*) is associated with the feminine, and the objective (house/*casa*/country/*país*) with the masculine. Yet this second formulation doesn't work so smoothly either. On the one hand, the domesticity of the house and conventional notions of masculinity do not easily coincide; on the other, *patria*, with its masculine root, is unbounded space to which women have traditionally been denied access.

The building of the structure that is the house, however, is "men's work" — at least in the European tradition that marks the literary texts of the Southern Cone. Building the house is analogous to building the nation, and the deterioration of the house is a symbol of societal decline. Think for example of the house built by José Arcadio Buendía in *Cien años de soledad* (*One Hundred Years of Solitude*), or the hacienda at Tres Marías resurrected by Esteban Trueba in *La casa de los espíritus*) (*The House of the Spirits*). In both cases, women get into these houses and rearrange them: they build additions, close off rooms or furnish them, have babies, and generally turn the stark space of the physical structure into the occupied place of home as *hogar*.[10]

Patria, for its part, is marked by its masculine root. It would be a mistake, however, to assume the patriarchal sounding *patria* is best translated as "fatherland," a term with unfortunately Teutonic and militaristic overtones. During the period of dictatorship, the military governments of the Southern Cone certainly did conscript the term *patria* to evoke an obedience born of loyalty and, extending the doctrine of national security developed in the 1950s, to discern an imagined external threat of outside communist influences that would rot the core of those exposed to it. Nevertheless, as an abstract noun, like "justice" and "wisdom," *patria* is often represented symbolically by a feminine figure. José da Cruz ridicules the masculine militarization of *patria* by appropriating and parodying the motto *o patria o tumba* (either country or death) of the Uruguayan national anthem as the title of his novel *Sin patria ni tumba* (With neither country nor death).[11] Mexican school texts carry an illustration of "la Patria" in the form of a woman draped in a Grecian-style tunic, and Chile was founded as a nation under the protection of the maternal Virgen del Carmen, before whose image O'Higgins and San Martín incongruously knelt.[12] Moreover, for the people, *patria* never lost its feminine edge. Luisa

Valenzuela renders *patria* as "motherland," and Angel and Isabel Parra, the children of Chilean icon Violeta Parra, sing of "madre patria, madre revolución" (mother country, mother revolution). Over and over again writers evoke mother as metaphor, or perhaps metonym, for *patria*. Pablo Neruda writes:

> Country, my country, I turn my blood in your direction.
> But I am begging you the way a child begs its mother,
> with tears:
>   take this blind guitar
> and these lost features.
> I left to find sons for you over the earth,
> I left to comfort those fallen with your name made of snow,
> I left to build a house with your pure timber,
> I left to carry your star to the wounded heroes.
>
> Now I want to fall asleep in your substance.
> Give me your clear night of piercing strings,
> your night like a ship, your altitude covered with stars.[13]

In this poem the son claims his identity as hero and adventurer — the healer of fallen patriots, the builder of houses, the singer of hope; but he also wants the comfort of the mother/infant dyad, to sleep in the substance of the mother/land. He wants her to sing to him, to return to her materiality, to the oxymoronic bright darkness (*clara noche*) of undifferentiation between himself and the maternal body.

More recently, in a less beautiful but more complicated rendition of the Chilean *patria* as mother, novelist José Leandro Urbina gives his protagonist, a Chilean exile in Canada, a mother who is both loving and tyrannical.[14] She is attached to him in the classic manner described by the orthodox Freudian theory of mother-child cathexis. But, in her zeal to keep him from what is in her view a politically dangerous sexual liaison with an older woman, the mother allies herself with the repressive forces of the dictatorship her son is committed to opposing. Nevertheless, when his mother dies, the protagonist feels it is his responsibility to go to her funeral, to return to the mother's, and the country's, dead and deadly body. The figuration of the homeland as maternal, where the nation vacillates between the sentimentalized mother the child left behind and the phallic mother who threatens her child with engulfment, who has betrayed that child by becoming the repressive, smothering dictatorship he had to leave, is particularly resonant for male exile writers. It is not the only version of woman-as-nation in a situation of threat and loss. In cases of foreign invasion, the more common trope is that of the violated woman. Invasion becomes comprehensible as rape. Just as the nation-as-mother is a problematic construction, meaningful primarily within an androcentric system, the violated nation-woman, as Mary Layoun points out, relies on already repressive notions of women's agency and sexuality.[15]

In José Donoso's *El jardín de al lado*, to which Urbina pays homage in the title of his novel *Cobro revertido* (Collect call), the trope of the maternal nation is again varied slightly: the exiled protagonist's mother/country is not quite dead; rather she is moribund.[16] Here the mother, a metonym for Chile in extremis, is dying slowly of anorexia nervosa. Wasting away from self-starvation, through the first two-thirds of the novel never quite dying but always on the edge, she is a particularly apt metaphor for Chile under dictatorship, its nourishing cultural core — the exiled artists, writers, and intellectuals who populate the novel — drained away. (I realize I am collapsing two different kinds of trope here, but the figure of the mother/country is, I believe, metonymic for these men writers, while it remains metaphoric for the woman reader.) The writer-protagonist cannot or will not return to attend his mother's death. Without the dreaded *L* on his passport, which would mark him as an enemy of the state, he can return; without money it is difficult for him to do so. But he admits that what keeps him from returning is his fear that she will continue not to die, and that he will be trapped in and by her interminable dying.

Insofar as *patria* is figured as the maternal body — dead and no longer able to nurture or thwart her child, as in Urbina, alive but fixed in place as in Neruda's poem, or dying and entrapping in Donoso — masculinity is identified with the maturing process defined as separation from mother/homeland. But it is equally marked by the infantile desire to return. In the gendered dyads that structure the Western imaginary, the exile occupies the masculine position — or at least one of them — of child in the process of separation, while the feminine position is the maternal place left behind.

This powerful metaphor has become so common in exile literature written by men as to have become almost predictable. It appears, for instance, in Juan Rivano's *Época de descubrimientos* (Age of discoveries), a novel of Chilean exiles in Sweden, in which the mother's death closes the novel, and once again marks the now irrevocable separation from home.[17] Daniel Moyano makes use of it in *Libro de navíos y borrascas* (The book of ships and storms), where both the homeland and the ship carrying the protagonist into exile are figured as the maternal body. Here the body is amplified, as the stars (by which figuratively, at least, the ship is navigated) connect the exile to the universe as an "umbilical stairway" (*escalera umbilical*). Disembarkation is a troublesome birth, "a birth, a departure with forceps, but a departure, imminent childbirth, after all."[18] Much later, acclimating to exile, the narrator refers back not to the ship but to the homeland as the mother, and this time he is the child proclaiming his decision to separate from the mother's body: "an Argentinean taken from the breast who decides to break formally with his mother."[19] The tension between passive and active behavior here is noticeable: the child, identified via the national adjective, is removed from the breast (*argentino destetado*) and then "decides," "formally," "to break with" "the mother," unnamed but presumably the originating proper noun ("Argentina") that gives birth to the adjectival *argentino*.

As I noted earlier, the mother as home and nation is closely identified with the family's dwelling place. Julio Méndez, José Donoso's writer in exile in *El jardín de al lado*, is afraid that when their mother dies his brother will want to sell the house where he grew up. When she finally does die, his fears are realized, and he finds himself justifying his desire to keep the house, in the face of enormous costs to maintain it and the huge amount of money they will receive if the house is sold. His refusal to sell the house is neither madness nor nostalgia, he argues: "It's deep-seated roots, history, legend, metaphor, one's own ground, a place where the heart lives."[20] Here house, home, and mother merge in a masculinist idealization of "place" as "home."

The returning exile, however, is faced with the desecration of the (no longer maternal) house/nation. In *Una casa vacía* (An empty house), the eponymous house of Carlos Cerda's novel has been sullied by its use during the absence of the protagonist.[21] Having been recruited into the state apparatus as a torture center, the house is no longer usable as a metaphor for maternity. It instead becomes associated with the father, who uses it at first speculatively, as real estate he buys cheaply after redemocratization has closed down such places. He then utilizes the house in order to uphold a patriarchal domesticity he maintains by means of coercion of the daughter. The house is corrupted and is no longer functional as a domestic space; the marriage it is supposed to salvage is similarly rotten at the center. The father's heavy-handed tactics (he gives the house to his daughter and son-in-law on the condition they do not divorce) echo the brutality of the military state and in fact derive from it. The daughter will do as she is told, just as the country has been expected to do. The patriarchal prescription is morally, politically, and emotionally bankrupt, however. When the father — either in the guise of the state that takes over the house to use as a site for torture, coercing the complicity of the protagonist, whose family's safety as well as his own economic survival depends on their agreement to let the military occupy their home, or in the form of the pater familias who demands filial loyalty from his daughter — takes over the house, the maternal is evacuated. At the center of this novel is the empty space left by the absence of the angel (no longer) in the house.

Geographer Gillian Rose argues that humanistic geography longs for a prediscursive space that it associates with the mother, and that "[p]lace is represented as Woman, in order that humanists can define their own masculine rationality."[22] She suggests that the entire scholarly enterprise

of humanist geography is ruled by this trope. Furthermore, the confla-
tion in "home" of "woman" and "place" is invoked not only by those still
held in thrall by androcentric ideology, but by some feminists themselves.
Danish psychologist Inger Agger, who worked with women who had been
political prisoners in Latin America and the Middle East, invokes "a ther-
apeutic space," "the house of the woman exile," consisting of a number of
"rooms" in which different traumatic scenes are played out.[23] This house
is the body not of the exile's absent mother but of the woman exile herself. Agger's stated intent is to map a psychic geography of the exiled
woman. The map, though, becomes a blueprint of a house, whose rooms
are figured as the enclosed spaces of childhood, heterosexual coupling,
motherhood, and torture.

Women exile writers themselves tend not to (con)fuse the maternal
body with the lost homeland. References to the mother are rare, and when
they do occur, they avoid the infantile representation of the mother who
exists solely in relation to the child. Ana Vásquez's Mi amiga Chantal (My
friend Chantal), for example, contains no mention of the narrator's family
of origin, and Chantal's mother is presented primarily in relationship to
her husband, a relationship Chantal is determined not to imitate in her
own life.[24] Ana, the novel's narrator, is a mother herself, and although
her children are important to her, they constitute just one aspect of her
life. Vásquez depicts the mother as political actor and worker, and only
secondarily as a mother.

The politically active mother turns up in Marta Traba's texts as well. In
Conversación al sur (Conversation to the south, translated as Mothers and
Shadows), Irene comes to political consciousness largely as a mother, but
she has a professional life as an actress.[25] Dolores seeks Irene out in part
because she is a mother figure, a mother whom the younger woman sees as
a more congenial model for her as a political actor than her own mother.
In Traba's posthumously published novel, En cualquier lugar (In any place),
Luis's mother is far more committed to her Marxist press than to caring for
her grown son's needs.[26] The mother in Cristina Peri Rossi's "La influencia de Edgar Allan Poe en la poesía de Raimundo Arias" ("The Influence
of Edgar Allan Poe in the Poetry of Raimundo Arias") is indeed left behind, but that is because she is a member of the insurrectionary guerrilla
movement.[27] Her association with the armed struggle in the homeland
is precisely the inverse of the mother as the homeland we encounter in
Neruda, Urbina, Donoso, and others. Not incidentally, the child exile in
this story is a daughter who, despite the fact that she has yet to reach
puberty, is primarily concerned not with her mother but with her own
and her father's survival in exile. In contrast to the infantilized adult male
exile, Peri Rossi's Alicia is a preternaturally mature little girl.

In Traba's Conversación al sur, Irene, an Argentine, fiercely defends herself against the knowledge that her son and daughter-in-law, who went

to Santiago to study, are being tortured somewhere in Chile. This text records the end of the period between the early and mid-1970s, when Chile, Uruguay, and Argentina served as a refuge from each other. Going from one of these countries to another was certainly a palpable move — national identities and rivalries had been fostered for generations, first by border wars and later by soccer team loyalties and jokes; still these border-crossings felt within reach of home.[28] But once Argentina fell to the generals in 1976, the governments began cooperating in the detention and disappearance of each other's dissidents, creating the need for a more substantial exile — for greater, safer distance from home, always understanding that absolute safety was never guaranteed: Chile's DINA assassinated Orlando Letelier in Washington, D.C., and planned to do the same to Volodia Teitelboim and Carlos Altamirano in Mexico City.[29]

Before she died, Traba meant to write three novels of the repression. The second, *En cualquier lugar,* moves outside Latin America to take place in a European exile that, from the point of view of the host country, mutes the differences among Latin American nationalities. In Spain, Latin Americans are all *sudacas,* a term that occupies approximately the same vile register as "nigger" does in English. In the countries of northern Europe, one dark head is very like another and might as well be from Iran or Turkey as from Argentina or Uruguay.

Exile from Uruguay and Chile in 1973, like exile from Argentina in 1976, was pretty clear-cut. People involved in progressive politics, from labor unionists and sociology students to urban guerrillas, were targeted for detention, which most often meant disappearance, torture, and, in thousands of cases, death. As Mario Benedetti points out, there was little choice involved in going into exile. Large numbers of people were forced out of their homeland. Some escaped before getting caught; some were released to a precarious freedom after detention, interrogation, and often torture; some were taken from prison directly to an airport. Others found themselves outside the country at the time of the coup, unable to return. Nevertheless, as political scientist Yossi Shain has noted, it is often difficult to distinguish exile from other forms of separation from one's country of birth.[30]

"Exile," as I use the term, is always coerced. "Voluntary exile" is, I believe, an oxymoron that masks the cruelly limited choices imposed on the subject. Still, there were those who could have stayed but chose to leave and others who, outside the country at the time of the coups, would have found it risky to return. Moreover, in the literary examples I discuss, I impose no litmus test to discriminate between exiled and expatriate writers, since what I am interested in textually are representations of the process of exile, not the details of biography.

Luisa Valenzuela distinguishes between exile and expatriation in an original way, suited to the circumstances of Argentina between 1976 and

1983. Valenzuela could have chosen to live quietly in Argentina, but instead she left. She acknowledges that she was not a political exile, in the strict sense of the term as I am using it. Yet she redefines "expatriate" as one who has had her country taken from her. In a 1981 interview, which took place just at the end of the darkest period in the dictatorship, as the *apertura* was about to begin, and before the war with Britain over the Malvinas put an end to the military's pretensions of being the country's salvation, Valenzuela said:

> My Argentine society does not exist any more; in many ways it is ended. I am not an exile; I am an expatriate in the sense that I do not have a homeland any more. They have managed to kill our country in a variety of ways, so it is a very painful situation to deal with, but at the same time it is a reality one cannot deny. So even if I went back to my country, which I could, being quite careful, it would not be the same place I used to love. My friends are not there any more, and people cannot speak freely. They cannot even think freely. That is terrifying. I don't know if I really left to be able to write what I wanted (which I still did there, even knowing that I would not be published there) as much as to be able to speak to people in another way and to recognize and acknowledge the awesome reality of torture and horror. In some ways, one has to keep a distance. One has to get a perspective, because when you are immersed in pain, I don't think you can see it so easily.[31]

Julio Cortázar writes of another sort of exile. An expatriate who was always nourished by the language and presence of his Argentina, Cortázar kept the line of language and communication open through travel and, more important, the capacity to have his texts read and known in his native country. His sense of himself as an exile came about as a textual matter, when the government banned one of his books. Not being able to be read in his homeland constituted exile for Cortázar. Notwithstanding the privilege of this position, or its narcissism (not, "I am rent from my country," but "My country cannot have access to me"), Cortázar raises the specter of the cost of exile for the homeland as well as for the self.[32] Valenzuela similarly notes the distress of not being able to publish in the Argentina of the generals, but for her it occupies space not at the center but quite literally as a parenthetical aside.

Meanwhile, those who remained did not always do so happily. Of them, many experienced what has come to be called "inner exile," or what some have called *insilio*, characterized, according to Carina Perelli, by dissociation, by the lack of "guarantees inherent in a universe in which being and acting are dangerous activities," by self-censorship, and by fear.[33] Yet this inner exile necessarily remains a metaphor in one real sense. Exile is a removal in space as well as in spirit. It is a physical uprooting, an individual's removal from a familiar place to a new space that has, at least at the beginning, no recognizable coordinates. Geographer Yi-Fu Tuan conceives of rootedness in a place as so absolute as to be unconscious — he differentiates it for that reason from the self-aware sense of place. Uprooting in this sense involves bringing this change to consciousness in a particularly painful manner.[34] This process of uprooting is a literal *desarticulación,* a term that evokes the physical processes of both speech and touch.

Gabriela Mistral, an expatriate who wrote of exile, describes the new space, which is also clearly an inner landscape, as a "land of absence":

> Land of absence,
> strange land,
> lighter than angel
> or subtle sign,
> color of dead algae,
> color of falcon,
> with the age of all time,
> with no age content.
> . . . .
> It was born to me of things
> that are not of land,
> of kingdoms and kingdoms
> that I had and I lost,
> of all things living
> that I have seen die,
> of all that was mine
> and went from me.[35]

Cristina Peri Rossi echoes that characterization in her parable "Las estatuas, o la condición del extranjero" (Statues, or the condition of the foreigner), in which the narrator describes the town square as empty of all the things that usually give such a place its life. In his delineation of the difference between space and place, and the process by which the former becomes the latter, Yi-Fu Tuan argues that place is filled with affect. It is known and understandable.[36] All the familiar landmarks of home — food, smells, the flora and fauna even of the city, the sounds of a familiar language, the fixed points on the internal map of your neighborhood, the knowledge of the time it takes to travel certain distances over certain routes, the kinetic knowledge of the place that is your home, *where* you can feel safe, *what* signals danger — all these vanish in the condition of foreignness, to be regained slowly, perhaps incompletely. The abruptness of exile can only intensify the experience of displacement. When familiarity is finally achieved, it can be a source of intense pleasure, even of rebirth. The elderly Don Rafael in Mario Benedetti's *Primavera con una*

esquina rota (Springtime with a broken corner) makes the space of exile
his own by walking it, marking it, and internalizing that route.[37] The act
rejuvenates him; he gets rid of his cane.

Don Rafael's appropriation of exile space belies the assumption, so
often made, that exile is somehow a fixed thing. Even such a subtle
thinker as Rosi Braidotti sees exile as unitary, utilizing it as the fixed
term in a metaphor as she criticizes a too-simple "identification of female
identity with a sort of planetary exile" among feminist thinkers.[38] Exile,
however, is complex, a nonlinear process — two kinds of noun, as well as
a verb and an adjective. The first moment of exile, when one is exiled,
becomes an exile, is a moment of trauma. The subject's forced break from
the homeland is quite literally a physical rupture. The first description
in the Hispanic literary tradition of this initial moment of political exile,
and the occasion of the earliest simile in Spanish poetry, tropes exile as
a physical injury that recalls a classic torture. The poet evokes the pain
of Rodrigo Díaz and his family when, banished by his king, El Cid takes
leave of his wife and daughters:

> Crying their eyes out as you have never seen,
> thus they part from each other, as the fingernail from the flesh.[39]

Yet exile's initial rupture may be an exhilarating moment as well, a
moment of knowledge of survival, of new opportunity. Two of the poems
in *Descripción de un naufragio* (Description of a shipwreck), Cristina Peri
Rossi's lyric disquisition on the end of democracy in Uruguay and the
subsequent death and exile of many of her compatriots, concern a woman
who jumps overboard and does not look back. In the first, the woman's
husband speaks:

> At the cry of "Every man for himself,"
> everyone made for the lifeboats,
> almost everyone, everyone but me.
> It was growing dark and the sea was choppy,
> we saw the bodies fall,
> slam against the lifeboats,
> like vanquished birds, one by one.
> My wife, among the first
> jumped nimbly — the bright beam of a lighthouse,
> her hands to the winds, open like sails,
> her legs in the air,
> a pair of hungry birds,
> behind, a multitude.
> She did not look back.
> As for her body, it alighted on the lifeboat
> a chattering bird, a fighter —

she, magnificent,
>dominating,
>>began to row.
. . . .
The lifeboats drew away
her arms were full as sails
and she rowed firm and sure
with the terrible instinct of mothers
and survivors.
>>In catastrophes, the strongest survive.[40]

For the husband, his wife's leap is pure, magnificent because of its absolute certainty. The woman tells a different story:

If I was bitter it was from sadness.
The captain cried, "Every man for himself"
and I, without thinking twice, threw myself into the water,
as if I were an avid swimmer
as if I had always been waiting for this moment,
the moment of supreme solitude
when nothing has weight
nothing remains
but the unshakable desire to live;
I threw myself into the water, it is true, without looking back.
If I had looked perhaps I would not have jumped
I would have hesitated looking at your great sad eyes
. . . .
"Every man for himself"
the captain cried,
life was a leap, a hypothesis,
to stay, certain death.[41]

The first moment of exile is that life-or-death hypothesis, but living exile takes a long time; and it is not always the same. In a later text, the novel *La nave de los locos* (*The Ship of Fools*), Peri Rossi once again makes use of the metaphor of the ocean voyage.[42] *La nave de los locos* is a complex novel, one of whose central themes is the long middle stage of exile, of living in exile as the human condition. At the beginning of the novel the space is undifferentiated; the Everyman protagonist, Ecks (X), is on a boat in the middle of the ocean, claiming he has never traveled before. Space begins to take shape as place as, first, the narrator plays with place-names. The nonsense cities — Psychos Aires, Merlin — recall real-life places, with only ludic references to history. Finally, toward the end of the novel, Ecks is located in London, a real place at a critical historical moment. Both Ecks and his friend Vercingetorix, who are political exiles (presumably from Uruguay), have specific memory of their homeland, which in Ecks's case manifests itself in his kinetic response to port cities. This is a departure from earlier Peri Rossi texts in which home becomes as hallucinatory as exile, so that the exile has no firm footing anywhere. Space in *La nave de los locos* is not hallucinatory, but it is not simple background, either. Later Peri Rossi novels, *Solitario de amor* (Love solitaire) and *La última noche de Dostoiewski* (Dostoyevsky's last night), seem both more rooted and more at ease in the space they occupy, as are diasporic texts by other writers. The two male protagonists in Marta Traba's *De la mañana a la noche* (*Cuentos norteamericanos*) (From one day to the next: North American stories), one a real student, the other hanging around the periphery of academic life, live in and travel through a New York that they have learned to navigate. Manuel Puig's protagonist in *Maldición eterna a quien lea estas páginas* (*Eternal Curse on the Reader of These Pages*) is similarly comfortable in that city, as are the writers of Luisa Valenzuela's *Novela negra con argentinos* (*Black Novel with Argentines*). Antonio Skármeta's novel *Match boll* (Love fifteen), written in Germany, was probably the last of his exile fiction.[43] It is about a man of fifty who falls in love with a teenage tennis player. The protagonist is a North American physician, married to a German aristocrat; exile is re-created as expatriation. Alberto Madrid, who calls *Match boll* a postmodern narrative, notes that Skármeta's usual style (colloquial language, "demystifying humor," cinematic elements, and so on), which before served a social-realism function, is now not about anything political or social, but rather about the pleasure of the text.[44] Skármeta's previous novel took place in Berlin as well, but it was about the condition of the exile. This novel is simply set there. Its protagonist is comfortable — he has money and lives happily outside his native country, which he has not left traumatically but rather for convenience. Berlin has become just a place to set a novel.

Ana Vásquez's *Abel Rodríguez y sus hermanos* (Abel Rodríguez and his brothers), a grim novel of denunciation, owes much of its immediacy to the author's work as a psychologist with survivors of torture.[45] In *Mi amiga Chantal*, a later novel, Vásquez does not entirely abandon the political questions that drove the earlier novel, but the primary theme of *Mi amiga Chantal*, published in 1991, is the asymmetrical friendship of the narrator, Ana, with the grotesquely fat, ugly, and self-obsessed Chantal. The action takes place against the backdrop of Chilean politics and exile in the 1970s. Chantal's immense need for emotional support and her extraordinary talent for manipulation edge Ana's family life, political work, and work life nearly entirely out of the narrative, almost as if Chantal's physical bulk shut Ana's own slim body out of the frame. The work of Popular Unity, the coup, and the family's experience of exile can be glimpsed in this novel, but as Ana says of her husband's almost miraculous evasion of the military's roundup of leftist academics, "that's another story."[46] As its narrator, Ana claims to be an unwilling participant in Chantal's narrative, but she finds Chantal compelling enough and demanding enough that she allows her family life and her political work to be set aside. The rest of Ana's life does not go away when Chantal makes her demands, and in fact Ana resents Chantal's interruptions. But she also feels some sort of responsibility toward the woman's needs. There are other stories that impose themselves while the story of exile goes on, and those stories also need telling.

One way that men and women experience exile differently from each other may be this very sort of interruption that can, intermittently, take over a woman's time and attention. Other discrepancies, based on class as well as gender, also emerge in exile. These differences may have to do as much with intellectual capital as with material wealth. Few exiles show up on another shore with large amounts of money, although some are writers, musicians, and intellectuals, and the most successful of these enter into a transnational arena of publication, lectures, conferences, and performances. Visibility and mobility do not necessarily translate into easy living, however. Poet and storyteller Alicia Partnoy writes of doing her laundry in a crowded laundromat in her Washington, D.C., neighborhood in the morning and appearing before a group of former heads of state in the afternoon to tell them about human rights violations in Argentina; of having "barely enough money to eat one month" and being flown to England to appear on the BBC to talk about her book the next.[47]

Exile, as it is lived, presents a series of choices and opportunities em-bedded in a mass of exigencies. It may bring, as it did for Partnoy, a terrible celebrity. There are political and psychological reasons for retaining the stance of exile. People who were politically active before they left, who were deported for their political work, are not likely to desist once they are outside their country's borders. At the very least, one participates in solidarity work in order to justify one's own survival. I do not mean to be cynical here; recent exiles can easily experience a deep sense of guilt for having survived when others have not. Everyone who left, left some-body at home. Writers and intellectuals in exile justly claim a moral high ground from which to exhort an international community to pay attention to events in their homelands.

Guatemalan novelist Arturo Arias notes a change in this phenomenon from the earlier part of this century to the contemporary moment. When writers like Miguel Angel Asturias went into exile, they were read and revered as the soul of their country; now the writer and the intellectual are mere mortals. Moreover, they may be positively irritating. One partic-ularly offensive character in José Donoso's *La desesperanza* (translated as *Curfew*) is described as belonging to "this new race of I-was-exiled-and-so-I'm-better-than-you, invested with authority abroad."[48] South African novelist Breyten Bretenbach, who spent years in exile, is brutal about an exile's tendency to demand pity and attention:

I dislike the manner in which [exile] has been romanticized, with the exiled ones pitied and slobbered over by vicarious voyeurs. I abhor feeding the stereotyped expectations of exile as consisting of suffering and deprivation. . . . In the meantime the condition of exile becomes a privileged status from which to morally and emotionally blackmail the world with special pleading. It becomes an excuse for defeat. It is a meal ticket. And yet — isn't it true as well that exile is a chance, a break, an escape, a challenge?[49]

Later, in a more conciliatory tone, he says, "The exiled person is probably marked by a loss that he or she doesn't want to let go of" (71).

Still, Bretenbach makes exile a condition of his writing: "Exile gave me the motifs for my work" (75), and he is acutely aware of the physiological consequences of territorial exile: "Now you can never again entirely relax the belly muscles. You learn, if you are lucky, the chameleon art of adaptation, and how to modulate your laughter. You learn to use your lips properly." Bretenbach's reference to the mouth reminds us that writers, particularly, feel the loss of language in exile. What interests me in Bretenbach's formulation is the physical process, the somatization of exile, that is also part of the process of getting to "after exile" — or at least to the after exile of those who choose to stay, diminishing their foreignness to others, acculturating if not assimilating. This is an act of the body, of the belly muscles, of the mouth. For women it is also a learning of the ways to occupy space safely. As exile is a bodily experience, acculturation, which is part of the process of one version of *desexilio*, is also experienced bodily. This is not the *desexilio* Benedetti conjectured on, but there is another way of living after exile, in the choice to remain in the diaspora — indeed, the distinction between before and after exile for those who do not go back is the shift from exile to diaspora.

This transition from exile to diaspora has, until the present century, meant the irreparable severing of the collective subject from a home in which they may never themselves have lived but through which they have come to know their identity. Contemporary diaspora, still marked by the loss of the place of origin, contains an odd promise of return diminished by the impossibility of full restitution. Only memory, or perhaps the Messiah, can make repossession approach the absolute. The Africa lost by those condemned to the Middle Passage and their descendants has been irreparably changed by colonialism; biblical Israel cannot belong only to Jews after its modern history as Palestine. Beyond this, non-Israeli Jews, like Afro-Caribbeans, Afro-Brazilians, and African Americans, are, however precariously and complicatedly, part of the host cultures where their diasporan parents bore and raised them. Similarly, Chile, Uruguay, and Argentina are marked by the years of military control that will not soon cease to be a threat and will never fully be erased. The stories of these countries' exiles are bound to, and different from, the stories of those who stayed home. Diaspora contains the history of exile, but it now holds as well a certain degree of choice. Yet it is not easy to go home: people who have decent jobs in Europe or the United States may not be able to survive economically in the precarious economies of Chile, Argentina, or Uruguay. There are other reasons to stay as well: new families have been formed, and a new language is learned and made part of one's inner life. Heterosexuals may marry, have children who know no other home. Gay men and lesbians, perhaps now partnered with natives of the new place, may well find greater freedom to live somewhere other than in their former homeland.

One of the most reliable ways of navigating this shift from exile to diaspora, of learning a new language, new foods, new ways, is, as Peri Rossi's narrator in *La nave de los locos* archly tells us, to fall in love. Peri Rossi's irony echoes Bretenbach's denunciatory observations on the pity exiles inspire, but adds to it a deflation of the male exile's pretension by infantilizing him even as she pokes fun at the sentimentality and racism of the women who romanticize exile. Still, there is truth to be had here. Isabel Allende, whose first exile was to Venezuela, where she wrote a Caribbean novel, *Eva Luna*, went to California and married a North American lawyer. Her most recent novel, *El plan infinito* (*The Infinite Plan*), in part woven, she has said, from the strands of his life, is a reading of the American dream.[50] José Leandro Urbina's protagonist is accused of abandoning his friends and his political responsibilities when he marries the Canadian Megan, begins to learn French and English seriously, and enrolls at a Canadian university. Mario Benedetti's Don Rafael counsels, "The essential thing is to adapt. I know that at this age it's hard. Almost impossible. And still."[51] Something as simple as having one's experience understood can begin to make this adaptation possible, though never complete:

> And ever since then [an interaction with a student in which Don Rafael describes what happened in Uruguay, and why, and he is met with comprehension], every afternoon I go home a different way. What's more, now I don't go to *a room*. Or a house. It's simply an apartment, that is, a mock house: a room with things added. But I like the new city. Why not?[52]

New families, new language, new work, and new ways of living are complicated by a sense of identity that persists in connecting the individual with the homeland. Don Rafael's abode in exile may no longer be a sterile "room," but it is not a house/home either. There is a secondary history, a palimpsest that attaches itself to the first, that connects what was exile to diaspora. The exile's sense of identity and sense that exile is a u-topia (a no-place) with promise — the promise that one will survive, at least — transform into the diasporan subject's sense of being elsewhere,

some place, if not *the* place. Diaspora connects the exiles with intellectuals and writers who were already outside the country when the coups
happened, who also feel connected. Saúl Sosnowski's comment that "we
never left," referring to Argentines in the United States and elsewhere,
is a way of indicating that primary intellectual (and emotional) energy
was spent on the homeland. The tireless work of scholars like Sosnowski,
Hernán Vidal, and Marjorie Agosin, already established in the United
States, to tie their scholarship to the political emergency in the countries
they had long ago left attests to the validity of Sosnowski's remark.

Bretenbach speaks eloquently of "after exile": "An exile never returns,"
he writes. " 'Before' does not exist for 'them,' the 'others,' those who
stayed behind. For 'them' it was all continuity; for you it was a fugue
of disruptions. The thread is lost. You made your own history at the cost
of not sharing theirs. The eyes, having seen too many different things,
now see differently."[53] Moreover, those who remained may be reluctant
to acknowledge the pain of exile, recognizing instead only its opportunities, especially for financial advancement. Thomas C. Wright points out
that for some returning exiles interviewed by researchers María Angélica
Celedón and Luz María Opazo, this was their first chance to tell their
stories: "The subject of exile is prohibited in my family," says one of the
eight women Celedón and Opazo interviewed. "They don't want to hear
those stories."[54] The "privilege" of exile brings with it demands for success;
failure is shameful. Donoso's Julio Méndez feels unable to return to Chile
without a published novel and a decent job. Andrés, the protagonist of
Carlos Cerda's *Una casa vacía*, invents a lover left behind in Germany so
that he will not appear pathetic before his Chilean friends and family.

Chilean economist Ricardo Lagos, who left Chile after the coup, illustrates Bretenbach's observations in an anecdote he tells of his return to
Chile in 1978. Lagos, a member of an older generation of leftists, attended
a weekly workshop on the economic and social situation in the country
where a young woman, now an eminent professor, made a point of publicly ignoring him, distancing herself from what she clearly perceived to be
his dangerous behavior:

> For her that workshop (called VECTOR), which met every Monday
> from six to nine at night, was a dangerous activity. There I under-
> stood that there was a different way of understanding Chile among
> these young people who had grown up in the dictatorship and those
> who, a few years older, did not manage to adapt or did not accept a
> situation in which there were evident risks.[55]

The workshop anecdote tells us that there was a generational split in
the understanding of what could be done, how much could be risked.
Lagos makes no value judgment here. The excessive fear of his young
colleague is justified; the older generation is not braver — it was simply

reared in a moment when such activity was normal, and it is not easy to undo that sense of normality. Meeting regularly to discuss questions of economics and government was undoubtedly risky, but on some level it made no sense to Lagos that it should be so.[56] Uruguayan poet and critic Hugo Achugar, who lived part of his exile in Venezuela, also writes movingly of the impossibility of returning, at least to the place as it was before, as the person he was before, as he recounts his (in many ways painful) return to Uruguay. Between Sosnowski's never leaving and Achugar's and Bretenbach's denial of the possibility of return, all belied by their actual movements, we are faced with the impossible, utopic hyperbole of emplacement.

In the first years after redemocratization, much of what was going on in Uruguay, Chile, and Argentina was a struggle to recuperate recent history, often finding meaning where none was apparent before. Poli Délano implicitly rewrites the banal stories of the lives of university students and teachers in the 1960s in *Como si no muriera nadie* (As if no one had died).[57] In the novel's last chapter, narrated by a character who is now a political prisoner, fleeting details concerning political affiliations in the early chapters are catapulted into the foreground. Although sexual and professional intrigues are what most concern the characters narrating the text in the precoup era, all that is swept away in the brutality of the dictatorship, which killed, exiled, or imprisoned many of the characters. Apparently minor political differences in early chapters acquire entirely new meaning now, where they signify life or death. Mario Benedetti's more recent *Andamios* (Scaffolding) recounts the (mostly futile) attempt to reconnect the lives of former political activists after their release from prison and return from exile.[58] These characters cannot recapture the intensity of their politically motivated connection and must rely on the far less intense bonds of friendship, nostalgia, and sexuality, in a kind of reversion to the precrisis relationships Délano chronicles, relationships that had been transformed in the crucible of dictatorship.

Argentine cultural life in the time immediately following the fall of the Videla government was marked by a search for truth, what Kathleen Newman calls an "energetic confrontation with . . . state terror," but people were still afraid.[59] Although testimonies were collected in the Argentine Commission's document *Nunca más* (Never again), witnesses were often still too fearful to come forward to corroborate the survivors' testimonies. The need to remember what happened during the years of repression and exile seems overwhelming, but it is hotly debated. Sanguinetti came to power in Uruguay on a political platform that included what Aidan Rankin calls "a scare-mongering campaign against the opponents of a total amnesty for the armed forces."[60] All three countries have backtracked in the resolve to bring to justice members of the military responsible for abuses. Reconciliation was the goal, but amnesty seems to have been the method of choice for achieving it. At first glance it appears that those most insistent on remembering, on justice, are those who remained outside the country. Mabel Moraña speaks of an evening in Uruguay when she emptied a room full of Uruguayan intellectuals, a number of whom had, like her, lived in exile and were members of what she has called "la generación fantasma," by asking what was being done to get the murderers to trial.[61] Andrés Avellaneda writes about two generations of Argentine writers who refuse to link literature with politics, pointing to "the seduction of not-saying in a society that accepted a ferocious and indiscriminate punishment in the immediate past, and that in the present resists recognizing it."[62]

But the price of willful ignorance is high. Cristina Peri Rossi's short story "Lovelys" begins as an account of an obsessive-compulsive man distressed about the possibility that he might "forget something fundamental, a small, yet decisive, detail."[63] Knowing what to remember is a matter of keeping control, of maintaining personal safety, and also a matter of silence. The presentation of these worries, spoken to a therapist and in a state of apparently groundless dread, indicates that this is a story of an individual's intrapsychic problem. When we learn he is impotent, we are satisfied that we understand the important connections being made between psyche and soma. But the story does not end there; the event he is struggling to keep silent, to forget lest he forget not to remember it, is the military's kidnapping of his neighbor's family, which both he and his wife witnessed. His fear is quite real and quite justified, and, textually speaking, his impotence is only secondarily sexual.

Ariel Dorfman recalls:

What I found when I went back to Chile — a Chile that was democratic, where the struggle was not against a tyrant — was a struggle about what you do with the tyrant's legacy. What do you do with the past? I found myself in a country that, strangely enough, instead of fighting tyranny was discussing openly and circuitously what to do with its own past. I found most Chileans very interested in resurrecting part of the past, some of the horrors that had been done, but not so much that we would destabilize the regime again and bring back the military one more time. In other words, if you investigate all the torture done to everybody, you are going to have to put the whole armed forces on trial. And the problem is that they've got the guns and we don't, so the past was in danger of repeating itself. Living this profound process, the fact that most of my countrymen were willing to resurrect part of the past but not all of it, was very painful. . . . My community back home is as divided as yours was during the Vietnam War. And until we really confront that past we are not going to be able to create a different sort of community.[64]

Dorfman here points to the need to reestablish a national community, and he suggests that while remembering is crucial to that process, amnesty is the price of peace. Amnesty, of course, is quite literally the opposite of memory. And the past that is to be forgotten is precisely the past that has formed this phantom generation, who so badly need their past. To forget that is to deny a central piece of their understanding of who and what they are as argentinos, chilenos, uruguayos. But how, in the first place, does one get to think of oneself as belonging to a nation, being so much of it, in fact, that its adjective becomes a noun that one inhabits, that one *is*?

Chapter Two

SUBJECT OF NATIONAL IDENTITY

> Mi escenario no se restringe a ninguno de esos lugares geográficos que ellos llaman patria.
>
> [My stage is not restricted to any of those geographical places that men call nation.]
>
> — LUCÍA GUERRA

Contemporary distress over the formulation and perpetuation of national identities has perhaps less to do with fear of reification and postmodern rejection of subject-stability than with the real dangers of civil and border wars among groups heavily invested in the sense of themselves as a people. Rwanda, Sudan, former Yugoslavia, what once was the Soviet Union, Ireland, Israel and Palestine, the Koreas, Germany, and South Africa resonate with the power of the assertion of national identity. The questions of who and what the nation includes and who defines it are contested in all these places, as they have been in the geographical reference point of *this* book: Argentina, Chile, and Uruguay, where the war over naming and possessing the nation was brutally fought with the sadly familiar techniques of state terror, as well as with words and images. The struggle between the state's interest in forgetting those pieces of the past that threaten its own legitimacy and the oppositional individual's need to remember precisely what the state legislates forgotten is the problem embedded in the question of who, precisely, is the subject of national identity. National identity is most often theorized in terms of the nation itself, but it can as well be thought of as attaching to the individuals who identify themselves as members of that nation. Exile identity — the sense that one is deeply marked, known to oneself and others, as an exile — is a function of the self's being tied to a particular place where it belongs, however tenuously. Yet as Yossi Shain points out in his study of exile and national loyalty, as subjects located outside the national borders, exiles are rarely taken into account (by political scientists at least) in discussions of the nation.[1] The narrow definition of exile I have been insisting on contains as its principal elements forced separation and a politically construed place of origin whose governing institutions have the ability to impose that separation. Thus the "place one belongs" I am talking about has topographical features and enforced symbolic boundaries recognized — or contested —

by international bodies as well as by less formally constituted groups and by individuals.

What I want to do in this chapter is search out what happens within these boundaries to constitute national identity, or, more precisely, the subject's sense of an identity that is connected with nation, understood as both physical-geographic and symbolic-political space.[2] The nation's geographical features are by definition topographical, inscribed in the landscape itself. Most of them predate human existence on the planet. Its political features are human inventions. Political boundaries often honor topography — the rivers, mountains, oceans that form natural hindrances to access — but the lines distinguishing between contiguous nation-states are primarily the embodied will of one group or another, created by war, annexation, and treaties, and perpetuated by such institutions as border-crossings, customhouses, and language. Physical geography and politics, as avatars of material and discursive reality respectively, will be touch-points of this discussion.[3]

It is useful to keep in mind that the nation-state, whose correlatives in national culture and geographical space are determinant of identity, is itself a modern invention. Pointing out that political exiles have had a significant role in defining the object of political loyalty in Western history, from the city-state to the international proletariat, Yossi Shain argues that "their importance in defining the shift of political loyalty toward the nation became indisputable."[4] His argument suggests that "nation" is in part produced by exile:

> In the early nineteenth century, as the notion of a unified sovereign state striving to enhance its own self-perceived interests by expansion became closely connected with the idea of a culturally and demographically defined nation, political exiles throughout Europe, Latin America, and East Asia led the resistance to imperial rule, advocating national self-government in a recognized homeland.[5]

The nation, then, is to a certain extent an effect of exile, producing itself outside of its own borders.

Most contemporary discussions of national identity at the humanities end of academia concern the "identity" of the "nation," a double abstraction. Their point of origin is Ernest Renan's 1882 Sorbonne lecture, "What Is a Nation?" Renan's idealist version of nation, located in the realm of will and idea, appeals to practitioners of textual analysis, who valorize discursive formations. Renan's rehearsal of what is *not* important in the making of a nation — all the material things like geography or armies or even a common language, in favor of "an aggregate of wills" — is most congenial to us.[6]

Characterizing nation as idea enables us to think of nationhood in new ways; not incidentally, it enables literary scholars to shift the center of gravity toward what we are used to doing — reading texts, the texts in which nation is narrated or narrativized. Fredric Jameson certainly overstates the case when he asserts that *all* third-world narration is about writing the national allegory, but he points us in a fruitful direction: broadly speaking, the literary and national projects are, if not identical, at least connected. And the relationship between narration and nation appeals to literary scholars: Doris Sommer deconstructs the "foundational fictions" of Spanish American nations; Mario Vargas Llosa claims early on the wide open spaces ready for the boom novelists to write the nation and the continent; Francine Masiello elucidates the connections among "women, nation, and literary culture in modern Argentina," the subtitle of her 1992 book; Homi Bhabha cuts straight to the conjunction in titling his edited anthology *Nation and Narration*.[7] Bhabha, who writes about the "cultural construction of nationness as a form of social and textual affiliation," points out that even Julia Kristeva, who tends to work on the intrapsychic level, brings nation into her work as a "symbolic denominator."[8] He also notes that for Renan, nation is a "spiritual principle," assembled by common remembering and, importantly, forgetting.

The use of gendered metaphors in developing the idea of nation has been well rehearsed by feminist scholars, from Annette Kolodny's wonderfully titled *The Lay of the Land*, through Joan Landes's study of the creation of a modern France whose emblem is the suppression of the feminine.[9] Francine Masiello adds to this body of research and theory with her discussions of the ways women and nation are intertwined in the Argentine case. Her reading of Ricardo Rojas's *Eurindia* (1924), in which the virgin body of America is "penetrated by an invasive European force," recalls Kolodny's reading of textual accounts of the settling of the U.S. west.[10] Masiello is more conscious of the racial component of this discourse:

> Silent, communicating only through the impulses of her body, the woman is placed in the service of a national project whose meaning escapes her control; she also conflates European and indigenous traditions in the mind of her observer and forges a new aesthetic from the merger of different cultures.[11]

Masiello goes on to demonstrate how, in the view of the periodical *Inicial* (1923–26),

> a masculinist rhetoric corroborates virtue and patriotism . . . ; the vile elements of society are singularly debased to the sphere of the feminine. It follows that the masculine is the equivalent of self-control and restraint, whereas the feminine is viewed as inimical to the state.[12]

Masiello's focus on the period of Argentine modernization — which she reads through texts by two women writers, Norah Lange and Victoria

Ocampo, that "reverse the patterns of female participation in nationhood so rigorously defined by intellectuals of the early decades of the twentieth century" and "structure an alternative geography for national inquiries" — broadly coincides with the time frame of Renan's assertions.[13] These assertions, concerning the essential elements of a nation, came at a moment when the physical labor of building the modern European nation was coming to an end and when the countries of the Southern Cone were establishing themselves as nations. "Building the nation" denotes the creation of institutions and infrastructure — developing communications and transportation systems, writing constitutions, minting currency, designing a military and putting it into place. All this activity sounds vaguely archaic — the stuff of the eighteenth and nineteenth centuries. More recent discussions of nation-making, particularly in the field of literary and cultural studies, tend to eschew the concrete term "building" in favor of "construction" or "production," terms that have become part of the rhetorical repertoire of cultural studies, feminist theory, and postmodern analysis, as in "the cultural construction of gender," or "María Luisa Bombal's literary production." As metaphors, these words *evoke* but no longer *signify* physical labor.

Benedict Anderson, who dubbed nation an imagined community, is probably the most influential of contemporary cultural critics on the subject.[14] The question remains, however, how and why does the individual subject imagine him or herself into this community? To return to Renan, we may ask: What produces the aggregate of wills? Why and how do individual wills sign on?

The easiest answer, perhaps, involves the nostalgic notion of the organic nation that emerges from an unconscious, collective knowledge of unity. The "people" are inevitably invoked in this version of nation, and in order for it to work they must be taken to be homogeneous, identical subjects striking the same note. The countries of Latin America, however, are notoriously nonhomogeneous, and to fit them into the Procrustean bed of unitary identity requires the same kind of painful adjustments the robber of Attica required of his overnight guests.

The nation is patently nonorganic in America. Any one group's interpretation of nation is always going to be partial, given differences among those claiming title to its meaning. Under the military dictatorships of the Southern Cone of the 1970s, the state took as its task the absolute and complete assimilation of the nation to its definition of itself, emphasizing the subjection of the individual to the state in the term "national subject." It manipulated the technologies at its disposal (television and radio, for example) to catechize the citizenry. The opposition, not surprisingly, used alternative means (writing, song, art, street actions) to undermine the dominant pedagogy and offer an alternative.

Sergio Badilla, Vlady Kociancich, and Miguel Enesco all attend to the paraphernalia of citizenship as it is controlled and apportioned by the state. Badilla's poetry collection *Terrenalis* (1988), published in Stockholm shortly before he left Sweden and returned to Chile, contains a series of visual images, or picture-poems, all of which call into question the intelligibility of language, and some of which reproduce such official identity documents as the poet's birth certificate and passport, ironically altered.[15] In Kociancich's *Los bajos del temor* (The shallows of fear), the bureaucrat Kohen presides over the civil registry but is unable to control the slip-sliding name changes of his friend and even his own daughter, which are only one of the signs of impermanence and undecidability of reality in the novel.[16] In Enesco's novel *Me llamaré Tadeusz Freyre* (My name will be Tadeusz Freyre), identity for the protagonist resides in the passport, that is, in the legitimation conceded by a government and a document. His entire existence is tenuous because he never achieves that legitimation. The novel, like the protagonist's life, hangs on endless deferral.[17]

John Agnew and James Duncan, writing about race and nation, point out that "those who already 'possess' the nation can control who is to be admitted within its borders, as Enesco's protagonist well knows."[18] Agnew and Duncan's insight can, however, just as well apply to the demonization and subsequent ejection of those who were once within, as happened during the dictatorships. We can similarly modify their assertion that "where an equation between a distinctive people and a fixed territory or place is part of the vision of the nation, the ascription of 'race' becomes a basis for exclusion" to note that the ascription of menace, or disease on the body politic, can serve the same function, where the vision of the nation depends on an equation between a distinctive set of behaviors and that fixed territory.[19] The erstwhile "possessors" of the nation endeavored to silence and blot out all claims of nation that were not their own. Their ferocious imposition of nationality is an extreme example of what Homi Bhabha calls "[placing] the people on the limits of the nation's narration," that is, the marginalization of the people in the effort to make the nation.[20] This narration is not just talk; it includes the physical removal of people who threaten state power. In the implementation and imposition of a national identity by a repressive state, the hand of power becomes visible. We can discern people — even if, paradoxically, they are people being expelled from the body politic, as well as the people in power doing the expelling in order to ensure their own place.

But how do those expelling manage to limit the notion of "people" in order to get those who are left to consent to, or at least not oppose, the expulsion? How do they challenge the right of native-born people to "belong" to the nation? The answer has to do with a strategy of disappearances, torture, and murder that terrorizes the general populace into submission. Concurrent with this strategy is an ideological campaign designed to make the victims of state violence appear to be the true villains, who harm the nation and are a danger to its true citizens, and who therefore deserve to be expelled or otherwise dispensed with. These two tactics work effectively together: fear leads to a complicity that such propaganda offers to justify. Any number of ordinary people found themselves convinced by the specious argument that those who were being picked up by the police — to who knew what end — must have done something to provoke the state to its murderous political cleansing of thousands of its citizens: "Por algo sería" (It must be for something). Thus, far from proposing a native-born inhabitant's natural connection to nation, repressive regimes such as Videla's in Argentina and Pinochet's in Chile enforce their own performative, and often racialized, versions of who belongs to the nation, and, by reciprocity, to whom the nation belongs.

The democratic, heterogeneous nation determined to reconcile differences or celebrate them, rather than stamp them out, must be more consciously assembled. Certainly in the multicultural, multiethnic countries of Latin America, this inclusive nation is the only one that can bear all the actual people who might claim it. Ideally, it would be the site of friendly contestation and harmonious interaction. But when the subjects of national identity are not identical to each other, no one can be a perfect representation, or representative, of the nation itself.

Still, national identity and the identity of the national subject are not entirely unconnected. León and Rebeca Grinberg remind us that Freud's only mention of identity was in a psychosocial context, from which Erik Erikson derives that "the term identity expresses 'the relation between an individual and his group.'"[21] Of the psychic structures and social institutions in and through which the relation between individual and group/ nation is forged, citizenship is certainly pivotal. The excision of certain people and groups from presence in the nation to create a version of nation congenial to the goals of a repressive government makes the legislative conferring of citizenship seem benign, almost natural, in contrast. Yet citizenship is the aspect of national identity that is most strongly legislated: it is official, subject to law and in some cases to revocation. Moreover, ideas of what constitutes citizenship vary in different parts of the world. In northern Europe there is a continuing racial/ethnic presumption — that the folk are born to the place, though not necessarily in it, by virtue of blood. This notion is codified into law by conferring citizenship as a matter of parentage, not place of birth. In the Americas, place of birth is of equal weight. One is Chilean or Argentine by virtue of being born in one of those nations. Territory so recently claimed in conquest by outsiders and wrested from their control by revolution by their own descendants, and then adopted by new immigrants, cannot rely on ancestral rights, which would logically revert to the indigenous people on whose land and backs the nation-state was founded. Possession determines belonging — and is determined by physical presence.

Homi Bhabha's essay "DissemiNation," though primarily about the production of the definition of the nation, includes a discussion of the woman or man whose sense of self is at least partly bound up in a consciousness of nationality. I amused myself briefly by thinking I could pay an irreverent tribute to Bhabha by calling this chapter "InsemiNation," but I decided against it, even though it is a pretty good pun. "InsemiNation" points to the individual subject by referring to the intimate act (really series of acts) upon, and in intercourse with, that subject; it is the source of the reproduction of the national, and it contains its own reference to the (reproductively) sexed and, by extension, gendered aspects of the process of producing national identity, and the identity of the national subject. "InsemiNation" suggests a shift in focus from national identity — the nation as it is created in and through stories told (I almost wrote, "stories it tells about itself," but how does an imagined community or a symbolic denominator tell stories? Where is its mouth? Where does it keep its word processor?) by its own subjects — to the subjects of national identity. Such subjects are always imperfectly identified with (or by) the nation; multiple "identitemes" don't always coexist happily. Feeling oneself to be Uruguayan is to have very specific connections to the country, not necessarily all the elements that the idea of "Uruguay" bears. Normative national identity projected onto national subjects is an imagined thing; no person fully fits. Put another way, the imagined community is imagined differently by different subsets that comprise it.

Nation is an abstract figure, and its identity is doubly abstract, whereas human identity has to do with subjectivity, and only indirectly with an amorphous notion of a nation's identity. A person is a physical entity, and also one who experiences consciousness and therefore whose identity is somewhat closer to tangible and is based on material stuff — sights, sounds, smells, presence in a place, and memories of all these. Not only is the individual's identity as a national subject different from the nation's identity, but the former might be called into being only as a result of national catastrophe that impinges on individual experience. Consciousness of self as a national entity may be triggered by separation from the place and from others whose language and behavior are familiar. Someone who has never much thought of herself as Argentine might begin to do so when the country is threatened by military takeover, and she may have that sense of nationality consolidated when expelled from the country and confronted with a perhaps hostile, and certainly unfamiliar, place. The moment of othering can take place within the nation as well. Vlady Kociancich's novel *Los bajos del temor* puts into play the very possibility of establishing identity in the tangles of conflicting and competing levels of representation. Byrne (aka Teddy Coper), its protagonist, experiences this sense of first awareness, not just of national identity but of nationalism, in conversation in Buenos Aires with North Americans who treat Argentina with disdain:

"How much does Martel pay? In dollars, a pittance, in pesos, I don't know. My guess is that he pays you the minimum. That Martel is no fool. But he was born in the wrong country and he's too old to be changing his ways."

"If it's about ambition, we were all born in the wrong country," said Coper, with an anger that surprised him. The [American] nun and Dickens managed to light a spark of nationalist fire where none had ever been before.[22]

To put it more strongly, and more generally, identity as a national sub-ject depends on friction and is often tied to loss, lack, and longing. Perfect self-identity would be unconscious, self-referential, with no outside coor-dinates. It would not betray its having to be learned. The pedagogical aspect of identification with a nation — what we might call citizenship training — begins with a system of institutions (school, army, perhaps fam-ily) in which the nation is already inscribed as an idea(l), institutions that educate the subject in national virtues and national traits. Loyalty and history are transformed into identity. It is the task of the institutions to encourage or legislate performance as a national subject, binding abstrac-tions of nation to those fragments of knowledge and experience that the subject internalizes. But this all presupposes a gap between the ideal and the material. The institutional meaning of nation and the subject's role in it must be projected onto individuals whose own history, agency, de-sire, experience, and social location make them elusive targets. Manners and mores, even what is considered human nature, are produced locally and can be brought to consciousness by the contrast between home and elsewhere.

Identity, then, has to do with memory and with control of discourse.[23] For postexiles, national identity is very much about individual identity, forged in exile and in resistance to "othering." The reconciliation of self under these circumstances is a complex task; the postexile who does not return is always something of an outsider. As is the one who does return. Jorge Abril Trigo writes about the impossibility of national iden-tity — a concept that presupposes its opposite — in an article whose title, "Fronterías: Liminaridad: Transculturación: Para una hermeneútica de la neomodernidad posuruguaya" (Borderistics: Liminarity: Transculturation: Toward a hermeneutic of post-Uruguayan neomodernity), parodies the no-tions of space and history we take so seriously.[24] The piece reads like a series of displacements on the problem of displacements, history becoming nostalgia for what was not, for what would be a falsified view of the nation if there was something akin to a true view of the nation, which there also is not. Abril Trigo describes a history and a space that are nostalgically hallucinatory. In an almost comically Freudian gesture he maintains that the problem is not so much about Uruguayan national identity but about size and placement: "la integridad y la (in)definición territorial" (173), of living in a nation that is small, so marginal.

Luisa Valenzuela's dense and complex *Novela negra con argentinos* (*Black Novel with Argentines*) plays with any number of identity formations: gender, profession, class.[25] Over and over again, identity depends on issues of performance and nonperformance. Roberta and Agustín are writers who do not write. The novel poses a series of interrelated questions: What produces certain acts? How are we responsible for our actions? (What happened inside and outside of Agustín to "cause" him to kill Edwina?) How do our actions determine who we are, or how does who we are determine (the meaning of) our actions? What difference does context make? What, specifically, is the relationship between political torture in Argentina and the sexual torture of willing victims in New York? Disguise is central to the text and to the characters' lives, and a change of hairstyle or color, shaving a beard, or revising a wardrobe are all enactments of self, performances that constitute not just plot but personality. Nevertheless, the one identity that is not called into question is the protagonists' nationality. It is prominent in the title, and Agustín and Roberta always know themselves to be Argentines. This is a core identity, one that would not need to be named but for the fact that they are displaced. The displacement is not, however, emblematic of utter alienation. Roberta, especially, knows her way around New York. She is a foreigner, but no longer a stranger. Agustín trusts her because she is in a way his double, and she is his double in large part because, in New York, she is the one who can differentiate between "Latin American" and specific nationality, and share that nationality with him. But as a woman, she cannot be his perfect double, and in fact his fear of her sexual jealousy keeps him from telling her the whole truth about the murder he committed: that his victim was a woman.

In Valenzuela's novel both Roberta and Agustín are the self- and externally identified Argentines of the title. This equal bestowal of citizenship on differently gendered individuals is worth mentioning, for it is not self-evident that the identification with nation is to be produced universally among those born there. These two characters are differentially able to acculturate to New York, suggesting a certain underlying asymmetry in their relationship to Buenos Aires. Not all wills are to be equally aggregated under the banner of nation. A return to Renan reminds us that the subject, as originally construed, is relentlessly male and upper-class. In the Parisian university of the late nineteenth century, Renan spoke of men to an audience he addressed as "gentlemen."

But closer to the truth may be that, despite the perhaps inadvertent exclusion of women by theorists of nation and their more explicit exclusion by designers of national constitutions, women do feel themselves connected and have been conscripted to the project of nationhood. This has been accomplished most overtly and obviously in the ideology of re-publican motherhood, but it occurs in other, more subtle, ways as well. Femininity is widely enlisted to allegorize the nation. This gesture, which makes of (abstract) woman the carrier or emblem of the nation, need not mean that she is also thereby accorded citizenship, but it can serve to en-gage (real) women's affective connection to the nation in whose emblem they see themselves. Francine Masiello has argued elegantly and persua-sively that from the beginnings of the nation in the nineteenth century through the 1930s, Argentine women writers graph a response to what it means to be conscripted to the national project as symbol rather than subject, wresting back a subject position from which they write a more complex story of nation that depends on internal fracture and difference.[26] Writing about Juana Manuel Gorriti, Rosa Guerra, and Eduarda Mansilla, Masiello notes that "though disparate in their projects, they were joined by a common wish to link women's perspective to a new national dis-course in formation and to enter the public arena through the privileges of authorship."[27] Later she says:

> The urge to heterogeneity [in the face of the unifying project of nation-building] is reflected in the writings of these women as a signal to defy the linguistic authority of the state and advance a voice of their own. . . . The double messages of cross-cultural insem-ination, the clash of oral and print expression, and the confusion of Indian and colonizers' discourses (in which the woman is identi-fied invariably with the concerns of Indians) are brought to bear on the confrontation of dominant and oppressed groups, with women serving as mediators in such struggles.[28]

Women during this period had a markedly different view of the way the nation was to be envisioned, insisting on gendered difference and valuing it. According to Masiello, Norah Lange's and Victoria Ocampo's feminine figurations of nation-building contrast markedly to

> Ricardo Rojas's silent dancer, who melded indigenous and cos-mopolitan Americas by the rhythmic impulses of her body alone. . . . Drawn into the intimacies of family exchanges and personal-ized by the dynamics of female subjectivity, the map of Argentina is reshaped [by Lange and Ocampo] to celebrate an autonomous territory belonging primarily to women.[29]

Masiello also discusses socialist women of the period, who "issued a dramatic call for their participation in national events."[30] They take up questions concerning such oppressed groups as indigenous peoples, workers, and women, insisting that these be part of the national agenda.

Clearly, if we take woman as our starting point, the question of how the subject of national identity is formed runs into trouble. The institutional means — soldiering and willingness to die for the nation, political participation through the vote, and candidacy for office — were not available to women, who have had to fight long and hard for the privilege of even a portion of these responsibilities. Virginia Woolf averred that women had no country — their nationality, like their name, was that of a father or husband, not their own. Therefore women need have no loyalty, no patriotism. Yet Woolf was nothing if not British, constituted as such via family, language, and the society she kept. Writing in the same period as Woolf, the Argentine novelist Norah Lange similarly questions the principles of nation and state, while her compatriot, educator-writer Herminia Brumana, rejects any patriotic call to arms. More recently, the narrator of Lucía Guerra's novel *Más allá de las máscaras* (Beyond the masks) takes pains to point out that her story, which takes place in an unnamed country that reads very much like contemporary Chile, "is not restricted to any of those geographical places that [men] call nation [*patria*]," suggesting that the very concept of *patria* is a masculine invention.[31]

Starting from woman virtually requires us to find another path to the establishment of a subject that identifies itself with reference to nation, for that women do so is incontrovertible. Whether women *should* identify nationally or not is another issue. Many politically and culturally active women have, in the modern era, been drawn to international politics and transnational formations. Victoria Ocampo's literary review *Sur*, often excoriated for its elitism, for example, may as well be understood as a gesture that is less about the disparagement of Argentine national culture than an appeal to an internationalist perspective that in fact would draw Argentina to the attention of Europe. Mistrust of nationalist provincialism does not obviate the fact that women think of themselves nationally and furthermore indicates that an important distinction can and should be drawn between national identification and nationalism.[32]

Without discarding the effect of a pervasive national ideology that contaminates even those who do not enjoy full citizenship, I would like to suggest another basis for identifying nationally: specifically, the physical connection to place. Agnew and Duncan argue that place "serves as a constantly re-energized repository of socially and politically relevant traditions and identity which serves to mediate between the everyday lives of individuals . . . and the national and supra-national institutions which constrain and enable those lives."[33] National identification depends on a sense of place and of belonging to that place. Although Roberto González Echevarría is referring to the abstract notion of national identity when he recognizes the prevalence of landscape metaphors in the writings of the creators of the nations of Latin America, this connection is a crucial element in the production of the subject of national identity. It is the stuff of place, and also of language and of memory.[34]

Access to the landscape — freedom and means to travel and to claim ownership — is differentially apportioned by reason of economic, political, and gender disparities. The free subject's sense of entitlement to the landscape contrasts with the bonded peasant's legal inseparability from the land (in the Spanish American context, we can think in terms of the *latifundios*, whose native populations were part of the property deeded to the new Spanish owners). What they share despite the enormous disparity between them is the sense of connection to the land. The inveterately urban Ocampo, whose family owned significant territory in the countryside, stakes her claim to being not only Argentine but American in part via her identification with the flora of the pampas.[35] Mary Louise Pratt discusses the way class and gender difference play out in one's sense of relation to the landscape and how that manifests itself in literary texts. She contrasts the promontory stance of Pablo Neruda's godlike purchase on the heights of Machu Picchu with Gabriela Mistral's meanderings, hand in hand with an Indian child, through the Chilean landscape in *Poema de Chile* (Poem of Chile).[36] For Pratt, the poet's gender is central to the difference in the representation of landscape and the speaker's relationship to it. The woman speaker is not symbolic of the land, nor is she insentient as the land; she is, rather, its knowledgeable inhabitant, imparting that knowledge to the child who walks with her, who himself is far from a passive recipient of her teaching. Mistral's woman in the landscape finds a contemporary echo in Alicia Partnoy's "Ars Poetica," also a poem of movement — these women are not static — that eschews heights:

> That which flies close to the ground
> is my poetry.
> Tracker of scents
> among the weeds.
> I do not seek lofty heights.
> Heights make me dizzy.
> So I charge down on distance
> flying low.[37]

Partnoy's poetry, like her prose, is entwined with her human rights work and is in many ways born of her own imprisonment, torture, and exile. The national subject, particularly one without institutional ties, or who is oppositional, develops a sense of national identity via a sense of belonging to a place.

Most often that place is a fragment of the space the nation occupies, and indeed the notion of the *patria chica*, the region or province or state or town to which one belongs, is of long standing in Hispanic cultures. Often the subject's sense of connection to place is not conscious until s/he has been removed from it. For exiles, place, which "represents both a context for action and a source of identity,"[38] is crucial to identity and action, because they are separated from it. Andrés Avellaneda points out that once exile becomes an issue, especially in the context of postmodern sensibility, the place one speaks from acquires singular importance:

> Thus, as soon as we leave aside the traditional notion of the produc-
> ing subject — unity and center of meaning — the exile of the Latin
> American intellectual requires us to pose the question of the wider
> project into which cultural work is carried out. With the intellec-
> tual person understood as a social entity, and cultural discourse as a
> code produced in relation to other codes and discourses, *it becomes*
> *especially important to consider the place from which one speaks,* the
> means of articulation of discourse and of intellectual labor. *Forced*
> *geographical relocation produces fractures and disalignments in literary*
> *projects that should be analyzed in detail in order to reveal the totality of*
> *what is intended to be isolated as the "matter of the nation."*[39]

The characters in Marta Traba's *En cualquier lugar* (In any place) and José Leandro Urbina's *Cobro revertido* (Collect call) re-create a home culture in exile, consisting of individuals who might not have found them-selves in proximity at home at all. But the relation to place may surface in oblique ways for the exile, as in Peri Rossi's "Las estatuas, o la condición del extranjero" (Statues, or the condition of the foreigner), where the site of the tale lacks meaning for the protagonist, or in *La nave de los locos* (*The Ship of Fools*), where exile is explored as the human condition, and there is an overriding sense of uprootedness. The identification with place is refracted in the richness of the off-center geography in expatriate nov-els such as *La casa verde* (*The Green House*) and *Cien años de soledad* (*One Hundred Years of Solitude*) and in Cortázar's making the reader imitate, however palely, Oliveira's sense of imbalance between countries, between languages, and between one window and another, by flipping the pages of *Rayuela* (*Hopscotch*).[40]

Embracing exile identity presupposes some sense of what one is exiled from, that there *is* exile. But it does not necessarily follow that there was another identity just as strong, the identity of the self as a national subject within the nation. That sense of national identity may, as I have noted above, emerge precisely at the moment it is called into question, and the awareness of the self as other in another place is what requires conscious-ness of the self as self somewhere. Exile may precipitate, or intensify, a sense of nationality. Political exiles must counter the claim of those they are escaping, or who put them out, that they are not authentic nationals. The individual's sense of dislocation in exile probably intensifies the sense of self as a part of a nation. Activism in a resistance movement may well be predicated on a sense of belonging to the nation, presupposing some sort of national consciousness, some claim on the nation, even a form of patriotism. Such symbols of resistance as indigenous music, the unfenced land, and the revolution as mother tie family, racial identification, and geography to a communal project based on a myth of connection that is common purpose. National identity in exile foregrounds difference from the host country and intensifies identification with others from home. Expatriates may also have heightened national identity as a defense against the normativity of the host place that threatens them with erasure. It is disconcerting, for example, to find oneself explaining, interpreting, and even apologizing for American behavior that one would criticize at home.

This sense of oneself as Chilean, Uruguayan, or Argentine may consist of preexisting elements of identity that assemble themselves a posteriori, in memory, like metal shavings around a pole magnet, or as in the process of crystallization:

> the space in which we have moved, the familiar
> landscape
> common knowledge, popular culture
> schooling, experience in shared events
> smells, flavors, sounds.

There is a certain concordance between the Derridean insight that definition depends on difference and lack depends on what is left out, and Renan's pronouncement that national identity is based on a collective will to history that is itself predicated on a common agreement of what is to be forgotten. These theoretical notions come true in painfully brutal ways in the will to reconstruct and heal the nation after dictatorship in the Southern Cone. For the opposition, it is crucial to denounce the dictatorships and the state terror that held them up. For those in prison or in exile, for the families of the detained and disappeared, not only memory but also punishment of the perpetrators of the crimes of torture, murder, harassment, and exile are the minimum price the country needs to pay to atone for its sins and to discourage others from behaving that way in the future. Amnesty (literal forgetfulness of the crime so that punishment becomes nonsensical — if we do not remember there was a crime, how can we punish it?) is anathema. Amnesty is a cover. Neither the perpetrators nor the victims forget. It is they, and particularly the perpetrators, who might reactivate their programs given the chance, who are amnestied, but the forgetting is a sham because it is incomplete.

If memory is a key to nation, Renan points out, there must be as well some consensus concerning what is forgettable, in fact what must be forgotten, to consolidate the nation. This observation resonates ominously with the project of amnesty, official forgetting, in the nations of the Southern Cone. The argument has been made that in order for normal life to proceed, the past must be put behind; there must be a national reconciliation predicated on amnesty for those who carried out the Dirty Wars. Tulio Halperín Donghi talks about a structural need to forget:

It is this situation, unprecedented in Argentine history, that perpetuates the need of a version of history that will cover almost all the past beneath a thick blanket of silence, now to better assure its compatibility with those two versions, themselves perfectly incompatible, loaded down with the factious memories of two political movements whose rivalry, which they try to forget, fills the last forty years of our history, and that in addition define in radically different ways their ties to previous history.

But this same mutation affects in perhaps a less negative way the forces that are not oriented toward expurgating the past from memories that are dangerous for the fragile agreement that is now being born, but that instead try to see history from the point of view of a present that is no longer that of 1976, but that can no longer be that of 1973 either.[41]

Halperín is what the papers call cautiously optimistic, saying that at the moment of his writing it seems that "we find ourselves facing the first attempt at a new image of Argentine historical experience."[42]

Although the strategy of selective forgetting may work for many of those who remained at home, who were at least grazed by, but also shielded from, the realities of terror while living in its midst and in the midst of official obfuscation, most of those who were in exile are repelled by the very idea. The question of justice is paramount here, but because it is also self-evident, I will bracket it for a moment to try to attend to the difference in perceptions concerning amnesty. People who remained at home and who did not get caught in the net of state brutality experienced a continuity lived in the dailiness of their lives with no particular need to confront and question their national identity, accommodating, with whatever difficulty, to repression in order to survive. For them, who did live it and did survive, there is no psychological need to relive it in order to put it behind. Those who were in exile constructed a sense of self-as-exile inextricable from the sense of self as national subject, itself dependent on a construct of the nation consisting of memory. The past that the conciliators demand be forgotten is precisely the past that has formed these exiles and their nation; it consists of the critical events that ejected them from home and refused them return. To forget them is to deny a central piece of their understanding of who and what they are as Argentines, Uruguayans, and Chileans. National identification for those who suffered exile is *not* predicated on embracing the political hybrid — the reconciliation of the murderers and the survivors of their terror, or of the difference between themselves and others beyond the national boundary. It is about internal differentiation, about returning to reclaim a social and political space that has inevitably changed during their absence, in order to displace, to whatever extent possible, the generals and the culture of fear. During the dictatorships the military state waged an ideological battle, fought on discursive ground, concerning the meaning of nation, of patriotism.[43] To surrender memory of that battle is to risk having its (temporary) victors keep their discursive territory, so that they still name who is a real Chilean, who can claim authenticity as Argentine, who counts as Uruguayan.

However, pragmatically speaking, as Dorfman says, the military, who were the perpetrators, still have access to the guns that made them so dangerous in the first place. If they perceive themselves threatened, they will likely retake power. Amnesty, then, is not the road to happiness; it is simply the best way to defuse a frightening and perilous situation. It leaves the structures that allow abuse of power in place, because they are too dangerous to dismantle, much like a mine that is best left alone rather than tampered with — the chances of a new explosion if defusing is attempted are far too high. But the mine could go off anyway.

Add to this the preference to put the past behind, the deep need to deny complicity, and the understandable desire to try to get on with a life that feels normal, and the impulse to forget is more than understandable. The opposite desire is also fully comprehensible from the point of view of those who suffered prison or exile in their own bodies, or whose friends and family did. For them the wounds stay open and running until some closure is put to the period of state terror and the criminals are brought to justice. This is not just a case of contested meanings, but of contested *means* to get past, to get over, the time of rending. If only those who are victimized, or who are potential victims, forget, then they are prime targets for having history repeat itself on them. But "amnesty" is a different word from "forgetting" precisely because the forgetting is figurative, and because it always refers to a kind of loaded memory, the memory of some wrong that is being forgotten as a way of avoiding its being forgiven.

The *desexiliados* must reconcile the different lives they lived elsewhere to the life that went on at home — reconcile not in the sense of making peace between the two but in bringing them together and making sense of them as necessary parts of a whole. People are bearers of place; the elsewheres the exiles lived became a little Latin American because of their presence; what they remembered as marking home changed as a result of their leaving, of the dictatorships, and of the inevitable metamorphosis any complex living organism, whether individual or nation, undergoes with the passage of time.

Chapter Three

FROM SPACE TO PLACE
The Processes of Exile

Allá, siempre había hecho el mismo camino para volver a casa.
Y *aquí* echaba eso de menos. La gente no comprende ese tipo de
nostalgia. Creen que la nostalgia sólo tiene que ver con cielos y
árboles y mujeres. A lo sumo, con militancia política. La patria,
en fin. Pero yo siempre tuve nostalgias más grises, más opacas.
Por ejemplo, ésa. El camino de vuelta a casa. Una tranquilidad,
un sosiego, saber qué viene después de cada esquina, de cada
farol, de cada quiosco. *Aquí*, en cambio, empecé a caminar y a
sorprenderme. Y la sorpresa me fatigaba. Y por añidadura, no
llegaba a casa, sino a la *habitación*.

[*There*, I had always taken the same route home. And *here* I
missed that. People don't understand that kind of nostalgia. They
think nostalgia only has to do with skies and trees and women.
At most, with political militancy. The country, when you come
right down to it. But I always had grayer, more opaque, nostalgias.
That one, for example. The route home. A tranquillity, a calm,
to know what comes after each corner, each lamppost, each
kiosk. Here, however, I began to walk and got surprised. And the
surprises made me tired. And what's more, I didn't arrive home,
but to my *room*.]

— MARIO BENEDETTI

When democracy was restored to Uruguay, Argentina, and Chile between
1983 and 1990, people in exile could, juridically speaking, go back home.
Some did; others have remained in the Latin American diaspora. Where
return is possible, diaspora is a version of what Mario Benedetti has famously called *desexilio*, and the passage from exile to diaspora is as well
worth charting as the one from exile to repatriation. What accounts for
the decision to stay or to return depends to a certain degree on what
happens during exile, for exile is not a single experience, either across
populations or over time.[1]

In this chapter, I turn my attention to the processes of acculturation
and alienation that ultimately engender the "voluntary" diaspora or impel and enable return. Acculturation moves along axes of transition from

space to place; alienation, effected both internally by keeping oneself apart and externally by being perceived as "other" or not at all, is the drag on the process. Seen in this fashion, it is clear that alienation and accultura-tion are not mutually exclusive. Nor am I suggesting that exile experience is exhausted by alienation and acculturation. For example, José Leandro Urbina's *Cobro revertido* (Collect call) as well as being a tale of alienation and acculturation, is also a story of the struggle between the fear of return and longing to do so.[2]

Don Rafael, the superbly self-aware character in Mario Benedetti's *Primavera con una esquina rota* (Springtime with a broken corner), muses on the complex meaning and experience of exile:

> Am I a foreigner? There are days I am sure I am; others when I don't give it the least importance; and finally still others (to be more precise, they are nights) when I in no way admit this foreignness to myself. Could it be that the condition of being foreign is a state of mind?[3]

Javier, the protagonist of Benedetti's later novel *Andamios* (Scaf-folding), demonstrates the push-pull of the processes of alienation and acculturation in a description of the stages of his exile:

> The first, the one where you refuse to unpack your suitcases... because you have the illusion that you'll return tomorrow. Every-thing seems strange to you, indifferent, unconnected.... The second stage is when you begin to get interested in what's going on around you.... [F]inally, the political bars that kept you from going back begin to fade. Only then does the third and definitive stage begin, and that's when you get the lusty, almost absurd itch, the fear of losing your blessed identity.... [T]he return home starts to become absolutely necessary.[4]

Javier speaks as though these three stages are universal, as though the desire to return must arise in any exile. Yet his own wife and daughter choose to remain behind in Spain when he goes back to Uruguay. Only at the end of the novel do they decide to join him, a decision that seems unmotivated on their part but necessary for the novel's sense of comple-tion. In fact (as well as in other fictions) the desire to return home on the part of one individual in a family always implicates the rest of the family, but it does not necessarily mean all will return.

In considering the processes of exile, I believe it is essential to track the ways in which they are connected to the material world. Here I again expose my desire to get beyond representation, behind metaphor, to what Adrienne Rich has called "the wreck and not the story of the wreck / the thing itself and not the myth."[5] It may seem perverse to try to do this by invoking metaphor and reading novels and short stories, but the literary text's knowledge of itself as a fiction can point the way to the place where body and territory, as well as both of these and representation, meet and part ways. My focus, then, is on the literal, territorial exile that is a removal in space as well as spirit and on the representation of physical uprootedness, of the individual's removal from a familiar place to a new space that has, at least at the beginning, no recognizable landmarks. And language never escapes its function as representation.

Yi-Fu Tuan opened the discussion of space and place in 1977 with his book of that title.[6] For Tuan, space is place without meaning, or to reverse the terms, place is space that has been given meaning by the human mind through a process of narrativizing. Let us, then, begin with text. The very idea of literary or textual space is a metaphor; and, strangely, it is space we talk about in literary texts, not place — except in such idiomatic expressions as "this novel takes place in Santiago, in 1973." But what is the space of the text? the volume we hold? worse, the erasable lines on a computer screen that remain contingent until we tell the machine to convert them into hard copy? or the already metaphorical mental space of the electrical connections between eye, brain, and memory? How did we get back to space, the unbounded, provisionally prediscursive, here? The space of the narrative text is supremely discursive. Tautologically discursive.

Literature itself is called a space; it is one of the "sites" oppositional notions "occupy." Beatriz Sarlo writes, "In a hard-to-occupy space during the years of the dictatorship, literature tried, not to offer complete and articulate answers, but to surround this resistant and awesome nucleus that might be named 'the real.' "[7] In Sarlo's figuration, literature takes on physical proportions, not just as printed books but both as a zone buffering the precious nucleus of reality and as the material occupying that zone. Language makes the nucleus visible. By filling, enlarging, and protecting it, language represents, elaborates on, and even becomes that reality.

When space is used as a metaphor, it accrues value and meaning of its own. In an article on the multiplicity of languages under dictatorship in Argentina, Francine Masiello tells us that writing occupies metaphoric spaces, with oppositional writing occurring in the periphery:

> The enterprise can be defined in the expansions and contractions of permissive public spaces, a new topographical mapping of the battlefields in favor of a cultural expression and opposition. Torn between the center and the periphery, between the dominant discourse and the possibility of something different, Argentine writers and artists cultivated the marginal space that offers an alternative to the centralizing immobility of the regime.[8]

Masiello's analysis is, appropriately, replete with spatial imagery. She writes of the massive exile resulting in "a nation separated from itself," of how "a new territory is defined," and of how "dissidents were rendered invisible, evacuated from the place of human dialogue."[9] She makes a connection between physical (that is, spatial) isolation and discursive isolation and notes the multiple sites of writing: from within Argentina (Piglia), from exile (Martini), and within an "international circuit of interchanges" (Traba).[10]

When spatial notions are applied to objects that have no physical boundaries and no actual spatial relationship to each other, they confirm and produce meaning for those terms when they have to do with actual space. T. S. Eliot called the grounding term of metaphor the objective correlative, but the correlative is not objective at all. It depends, rather, on culturally sanctioned beliefs, codified, in however covert a way, as ideology. Masiello's spatial metaphors testify to power relations in sway during the Videla regime. Other spatial metaphors go further than confirming reality; they constitute it. Those dealing in the distinction between public and private, for example, relating them to men's and women's spheres respectively, have codified distinctions based on class privilege (only some women can afford to remain out of public commerce) and have held sway even after it became clear that they did not hold in reality. Even visual representations shore up hegemonic notions of spatial relations. Writing on cartography and reality, Eduardo Galeano says, "Even the map lies. We learn world geography on a map that does not show the world as it is, but rather as its masters demand that it be."[11]

The forced consensus of the map suggests to what extent the codification of space requires consent. Such consent is produced not only via representations but also by the experience of place. Maurice Halbwachs considers how both individual and collective memory take their "anchoring point on spatial images" and, more specifically, on the "material environment," "the home," and "the material appearance of the city," so that "[t]he place...has received the imprint of the group, and vice versa."[12] This imprint becomes part of the identity of the group, the individual, and the place, binding the three together. The expatriate Byrne, who abandons one identity to take up another in Vlady Kociancich's *Los bajos del temor* (The shallows of fear), claims not to miss his country, but he goes on to say that he remembers his youth only as "the profile of the city that you see from the Río de la Plata" and continues to link that to a collective experience of an amalgam of personal memories and places:

> Despite my good intentions, I cannot envision that side of my life except as the profile of the city that you see from the Río de la Plata. In the proud, gray, lofty face of Buenos Aires, the city's people are no more than the shadows of a few mutable strokes. I, myself, although I was too aware of the minutiae of my youth, fell victim to the city's alchemy, which fuses personal stories in the retort of

its own story, streets and loves, neighborhoods and enmities, voices and noises, passions and coffee, an indestructible amalgam. I do not even remember in what stretch of those days in November I stopped being Teddy Coper and turned into Byrne. But I remember vividly the details that were being left behind.[13]

Teddy Coper gives up his identity and leaves Buenos Aires willingly, but when the individual is rent from the collective, memory of the lost place may be too much to bear. The lost place of origin needs to be contained, to become manageable *as* memory. Elsa Repetto's narrator in the short story "Destierro" (Exile) finds that this intimate knowledge of self and space needs to be tamed — to *become* memory in fact. Before that moment, the idea of succumbing to thoughts of Buenos Aires is overwhelming, threatening the speaker with a kind of obliteration of the self: "A country destined to oblivion in time and space, that you fear has been forgotten on the other side of the ocean, existing only in memory. For a long time I could not remember you, I was afraid that nostalgia was death, entangling me like a spider's threads, like the quicksand in a bog."[14] The place the narrator left is no longer fixed and secure: the Spanish *olvido* is etymologically linked to oblivion and obliteration, so much stronger than the English "forgetting." Furthermore, memory is linked in the narrator's mind to nostalgia, itself figured as quicksand and bog — the instability of the very ground — or the spider's web. The space of home, so tightly bound up with the exile's identity, not only has lost its fixity but has become a site of engulfment. To invoke the space of home in this state is to risk shattering an already precarious sense of self. It is only when the speaker can reestablish the solid contours of the lost place, to restore it *as* memory, that it is safe to let it come to consciousness: "It was like this, simply, when I saw you appear...that I knew I could finally remember you, that your time had come, and mine as well, when I could turn you into memory."[15]

The historical and psychological context is crucial to the experience not only of the place left behind but also of the site of exile.[16] Laura, in Poli Délano's *Como si no muriera nadie* (As if nobody died), once lived and studied in London, which, at the novel's end, becomes her place of exile. She writes:

> This journey is not like other journeys. I am in the same place I was before and it is not at all the same. London cannot have changed much, but I can. . . . London is prison, exile, the place one must be but does NOT want to be, because absolute and quick return is the only answer we have, the only battle cry, the only way of knowing that we were destroyed but not defeated.[17]

London for Laura is doubly "not-same." The trip is not like other trips, and the place is not as it was before. As the emergency home during exile, it is not the same as the real home, and as what for the foresee-able future is her only possible home, it does not allow for the liberating superficiality of the visit. The difference Laura finds in London is not so unlike the radical changes in the sense of space undergone by Renata, the character who repeatedly refuses the opportunity to go into exile in Vlady Kociancich's *Últimos días de William Shakespeare* (*The Last Days of William Shakespeare*).[18] The defamiliarization of Renata's space takes the form of a tunnel in a Buenos Aires park that becomes the conduit to a mysterious and dangerous space where people disappear and probably die, a not-so-subtle reference to the terrifying clandestine disappearances that took place in the once familiar territory of Argentina during the 1970s. Simi-larly, the National Theater hides in plain sight. It occupies a city block, but it is virtually impossible to locate. The uncanny park and theater, like Laura's experience of space in both London and Santiago, have become unreliable, in instances of what Anthony Vidler calls "false permanence."

Vidler's notion of the false permanence of space names "the problem ... of spatial models conceived to center and ground the subject that are used to comprehend conditions where this subject is neither originating nor present."[19] Vidler speaks metaphysically here, about the human con-dition, concerned with the instability of the subject in the postmodern context. But as Délano's Laura shows, Vidler's words can be brought to bear on the very material reality of the exile subject, who, as exile, is either the subject not originating or the subject not present, but never both at the same time. The exile, spatially, originates somewhere and is not present there or is present somewhere from which s/he does not orig-inate. Moreover, there is always the problem of the residual in the exile subject: the stuff that is borne along from the place of origin, what accrues in the present place. Laura finds herself in London, waiting for the famil-iar buses of Santiago, unconsciously projecting herself into that space. She emphasizes the primacy of place memory over other sorts in relating her sense of loss: "I am incapable of expressing all I feel, or of communicat-ing as I would like the furrows carved into my soul since I lost my land, my center, my firm foundation, my whole context. Not the empanadas, Armando, or chicha in September, or the pastel de choclo. It's something else, y'know?"[20]

Space, for Laura, is *also* material, not only discursive. Yet there is reason to pause at the notion of the discursivity of space. Consider, for example, this irresistible missive from a dying hand: "Space may be the projection of the extension of the psychical apparatus. No other derivation is prob-able."[21] Space in these deathbed jottings is tentatively a product of mind, and makes mind itself responsible for the vastness, or limitation, of space. What other benediction than this — Freud's final observation — do we need to conjoin space and psyche?

Space is an abstract term, an idea with a history, as Victor Burgin and Anthony Vidler have maintained.[22] For Edward Soja, it is a cultural construct in need of analysis. Soja argues for a theorizable space, space that has been constructed and is not simply the ground on which history transpires.[23] Postmodern histories of space tend toward an evolutionary model that goes something like "space/space-time/space-mind," but do not often take into account the residual ways of experiencing space, specifically "the survival of optical, perspectival models of spatial structure based on the cone of vision and the plane of representation, that are retained in the analysis of psychical spaces formed by projection and introjection."[24] That is, the visual keeps getting in the way of the mental. Space, as we know it, is, perhaps, a function of language; but space and the physical, material world it grounds and represents are also constructive of language. There *is* a physical world, of which we make sense by a kind of graphing and that remains even in our absence — to be graphed, differently perhaps, by others.

Once we have taken the crucial step of problematizing the gaze, the gazed-upon is loosened from the gaze's rigidity. It is free, if it is animate, to return the gaze; and even if not, other gazers may see it from different perspectives. As I noted in chapter 2, Mary Louise Pratt shows just how this is accomplished in her reading of two geo-graphic texts, one, Pablo Neruda's "Las alturas de Machu Picchu," in which the poet is located above the landscape and takes it in from a perspective of mastery, addressing an abstract interlocutor; the other, Gabriela Mistral's *Poema de Chile*, in which the poet-speaker is within the landscape, addressing herself to a specific Indian child, who is far from a silent recipient of her knowledge. If in Neruda's text the poet defines the gazed-upon, in Mistral's she interacts with it.[25] In the masculinist/humanist mode of modernity the gazer imputes all physicality to the gazed-upon in order to rid himself of it, and, at least in one of its aspects, the postmodernist mode evacuates all but the discourse that constitutes both gazed-upon and gazer. A materialist feminism, by contrast, can recuperate an embodiedness, a materiality that both the gazer and the gazed-upon share, and whose reality need not depend on permanence (by which I mean unchangeability, rigidity, ahistoricity). As Pratt suggests, notions of transcendence require (gendered) man to distance himself from this primal space, which is not only mother but also sexually desirable woman, who threatens to enmire him in a physicality that precludes history. Cristina Peri Rossi's version of this *belle dame sans merci* is a city/woman (they have the same diabolical name, Luzbel — Lucifer) who converge in a space devoid of time.[26] Travelers to Luzbel have no desire ever to leave; they are enmired in an eternal present. The story takes the metaphor connecting woman-as-body to its logical conclusion, supporting in passing, and by counterexample, Edward Soja's contention that space is not simple, unchanging ground, but a concept in need of theorization.

Soja finds evidence to illustrate the discursive nature of space in the literature of the Southern Cone, albeit in one of its more metropolized manifestations, evoking the magical space of Jorge Luis Borges's aleph in order to ratify Freud's space/mind formulation. But the strategy only works if the reader of Borges is a foreigner, both to literary language and to bourgeois Buenos Aires. Soja uses "El aleph" to reflect on the frustration of the awareness of simultaneity (all points existing at once, yet independently, in the point of the aleph) having to be recounted through the medium of language, which is sequential. He points out that two words cannot occupy the same space on a page (any more than one person can speak two words simultaneously? but a chorus can). Still, the words occupy the same page: there is in written language the possibility of disrupting the spatial relation of the words. Julio Cortázar does it in *Rayuela* (*Hopscotch*), telling us to perform differently the geography of the text. Ordinary narrative is sequential, but lyric poetry is not, necessarily. The words must be read in order, one after another, but the image invoked, or the state of consciousness achieved through the poem, is not a story that tells cause and then effect, or a past in relation to a present. One of the delights of "El aleph" is how very placed it is in the bourgeois geography of Buenos Aires. That the infinite aleph should be encountered under the basement stairs in a relentlessly upper-middle-class house in a city that, within the story, is evoked in all its referentiality is a pleasure of the text, a piece of humor that is lost on readers who have turned Borges into a stern visionary. These tend to be readers for whom the real space of Buenos Aires is meaningless, who make a virtue of their ignorance and do not pay much attention to the city's presence in the text. For the knowledgeable reader — the one who knows Borges's city — the play between mundane and magical is a good part of the fun.[27]

The study of the physical world, according to Victor Burgin, Edward Soja, Nicholas Entrikin, and others, is a matter not simply for laboratory scientists but for cultural theorists, philosophers, historians, and — why not? — literary critics. Once we recognize "that the gaze of the fieldworker is part of the problematic, not a tool of analysis," as feminist geographer Gillian Rose puts it, the critique of the study of place becomes not only possible but necessary.[28] For the physical world is manifestly and multiply represented by scientists (social or lab) and artists; and we are invited to read those representations.

The postmodern critique of studies of space contends that any notion of space outside of discourse is untenable, that space does not exist prior to discourse, and that, also, space is a function of the structures of language. Yet as a feminist literary scholar, whose training and proclivities as a reader of texts make discourse easy to argue for, but who is looking for roads into the material world, I am interested in the interplay of discourse and materiality in the experience and representation of space. Space to occupy is a precondition for the body. As Entrikin says, "place represents both a context for action and a source of identity."[29] For exiles, place is most certainly, even doubly, so. First, there is the place of origin, now split into the mental projection of the exile's memory and the geopolitical space the exile knows to exist and change even in her absence. Second, there is the still space-y place of exile, the new place the exile knows, at least at first, as undifferentiated strangeness, against which, not through which, he identifies himself. Moreover, the nature of action changes as its spatial context shifts. The space the exile militates from, or survives in, is not the meaningful space, and may not yet have become place, as it slowly achieves that name and meaning.

In the late 1990s, the limitations of distance and therefore ideas about space are under full challenge by nearly instantaneous electronic access via e-mail and the Internet. The Net promotes communication within a diasporic community and has wrought changes in the international political scene. The Mothers of the Plaza de Mayo have a Web page, and the ChileLindo Website has links both to official government communications and to information on obtaining U.S. citizenship. Nevertheless, the ability to tell our computers to "GO" was still restricted to a very few as recently as the 1980s, during the waning of the Southern Cone dictatorships. Although we cannot, for that reason, expect to see much in the way of overt, interventionary political action on the Net, computer technology now makes it possible for many in the diaspora to connect.

The links of the World Wide Web map a complicated geography located in the virtual realm of cyberspace, where anyone with a computer equipped with a modem can "travel" freely. Despite the quick access to information that electronic communication offers, however, cyberspace remains a metaphor. The term itself was coined by William Gibson in his now-classic science fiction novel, *Neuromancer*, where travel in cyberspace is the ultimate body-free experience, once the delight of Case, the novel's protagonist: "For Case, who'd lived for the bodiless exultation of cyberspace, it was the Fall. In the bars he'd frequented as a cowboy hotshot, the elite stance involved a certain relaxed contempt for the flesh. The body was meat."[30]

Case's disdain for the body was a luxury he enjoyed only when his body was whole and placed in accordance with his needs and desires. He had been able to disregard it because it did not present him with any problems. Once his body had been neurologically damaged, setting in motion the novel's action, he could no longer ignore it. Similarly, only those who have the luxury of not having to mark the space they are in, those whose sense of rootedness remains undisturbed, are free to experience cyberspace and its chat rooms, e-mail, and Websites fully as a virtual space.

In the end, a person cannot occupy cyberspace. When individuals use the computer to help them communicate, establishing and maintaining relationships with others from a highly valued and distant place, they experience cyberspace as a technology, not very different in kind from the written, published word in print. On-line journals, local newspapers available via the Internet, and e-mail get the message out faster and cheaper than print matter, but they remain fundamentally journals, newspapers, and letters. The major difference this technology offers is the promise of uncensored information, difficult (but not impossible) for a repressive government to control. Access to the Internet requires the use of relatively expensive, far from universally available, machinery.

The technologies of rapid communication do not repair the damage of exile. They merely have the capacity to make connection possible despite distance; they do not eliminate distance. When exiles are communicating through cyberspace, they are still in front of a terminal or a personal computer, a machine that is connected to another via telephone or wires, hooked up, link by link, cable by cable. And when they log off, or even when they look up from the computer screen for a moment, they are still in the wrong country, the wrong climate, surrounded by the wrong faces and hearing the wrong language. A site on the Web provides visibility, information, contact, interaction: the range of what communication offers. It does not keep you dry or warm, and you cannot cook your dinner or eat it there. The sentient body is located elsewhere, and to the degree that that elsewhere is an irritant, a reminder of exile and of difference, the illusion that virtual reality, or virtual presence, can substitute for real presence and material reality is disrupted. For despite Derrida's rejection of presence, physical presence is a necessary fact of life and agency. It is not the same as information.[31]

The exciting new work being done in critical geography on representations of space and place is useful for understanding the physical and psychological experience of the spatial dislocation that is the hallmark of territorial exile and the cultural meanings attached to physical presence in, or absence from, a place. This work, informed by the practice of poststructuralist textual analysis, has made its way back into the field of literary criticism via cultural studies. Much of this analysis focuses on the way colonial or exotic space is imagined and represented by the colonizer — novelists, playwrights, travelers writing their accounts, authors of guidebooks, explorers, and anthropologists — whose "imperial eyes" chart an exotic geography.[32] Looking at the writing of Southern Cone exiles in Europe and North America requires a shift in the lens to get to what the exoticized "other" makes of the geography of dominance — the nations, cities, and neighborhoods of the industrialized North that become their places of refuge.

To say, with Yi-Fu Tuan, that physical space is given shape by our telling stories about it (making maps, inventing nations and neighborhoods, and so on) means that space becomes (like) text. But what, then, of the representation of space in fiction, that is, the spatialization of text? In Marta Traba's *En cualquier lugar* (In any place), some of the characters direct a conscious effort to keep the space as nonplace for as long as possible. The political leaders of the exile factions keep their attention directed toward their home country and try to re-create it in the ever-more-permanent holding camp of an abandoned railway station, keeping thousands of exiles from coming to know the country that has taken them in.[33]

Cristina Peri Rossi explores this issue in *La nave de los locos* (*The Ship of Fools*), which traces the "emplacement" of its exile protagonist, Ecks.[34] The novel slowly spirals from the undifferentiated space of dream through the unnameable space of the ocean to references to unnamed cities ("A") and puns on named ones (Merlin, Psycho-Aires), to allegorically named sites (Pueblo de Dios), to nicknamed places (the Great Navel), and finally to a real metropolis: London.[35] That is, the characters' relation to the space they occupy becomes increasingly concrete as the novel progresses. In *La nave de los locos*, Peri Rossi sets in motion a reciprocal questioning of how space is textualized and how text is spatialized. Until the end of the novel, when Ecks turns up in London, Peri Rossi, her narrator, and her protagonist avoid representing "real" space, or rather a "real place." This apparent progression toward a connection to the real world contains an exploration of how space might be textualized. Peri Rossi's narrator describes dreams that refer to space (the dream voice commands: "You will come to the city — describe it") and parody it (spatial shifts in dreams don't work in the waking world).[36] S/he uses footnotes, which draw our attention to the spatial relations of the text as well as to what is beyond the text; furthermore footnotes need not tell stories, so they do not need to represent space and do not lend themselves to placialization. Peri Rossi's Ecks rereads Homer, and Odysseus's journey is more real to him than his own; for Ecks cities are "states of mind." The narrator recounts newspaper articles about real places that Ecks reads about in fictional works. The narrator lingers over pictorial images of real places: a print of what is probably a Canaletto painting of Venice is described in detail, making the place in the painting more real than the room and the street and the unnamed city in which it's found. Similarly, the interpolation of a series of essayistic chapters on the tapestry of creation in the Cathedral of Gerona, whose structure is "a composition of the world," is a sort of map that makes order out of chaos. As a metaphor for the novel, it is a structuring device that explains both its own appeal and the novel's: "What we love in any structure is a vision of the world that gives order to chaos, an hypothesis which is comprehensible and restores our faith, atoning for our having fled and scattered before life's brutal disorder."[37]

Ecks's wanderings in not-named places are thus set against a world of spatial representations — visual, literary, journalistic, intrapsychic — that makes the representations more realistic than reality. The forty-five-year-old pianist who is at a loss in unfamiliar cities seems only to need the right analogy to accustom himself to exile: Ecks tells him that places are like pianos — you have to play them gently at first; the pianist learns to play so well that he undergoes a transformation.[38] Analogy, as a form of textualization, makes it possible for him to come fully to terms with place. Peri Rossi spins these spatial metaphors into what seems like an infinite regression. Ecks has recurring dreams, which he calls "dreams of representation" (*sueños de representación*), in which he is in the wrong spatial relationship to representation: he is a spectator in a theater with his back to the stage, or facing sideways, or unable to find his seat, or on stage.

Spatial confusion in *La nave de los locos* is overtly connected to the theme of exile and the variations of displacement. Ecks is the reluctant traveler whose vertiginous sense of the contingency of space permeates the novel. He first appears dreaming about a place where he will, sometime in the future, arrive. Then we find him on a ship, at sea, the traveler with no destination. The displacement of exile becomes the human condition, rendered in spatial terms: the astronaut exiled from the moon, the political exiles on the move in Europe, the boatload of mad people abandoned at sea, the gay writer who hates and fears leaving his safe, small space but who, once he goes to the city, meets the love of his life — a small boy — and launches off on a journey to Africa with the child and his mother. There is a constant interweaving of space and displacement as metaphor and as theme. Ecks's friend Vercingetorix is disappeared, which means he becomes increasingly invisible, not apparent anywhere: his neighbors cannot afford to recognize him as he is being taken away, and once he is gone the cement factory where he is forced to do hard labor is officially nowhere.

The reader's knowledge of space in the real world, still connected to "optical, perspectival models of spatial structure based on the cone of vision and the plane of representation," is likely to be much more stable than Peri Rossi's "psychical spaces formed by projection and introjection," constrained only by the freewheeling syntax of Spanish and the generous logic of fiction.[39] Our understanding of space as historically contingent and psychically structured is one thing; our experience of it is quite another. In order to come to an understanding of what we see as space, we convert it into place: bordered, historical, narrativized.

The exile, typically, inverts this order, performing a spatialization of place upon first arriving at the place of exile. Some government offers her asylum or gives him a temporary place to stay. Papers are stamped; all the bureaucracy the state can muster is called to bear. The spaces of exile are saturated with meaning, overdetermined as places, if anything. A superabundance of meanings in competition with each other is what sets the exile machine into motion in the first place — an authoritarian state excises the opposition. Exile refers always to political entities — city-states, nations — whose spatial boundaries are in the first instance symbolic. Like poetry for Marianne Moore (imaginary gardens with real toads in them), national borders are imaginary lines with real armed soldiers on them.

The space of exile is very much a place from its own inhabitants' point of view. It is full of signs that can be read. But the language, behaviors, institutions, and belief systems that create place out of space are still unknown to the exile. Peri Rossi allegorizes this state of placelessness in "Las estatuas, o la condición del extranjero" (Statues, or the condition of the foreigner), whose protagonist is unable to see the urban landscape around him as anything other than colorless, silent, and lifeless. José da Cruz writes about this sense of imbalance, ignorance, and dislocation in a comic vein: he describes the new arrival at Stockholm's Arlanda Airport buffoonishly unable to negotiate his way out.[40] The process of narrativizing space into place, a central motif of frustration in *La nave de los locos*, is an undercurrent, invisibly but perceptibly chilling the waters of Marta Traba's *En cualquier lugar*. Traba's station-dwellers simply do not cross into the new space; they remain in the symbolic liminal space of the railway station, always ready to be in transit, almost literally neither here nor there.

En cualquier lugar is a virtual primer of exile. The characters appear deliberately to arrange themselves along the axes of alienation and acculturation in almost measurable intervals. That is to say, in this novel Traba explores the choices of exile in relation to political and personal desire and with regard to spatial location. Traba's *cualquier lugar* (provisionally, "wherever," "any place") recalls Giorgio Agamben's valorization of the singularity of *qualunque* (provisionally, "whatever," "any") in *La comunità che viene (The Coming Community)*.[41] Agamben takes *qualunque* as one of his key terms. For him, the very lack of specificity, particularity crosscut by generality (or as Agamben's translator puts it, "that which is neither particular nor general, neither individual nor generic"), is what opens the possibilities of a new community beyond identity. The community of Traba's novel, unlike Agamben's, however, is thoroughly grounded in ideology and egocentrism, to the detriment of its occupants. Traba tells the story of the indifferent *cualquiera*, of the refusal of the opportunity for singularity. It is precisely the promising "as suchness" of the exilic space that the political leaders reject. In Traba, the "whereverness" of the place is the very thing that paralyzes those whose desires reside in a very particular, lost place.

Traba depicts a community in which several thousand exiles live in an unnamed northern European country, one of the meanings of *en cualquier lugar*. More arrive daily. Most camp out in an abandoned railway station at the edge of the city; a few find jobs and are given housing; others, entrepreneurs, have begun selling handicrafts and are revitalizing a seedy commercial center. Whether one remains apart or acculturates appears to be a deliberate choice. Those who stay in the station — that is, who remain in the liminal space of travel (here made concrete: the station no longer functions as the border between travel and arrival or departure; it has been converted into a refugee camp, complete with bureaucracy and portable toilets) — do not make use of the opportunity to acculturate: to learn the language, get a job. The center of town is unknown to the vast majority of the residents of the station; when a bombing of a newspaper office makes them fear retaliation and flee the station, they are at a loss where to go. Their lives are on hold, and they cling to the hope and promise that they will soon be able to return home. The leaders of this group — principally the aging politico, Vázquez — have a stake in retaining this mass of people: they are their power base, and if they disperse there will be nothing to lead. Luis Cruz, Vázquez's lieutenant, who is also determined to keep the station-dwellers where they are, is incapable of seeing the city he is living in. Luis is described as a man who does not connect with places. For him, his country is the people, and he is convinced that rebuilding the country can only take place outside, in exile, and then be brought back home. The place of exile is of no concern to Luis, but neither are memories of home. Keeping the people together is his primary goal: "Unlike many other comrades, he felt no nostalgia, not for his neighborhood, or for that particular café, or for the local soccer field; for him the homeland was transported along with the people, and it was anywhere the discussion and the arguments between people and groups continued."[42] Therefore, Luis sees the entrepreneurial artisans who have gone over to live and work in the "shops in the East" ("las tiendas del Este") as traitors. But he also is the link between them and the station-leaders, and he spends his time on the telephone and going back and forth between groups and people to keep everyone informed and connected. Ironically, as the least spatially oriented character in the novel, he is more familiar than most with a diversity of spaces in the city.[43]

Mariana, married to Vázquez, moves toward some accommodation to the new country, making friends and working in the library, stocking it with books in Spanish and about the home country — never specified, but presumably Argentina, from the references to Sunday ravioli and Gardel. But she always feels radically disoriented. In the end, she goes home, telling Luis that there are only two possible ways to deal with exile: accommodate or leave. Luis, whose badge of nonaccommodation is his ignorance of the language, leaves as well. But, consistent with his disinterest in place, he goes to Mexico, not home. There he will continue his political work, but more effectively, as a speaker of the language. Still another character, the poet Alicia, sets out deliberately to make a new life in a new country for herself and her children. Ana Cruz, Luis's mother and an orthodox Marxist whose vision has always been internationalist, also remains and prospers. The people living in the station, once they find out they have a choice in the matter, choose to be dispersed and relocated. Vázquez subsequently moves downtown (al centro) and begins work on an international project — a real and metaphorical spatial shift from margin to center.

The station, which turns out to be the reified space of transit, no longer means transit at all, but has become, rather, the rat's nest where people are warehoused. Not until the end of the novel are its occupants humanized: Traba gives us a vignette of a family desperate to get out of there, and we see the extent to which Vázquez's ambition has been at the expense of his compatriots. In the end it is the airport that is the limbo we were given to believe the station was. From there people can actually leave the new country. The station must be obliterated, and it is. A demolition crew comes in and dramatically tears it down.

Whereas Traba sets her novel in a single, fictional European city with roughly mappable physical landmarks (river, bridges, downtown, the shops in the East), Peri Rossi's novel offers a series of locations interspersed with free-floating meditations or discussion, and chapters where foreignness as a concept is underscored, but with no reference to a larger space than a museum or boat — the structure in which the interaction takes place, not situated in connection to outside reference points.

La nave de los locos opens with the first version of the journey, a dream of anticipated arrival: "You will come to the city — describe it." This is the task of the exile, and particularly of the exile writer. It anticipates arrival; that is, it takes place in the hiatus between departure and arrival, where the city can only be projected, perhaps imagined. Description can only come with physical presence: "You will come to the city — describe it." The response is the only one possible: "How shall I know what is meaningful from what is not?"[44] That is, how does the subject in a new place, in space before meaning is assigned, order the sensory input and discriminate? This act of "distinguishing," of separating what has meaning from what does not, is the thing that must be done. "Orientation," knowing which direction is which, what the relationship is among them, comes after deciding, or learning, what constitutes the significant elements in a place. As metatext, this imperative is what the writer must do — describe it, make space where there is none, represent space so that the reader experiences it imaginatively.

The second paragraph confounds the task — the seemingly simple job of separating what is meaningful from what is not, the wheat from the chaff. Gender, the primordial distinction, enters in the form of "she" (the protagonist until this point is not marked for gender), who finds significance in the insignificant — a weed, a stone, a mouse (vegetable, mineral, animal, that is, all creation) can be invested with meaning; the narrator gives up in confusion. There is no real hope of dividing the significant from the insignificant in a communicable way, no less in a way that will be universally agreed upon. There is no God (the voice that commanded no longer answers), no final arbiter. Without the ability to make distinctions between meaningfulness and meaninglessness, it may never be possible to turn space into place, and certainly impossible to reconstruct the place as it is known by its natives — which is tantamount to not ever acculturating. At best, space is made place differently by the foreigner, for whom the wheat and the chaff are confounded, and mean different things and have different degrees of importance than they do to the native.

Acculturation and alienation in these texts are closely allied with sex and language. Peri Rossi, with lovely mild derision encasing serious critique, addresses acculturation by sex for the exile:

> The best way for a foreigner to get to know a city is to fall in love with one of its women, *so susceptible to the tenderness that a man without a country — that is, without a mother — inspires, and also to the differences in pigmentation from one continent to another.* She will trace a path that does not figure on any map and instruct *us* in a language *we* will never forget.[45]

Peri Rossi's stark identification of homeland with mother, her bland implication that the exile is always male, her apparently neutral observation of European women's eroticization of the racial other, and her presumption of universal heterosexuality, all encased in the language of sentimental romance, indicate that this advice be read ironically.

Politicians give the same counsel, without the ironic smile. Göran Johansson, labor adviser in Gothenburg, Sweden, speaking of the problem of joblessness among political refugees, is quoted as saying, "Those who made out best are the ones who quickly learned Swedish, married a Swedish girl, and left the group."[46] The affective route to acculturation tempers Herbert C. Kelman's useful distinction between "sentimental attachment" and "instrumental attachment" felt for the homeland and the host country, the former reflecting "cultural integration and national identity" and the latter "social and economic integration."[47] Accordingly, one of the wisest exile characters of all, Don Rafael in Mario Benedetti's *Primavera con una esquina rota,* whose first words in the novel are "The essential thing is to adapt" ("Lo esencial es adaptarse"), nevertheless also practices adaptation by intercultural coitus. Conforming to this familiar pattern of exile, he enacts his acculturation to "a country called Lydia."[48] Here Benedetti turns inside out the tongue-in-cheek advice Peri Rossi gives: fall in love with a woman of the place; it gives her a chance to enjoy dark skin. It is Rafael who is whiter than Lydia — she is *indiecita,* a term that combines racial and gender marking with affection. That is, he is feeling titillated and politically correct, just the way Peri Rossi's racist European women do. Rafael describes Lydia as having "her bit of Indian blood, thank goodness. Or maybe it's black blood, also well and good. Let's say her lovely skin is darker than Graciela's or Beatriz's, and even darker (and much less wrinkled) than mine."[49] Don Rafael's inversion of the racial politics enacted upon Southern Cone exiles in Europe is not unique. The Mexican perception, at least in the university, was that Argentine, Chilean, and Uruguayan exiles were taking over.[50] The third/first–world split that made Southern Cone exiles in the United States and Europe into a dark-skinned, second-class minority did not operate that way in Mexico, which is also Latin American, Spanish-speaking, and decidedly more racially mixed and indigenous. There Argentines, Chileans, and Uruguayans retained, and — at least according to their Mexican counterparts — capitalized on, their racial privilege. This phenomenon was fueled by the class distribution of exiles to various countries: one observer notes that "exile in Mexico could even be characterized as a brain drain (a repetition of the Republican exile from Spain)."[51]

In José Leandro Urbina's *Cobro revertido*, the trajectory of exile played out in acculturation and alienation is fully charted through the protagonist's relationships with women. *Cobro revertido* is an allegory of dissociation from the homeland that follows an unnamed male exile in Canada whose mother has just died in Chile. As Peri Rossi notes, being countryless and being motherless are, rhetorically and sentimentally, interchangeable states. The protagonist's Montreal is a city of refugees and exiles, but it also contains Canadian women through whom he can acculturate. In fact all his primary sources of identity and emplacement are women (mother, lovers, wife) connected via alliteration: madre, Magdalena, Megan, Marcia. It is still another woman who asks him the key question concerning identity: "Who are you?" This minor character falls asleep as he answers; Urbina goes out of his way to efface her so that the protagonist, who by way of an answer simply talks about Chile, is explaining himself to himself.[52]

The prelapsarian mother/son cathexis, which unproblematically identifies the son with the mother country as well (according to Peri Rossi's description and borne out here), is interrupted by the appearance of the other face of the nation. Sexual, aesthetic, and political transgression are joined in Magdalena. The political activism she prompts the protagonist to leads to his arrest; his mother's connections to the military rulers make possible not only his release but also his exile and the death of Magdalena, who, as an older woman, is a rival to the mother.[53] Exiled from Chile to Canada, the protagonist follows Peri Rossi's advice and falls in love with Megan, who, spanning both city, where she lives, and countryside, where she is from, represents Canada to him. We see his initiation into this new place, an initiation that is both affective and sexual, as a process: Megan first seems strange to him, and somehow sexless, but he finds her to be a wonderful lover. She is the emblem of a unitary Canada, which Urbina refines and corrects when the protagonist breaks with her and has an affair with Marcia, who, as a French Canadian, occupies an insider-outsider position that refracts his own. The final stage in the protagonist's exile odyssey, his possible death, is also associated with a woman: a Chilean woman who herself has assimilated, marrying a Quebecois and speaking French with an accent the protagonist does not recognize as Chilean until after her husband has stabbed him. Women are, then, unreliable bearers of nation. Like his mother, problematically associated with both the nurturing and death-dealing aspects of Chile, this seductive woman's refusal to stay within the group is deadly to the male exile. She is never overtly accused of betraying a cause (as characters in *En cualquier lugar* are) by preferring exogamy; it is simply a surprise to the protagonist that she is Chilean. He did not recognize the sounds of his own country when they were wrapped around the words of another language.

Acculturation, which ultimately leads to death in *Cobro revertido* — the symbolic death of Chilean identity — is marked by exogamic relationships. The self-imposed alienation in *En cualquier lugar* is for its part linked to endogamous ones. The inevitable change of partners that occurs in this novel happens exclusively in-group. Fleeting relationships with women of the new country are so meaningless that when Luis engages in them he does not even consider them real enough to ease his sense that he has become asexual. He presumably cannot understand the women because he never learns their language. Exogamy is tantamount to treason. One of the leaders of the group that has moved to the shops in the East, El Chajá, has developed a taste for the European women; this is one of the things that marks him as different from the other men, all of whom restrict their serious liaisons to women from home. Since the main characters are those who do not acculturate, acculturation by romance (or sex) is notable by its absence. The women, like the men, are endogamous, though more complicatedly so. Mariana's liaison with Alí is sexually charged but never consummated; the brutalized Flora, a recent suicide at the beginning of the novel, was not sexually active; she lived with her husband, Alí, and with Flores, who had tortured and raped her. The epilogue projects Alicia through four years of marriage with Alí to a divorce and remarriage to a European poet. Ada outlives her lover Vázquez. Only Ana marries endogamously and stays in the new country.

Both *Cobro revertido* and *En cualquier lugar* depend on traditional gender relationships as emblems of ways of being in exile. These conventional sexual arrangements and gender categories are connected to the conventional structure of these novels. Exile unbalances, destabilizing space, but familiar tales of heterosexuality anchor the stories. In contrast, Peri Rossi unsettles the ground of the novel, disturbing three categories: place, gender, and sexuality. The unsettling of exile is not resolved into either total alienation (figured by Mariana's return home in the Traba novel) or the tragically culminated acculturation of *Cobro revertido*.

In *La nave de los locos*, exile is the human condition, not resolvable, but displaceable. There is little hope of permanent emplacement or acculturation in *La nave de los locos*; Peri Rossi rejects a sense of belonging as a value. Even before exile, before the Fall, there was no truly welcoming home. The small children who write their versions of the story of Eve in Peri Rossi's novel make it clear that Eden was not paradise for Adam's helpmeet. Aby Warburg writes of "the acceptance of the unhomely in the homely, [from which] we may learn...that no amount of space or structure can make a home where no home can exist."[54]

The radical alienation of the protagonist in Sylvia Molloy's *En breve cárcel* (translated as *Certificate of Absence*) demonstrates Warburg's point.[55] The tight focus on the claustrophobic flat in which this character writes and remembers, the immediate space her body occupies and her memory recalls as the site of lovemaking, contrasts with the deliberate blurring of the nation-spaces she has so elaborately repressed. The protagonist's refusal to name these places is consistent with the interiority of the novel. Childhood memories intimating sexual abuse by the father, an identification with the sister bordering on masochism, and the brutal death of a beloved aunt undermine the generic requirements of the canonical exile text in which home is written largely, even if rarely entirely, as the lost paradise, and therefore as an object of desire. Correspondingly, the North American and European cities the protagonist has lived in are marked as if through fog or haze in which no more than a few details can be made out, significant only because these were the places where she met and knew the women she loved. The lesbian spaces of *En breve cárcel* are as tightly shut as any closet. Space outside is not occupiable in the world of the wounded protagonist. Not until the end of the novel can she even attempt to function in any but the most restrictive spaces.

In *La nave de los locos*, space is not brought under control, nor is place fixed, via naturalized heterosexual arrangements; they are, rather, complicated by the problematics of sexuality and gender. The end of the novel is the dream of the end of gender, the answer to the riddle that would free the princess from the incestuous grasp of her father by endowing her with her (or her lover's) virility. In his agoraphobia Morris inverts its elements and exiles the world — until he has to go to the city where he meets Percival and falls in love and winds up mixing his myths wildly and going off with the child of the holy grail, Percival, and the mother of us all, Eve, to Africa to see the giraffes. The downtrodden woman on the abortion bus that Ecks drives becomes a transvestite performer whose act is so seductively described that it entices even the heterosexual reader into complicity with its lesbian eroticism.[56] The stories implode; the tapestry remains unraveled. There is no neat return; the ending is not written.

The end of the novel instead nullifies a key ground — gender distinction. Anthony Vidler's desire for a "stance [that] would…describe a complex movement between space and the subject, place and inhabitation, vision and drive, projection and reflection, open to multiple constructions of gender, sexuality, and difference" comes to fruition in *La nave de los locos*.[57] When heterosexuality and traditional gender arrangements are also interrogated, nothing is firm in exile; its spatial instability turns out to be only one form of uncertainty. We may all be the vigilant madman whose only madness is his vigilance (his insomnia), watching the ship being abandoned — and, unlike him, welcoming it.

Chapter Four

EXILE AND THE EMBODIED PRODUCTION OF LANGUAGE

ahora
> estoy sola en el bosque y de mi boca
s a l e n   s a p o s   y   c u l e b r a s.
No me arrepiento del todo: ahora soy escritora.

now
> I am alone in the woods and from my mouth
c o m e   f r o g s   a n d   s n a k e s.
I am not entirely sorry: now I am a writer.

— LUISA VALENZUELA

Toward the end of *La ciudad ausente* (The absent city), Ricardo Piglia's protagonist, Junior, comes upon an island inhabited by a motley crew of exiles who, together, speak all the world's languages.[1] The remarkable thing is that they speak these languages sequentially. By some silent accord, the island's population periodically and simultaneously leaves off speaking one to take up another. It is as though language itself took up space, and no two might be in the same place at the same time. At around the same time that Piglia published his vaguely futuristic novel, Luisa Valenzuela found in the European folk tradition a story to retell in which words attain mass, filling the woods with reptiles and a palace with jewels and flowers. In both *La ciudad ausente* and Valenzuela's "La densidad de las palabras" (The density of words) language makes space and takes space.[2] Space acquires a discursive quality insofar as language is taken to *occupy* it in these texts, in a gesture related to the evocation of spatial metaphors that we saw in chapter 3, in which concepts and acts are figured *as* places. This mutual constitution of language and space — the figuration of a language that occupies space and of space as figure in language — is linked by analogy and practice to the experience of exile and its aftermath. The prediscursive sense of rootedness (in Yi-Fu Tuan's problematic formulation, noted in chapter 1) and the trauma of displacement, followed by learning new space, find their counterparts in the representation of fictional or poetic space, wherein language provides the means to establish as well as to recover a sense of place.

Like space, the subject may well be produced through language. But the human body, animated by a sense of self and perceiving space through sensorial means (sight, but also touch and hearing), also quite literally produces language. This may seem obvious, but I believe that the current notions of language, mind, and subjectivity erase, or at least efface, the body in ways that, as feminist theorists have shown, discredit and disenfranchise women and whatever is figured as the feminine, as well as all those other others who have been relegated to the realm of the physical.

Lacan's linkage of psychoanalysis with language is a paradigmatic, perhaps founding, example of this: Lacan notoriously disembodies his theory by enlisting the phallus, that most notably physical of appurtenances, as the very thing that cannot be had, or achieved. This is a boldly ironic and funny move, but it is a move made under the sign of Descartes. It is to take language as always already so disembodied that its lack of bodiliness can encompass that which is most bodily (and unmistakably gendered) and attach it to the structure of the psyche, which itself occupies no known place in the body, and to make of it a tool of masculinity — the constituting element of the law of the father.

Among literary critics and cultural theorists, language is most commonly thought of as a system of signs, on the one hand, and as a structure or metastructure, on the other. Grammar seduces us: Derrida writes of grammatology, and we follow him like children trailing the Pied Piper. We think about the ways language itself constructs us, in a synecdoche for mind. The structure of language turns out to be the structure of the psyche, which in one chronology is another way of saying that language structures the psyche. And without a doubt, the disembodiment of language has enabled an extraordinary corpus of enormously illuminating and suggestive theory, not least among feminist theorists who have labored to enhance or problematize this work by making gender visible in it.

Psychoanalytic theory, particularly as rewritten by Lacan and his followers, can be read to suggest that awareness of place (the sudden knowledge of the possibility of other places that somehow define the borders of one's own place, a knowledge that awakens one from some prelapsarian sense of rootedness or nondifferentiation) is linked to language and its acquisition. The psychoanalytic interpretation of separation from the caretaker (who is usually the mother or her substitute) attaches individuation and the loss of boundarylessness to the child's initiation into language. We have already seen how "mother" is figured as place, and rootedness, as Yi-Fu Tuan formulates it, defined by the subject's integration of self and place, echoes the position of the child before separation from the mother and before entry into language. Symbolically the beginning of spatial awareness may coincide with initiation into language, as language and space become known in juxtaposition, perhaps intertwined. Beyond the abstractions of "language" and "space," the specific language and the particular place — the Spanish of Montevideo, say — are constitutive of culture and identity.

Although it is far too easy to fall back on the binary that connects woman, mother, body, and nature in opposition to man, father, mind, and culture, with sex organs as signifiers (that is, markers of both difference and identification), the physical characteristics of language that I am stressing here do, in the early stages, attach to the relationship between child and caregiver, usually mother and, even if not mother, still most often a woman.[3] This physical aspect of language — phonology and to a certain extent lexicon — that attaches to mother (the "mother tongue" in so many languages) can be theoretically isolated from the structural aspects of language (grammar, syntax, semantics) that, though not specifically named, have occupied contemporary critics and theorists. This gesture produces a binary opposition that, unlike most gender binaries, takes the female (mother) as the first term. What the (generically male) child gains when he loses the primal attachment to her, since there has to be a payoff somewhere, is the not-mother of language. And in the already present binary system the not-mother is the father, who is standing there ready with his system of laws and prohibitions, but who in fact need not be anything like the biological or social father. So perhaps the fetishized phallus is not the ultimate signifier that has no signified. Perhaps "father," as the marker for the empty space that is "not-mother," is the ultimate, end-of-the-line signifier. What if the insistence that language's consubstantiality with the realm of the father is nothing more than compensation for the superfluousness of the father, a way to inject him back into the family, and as its dominant figure, for good measure? The Oedipal drama has, from Sophocles on, been written as tragedy, but entry into language has its happy aspects. The power of naming, the joy of pleasing the parent and being rewarded with approval, and the ability to participate in the community of speakers are among these, though none is entirely unproblematic, especially for the girl child. Still, the very incommensurability of language makes intervention — and invention — possible. The law of patriarchal power protests too much, divesting the mother — and all women, just to make sure — of linguistic power by severing language from body (with which this law aligns her). For women to reclaim language and the body within this system is to risk falling back on hackneyed notions of femininity as reproductive function whose very technology is antiquated: vaginal secretions, menstrual blood, and milk are to be our ink. When was the last time you opened a bottle of ink?

Language is also physical, but the physical, even when it is gendered, and even when it is sexed, is not limited to the reproductive, even if much contemporary theory would have us believe otherwise. Rosi Braidotti, for example, constructs her Foucauldian-feminist argument on the technologies of power, "starting from the assumption that the privilege granted to the discourse of sexuality and reproduction as the site of the production of truth about the subject is the trademark of modernity."[4] The collapsing of body, sexuality, reproduction, and femininity in modernity, to which Braidotti and others are responding, has done much harm to women. But insofar as the postmodern critique still operates under the privilege and the collapse, prying these terms apart is a politically and theoretically necessary activity. Lesbian theory is one place this active disengagement has begun, with its convincing argument against the homology of the female body and reproduction. Widening our notion of the bodily with reference to the production of language makes space for another wedge to be inserted.

Consider the Spanish term *desarticulación* — "dearticulation." It is about separating two things that had been touching, separating each from the other's surface: the removal of the exile from her country, for example. But articulation and its undoing also have linguistic connotations. In English, to articulate is to make oneself understood through language. To *be* articulate is to have the capacity to make oneself *well* understood. Articulation is a term concerning speech and communication and facility with language, which has its roots in the physiological aspect of language production as the site of anatomical connection. To articulate is also to speak clearly, to bring tongue, lips, and palate into the precise conjunctions with each other to make the sounds of speech. The Spanish *articulación* means, among other things, pronunciation.

Language is produced in the body, as sound; and it is heard by the body through the sense of hearing or perceived in its written form by sight or touch. Moreover, speech patterns are highly individualized; a voice print will identify an individual as readily as a fingerprint. In his memoir of his clandestine visit to Chile, Volodia Teitelboim tells of a friend who tries to dissuade him from making the dangerous trip. Linking voice to such other physical characteristics as baldness, weight, and gait, the anonymous friend tells the exiled former senator that he will be recognized immediately:

> "I'm going. I'll try to make sure they don't kill me. I'll be careful and follow all the rules. I'll get into the country without anybody knowing it's me."
> "It'll be hard. You're fat. You're bald. Your face is round. Your voice will give you away. You've been talking on the radio for years. The police know it well. No one can fake their voice or their way of walking. And your voice and the way you walk are too characteristic, slow, like those of a man who's not in a hurry. They'll know you a mile away."[5]

Language is punctuated and emphasized through gesture, gestures that are specific to individuals, but also to culture and to gender and class within particular cultures.[6] People have bodily responses to language, to tone as well as to words themselves. Harsh words can provoke fear; erotic language, read or heard, has the power to arouse us sexually. Language can evoke visual images; it can make your mouth water; it can make you cry. The very sounds of a language have the power to evoke memories in the form of physiological change. Heart rates change at the sound of certain accents or tones. Psychoanalysts León and Rebeca Grinberg tell of "one patient, a native Austrian, [who] used to say, 'In German, the word "urinal" smells of urine.' "[7] Philosopher María Lugones notes the power of the traces of Spanish in the spoken English of other Latinas to create an immediate bond between them, a bond that manifests itself in the spatial terms of physical proximity:

> Getting real close, like a confidence, you tell me, "Because certain individuals can get too accustomed to being helped." That snatch of mestizaje — "certain individuals" — the Southamerican use of "individuos" chiseled into your English. Makes me feel good, in the know. I know what you mean, mujer, Southamerican style. Just like my "operation." Claro que se dice real close, it's not just for everyone's ears. You make me feel special. I know, I know about "certain individuals." Like the "apparatus" you borrow from me or I borrow from you.[8]

In addition to the marked "certain individuals," "operation," and "apparatus," Lugones tucks still other linguistic hooks into this passage. Also aimed at a Latina interlocutor, they will be understood only by readers who know such secrets of Spanish as the meaning of "claro que se dice," the spelling of "Southamerican" as one word, and the use of "accustomed" in informal discourse.

Lugones's affection for the syntax of Spanish and the traces of its lexicon suggests the extent to which language *is* culture. The relationship between culture/language and the sensory experience of the body can be glimpsed in the way we tend to deal linguistically with food, for words for prepared food are on some profound level untranslatable. There are ways in which "empanadas" are not and cannot be "meat pasties." The experience of eating can be unmediated by language, and language always follows the experience of food (which may be why restaurant critics' metaphors often sound so far-fetched). On the other hand, the preparation of raw ingredients into food and the rituals surrounding the consumption of food are, as Lévi-Strauss and others have amply demonstrated, always a profoundly cultural act. The signified of food requires a culturally and therefore linguistically specific signifier, and both of them merge in a sign that is irreducible even as, or perhaps because, it is reproduced differently by every cook in every kitchen. The perpetual need of the organism for nourishment means that the platonic empanada, widely recognized as the symbol of Chile for its exiles, is endlessly made material and consumed. The empanada is produced, devoured, and reproduced with ingredients that only approximate those of home, where, in fact, not all empanadas are created equal either.

The power of language to evoke multiple bodily responses is echoed in the way the aural in its entirety has that power. Song has functioned not only to keep exile communities together but also to establish and maintain solidarity movements in Europe and the United States. Meaning, contained most overtly in lyrics, is intensified by the sensations produced and evoked by the music itself. Moreover, as Román Soto has noted, the experience of singing together with others — and later the memory of that experience — can function to evoke a sense of community and common purpose.[9] A few bars of Popular Unity's anthem, or of one of Violeta Parra's signature songs, call forth the whole for the knowledgeable listener, and with it multiple associations. The semiotics of Western and indigenous music, the meaning attached to major and minor, the familiarity of certain tunes, and the political act of instrumentation (in Pinochet's Chile, for example, indigenous instruments were banned as subversive) are all part of the relationship between exile, political action, and memory. For years, museumlike, Inti Illmani's music preserved the sounds of Allende's Popular Unity party and kept them alive in Europe and the United States.[10] It is no coincidence that Mañungo Vera, the protagonist of José Donoso's *La desesperanza* (translated as *Curfew*), is a singer, a kind of Víctor Jara who survived, or Inti Illmani as a solo, whose crisis of conscience and identity revolves precisely around the power of his music to elicit the hopeful, youthful moment of revolutionary change in which he no longer believes. He is ever more alienated from the community his music calls into being as it is sung and listened to.

Of course, despite the fact that language, spoken or sung, is transmitted and received in and by and through the body, language does not have the materiality of other bodily products. It is not like tears or blood, made of molecules. Words printed on the page are material representations of the sounds of language, made and received in intimate relations, the speaker and hearer in proximity. Mañungo, who had not missed the opportunity to take advantage of the sexual response he elicited during his concerts, makes his former lover Judit shiver when he sings to her. But proximity is not required in the case of audio reproductions, in the form of records and, even more, tapes, which, during the dictatorships, were also significant forms of connection, based on the aural/physiological response of the receiver, hard-wired to the emotions. Volodia Teitelboim writes of music that cuts through space, carrying a kind of solvent against dictatorship.[11] The sensuality of sound may be augmented synesthetically in the literary and musical text, where metaphors about language render it material substance, perceptible visually and tactically. The title song on

Daniel Viglietti's album *Esdrújula* is about the pleasure of the sound of words themselves.[12]

Desire and fulfillment reside in the gap between language as incommensurate system and the sensorial production and transmission of the sounds of language, the almost unconscious sense of touch in the mouth and throat and the vibrations to the ear. What the body can give and receive depends also on what the system is capable of, and it is not capable of perfect congruence. There may not be homology between signifier and referent, but we learn early how to make the leap from one to the other. Gaps in interpretation make for good conversation; they require clarification, more words. Startling combinations make new worlds possible. This is the motor that makes language as a communication system run, that, taken to another level, makes figuration possible and desirable, makes it possible for us to be moved by literature to tears or to action or to laughter. This is what we need from language, as Luisa Valenzuela's story "Transparencia" (Transparency) demonstrates. This little parable is narrated by God, who wants to start all over, create the world again, but this time with a transparent, single, world language. Metaphors have caused too much trouble. In the new language, a thing is what it is called, and what it is called is what it is. The cosmos will be a club, to which all who obey the rules may belong. The rules call for clear divisions, particularly between the sexes. And the new world order sounds decidedly fascistic.[13] Where there is perfect congruence between signifier and signified there is no place for either resistance or the astonishment of beauty. Nor is there room for the reader to participate in the creation of the text. Given the way Sylvia Molloy's protagonist — and her text — shuts out the larger world in *En breve cárcel* (*Certificate of Absence*), it is impossible to detect any but the most nebulous traces of reference to prison and exile as the material reality of a particular historical moment in the already metaphorical, historical, and syntactically skewed-for-poetry phrases ("*en breve cárcel*"/"certificate of absence") offered in the Spanish and English titles. Yet the tension between prison and absence set up in the text's two titles, however mediated by their immediate source in the poetry of Quevedo and Dickinson, cannot help but resonate when we juxtapose the English and the Spanish titles in the context of recent Argentine history. So perhaps I have been misguided in trying to get behind or beyond or out from under metaphor (which all these spatial prepositions are, of course). Certainly I have been unsuccessful, for to get to them I need words.

In their study on psychoanalytic aspects of migration and exile, Rebeca and León Grinberg, clinically oriented psychoanalysts, discuss the individual psyche under the stress of migration. Their work, grounded in clinical observation and in the everyday, is marked by an immediacy of purpose and recognizes the crucial role of linguistic dislocation.[14] Their chapter on language traces theories of language from Jakobson and Saussure to

Chomsky, Lacan, and Wittgenstein, but it also, importantly, attends to the social and psychological fallout of language difference. They wonder at the ability of the migrant to return, quite literally, to the position of the very young child on the brink of learning language. Here they recognize the distinction between behavior and responses traceable to infancy and early childhood and the traumatic fact of being infantilized, as well as the different ways the adult must confront a new language. They note that "the adult tends to acquire vocabulary and grammar in a rational way; but not accent, intonation and rhythm — that is, the 'music' of language — as a child does" (110). These elements are the physiological/physical/sensual aspects of language: the way sounds and tones are formed in the mouth, the way they sound to the ear. Phonology can be explained in logical and descriptive terms, but it still must be produced and received through the use of the body. It is phonology, much more than grammar, syntax, or semantics, that the adult has trouble with. The production of foreign sounds is not natural for an adult and has to be learned, as for a child it does not. Absolute mastery of the sound system is rarely achieved by grownups; accent is an unmistakable sign of foreignness. But, the Grinbergs insist, semantics and syntax, lexicon and grammar, take primacy in the emergency situation of exile:

> [T]he communication established by the immigrant with native speakers inevitably contains alterations in the semantic and syntactic fields (confusion and misunderstandings between respective signifiers and signifieds and improper use of verbal structures), which are echoed in the pragmatic domain through the immigrant's behavior and his reactions to messages sent or received from other dialogue participants. For as long as this lasts, the immigrant feels alienated from his surroundings. Some feel they are "in disguise" when they speak the new language, that they have lost the language in which they feel "authentic."
>
> But when these obstacles are overcome, the immigrant feels that he contains the new language, and that the new does not necessarily replace the mother tongue: he makes space within himself for more diversity, which enriches him and may enrich others. (112)

This passage suggests the possibility of change and enhancement. Writers, who may well learn to dominate the new language and be enriched by it, nevertheless have a special relationship to language insofar as it is the medium from which they deliberately create their art. Chilean novelist and psychologist Ana Vásquez, living in France, describes this phenomenon, explaining to an interviewer that she writes her papers on psychology in French, but her novels in Spanish:

> I have two languages: I write my scientific work directly in French and my literary work directly in Spanish. They are two worlds, be-

cause they are two languages; that is, I am bilingual but I cannot play with the French language the way I can play with Spanish. In Spanish I can write a dialogue with grammatical errors, but they sound right, because they are the ones Spanish-speakers make. In French it sounds wrong; it is a linguistic mistake.[15]

Uruguayan writer and critic Leonardo Rossiello, whose own exile has been lived in Sweden, notes the difference between knowing a language well enough that it is serviceable for everyday communication and knowing it well enough that it can be a malleable medium for a writer. It is not surprising that Rossiello, a sculptor as well as a writer, uses plastic terminology to talk about language: "After a number of years of apprenticeship and practice, he manages the new language, more or less well, without coming to feel it as a ductile and precise instrument."[16] Not coincidentally, this observation follows immediately on a reflection on the loss of the familiar landscape. The whole passage reads as follows:

For reasons that are easy to understand, the writer in exile in countries that do not speak Romance languages confronts, more acutely than others (for example, exiles in Latin American countries, or in Spain and France), the problem of whom to write for. He has arrived in the new country as an adult. The writer's "emotional background," of which [Spanish novelist] Pío Baroja spoke, is already formed by the experiences of childhood and adolescence. His landscape, the real landscape he identifies with and with which his interior landscape resonates, is far away. After a number of years of apprenticeship and practice, he manages the new language, more or less well, without coming to feel it as a ductile and precise instrument. During the first years, his natural referent and "source of inspiration" is not, generally speaking, everyday reality. He needs to go to his memory or to literature itself to seek it. He writes, for the most part, in his mother tongue, which, nevertheless, he does not exercise as he should or would like. And his immediate readers are his friends, his partner. The road to Latin American or Spanish readers, although not impossible, is long and complicated.[17]

Rossiello traces briefly the connections between landscape, language, imagination, memory, and audience. It is a pain-filled route, borne with the stoicism of the academically rigorous sociologist of literature. Similarly, Renata, in Vlady Kociancich's *Últimos días de William Shakespeare* (*The Last Days of William Shakespeare*), ties language to space and history in a representation of the tension between home and exile. Renata calls it animal loyalty. The physical pull of place, language, and the quality of light are all part of the sense of connection, culminating in the sounds of voices figured as a knotted embrace that she cannot imagine breaking:

What keeps me here? Perhaps just a kind of animal loyalty: the smell of these streets, familiar sounds, the area where I live now, the food I eat, a tree, a friendly face, my conversations with you, the café on the south side. I feel too an unhealthy curiosity about where the world I know is going, what will become of the Theater, how we'll put on the new version (in English and in furs) of *Hamlet*, when the attractive painter and set designer, Claude, will ask me out, etc. As you see, a feeble plot. . . .

It's the flow of the river, not its origins, that interests me, so I'll never find the fountainhead. But I swear to you, Emilio, that when I said goodbye to Marga, when I started walking back toward my house and saw the lovely autumn light in the streets and heard the bruised, piquant Spanish of this city weaving together the unknown voices of the people I passed, tying them up in a strong knot, in a tacit, involuntary embrace, I knew I'd made the right decision.

Don't tell me off if you disagree. I'm longing for your return so that I can explain to you in person my sentimentality, my stupidity, or my cowardice.[18]

Exile, Rossiello tells us, throws up a barrier between writer and reader. Writer after writer deals with this dilemma. In an early work, *Como en la guerra* (translated into English as the novella *He Who Searches*), Luisa Valenzuela elaborates an extended metaphor of the home country as an enormous house with treacherous and misleading passageways, false doors and windows that keep the inhabitants in.[19] Those who escape have, from the outside, the perspective to disentangle the puzzle that entraps those within, but communication is utterly cut off. The ideal, in fact necessary, reader is the one reader without access. In an interview conducted while David Viñas was in exile from Argentina, this novelist was asked who his ideal reader would be. His response recalls Valenzuela's house, severing writer from reader:

To the question about who, in his judgment, would be the ideal reader of his work, Viñas responded in 1982, "I don't know. When I lived in Buenos Aires — back there — I thought I had an approximate idea. Now, today, what do I know? Not in Denmark or in Mexico. I just write. Frankly? No ideal reader or work or judgment. Or 'would be . . .' "[20]

With no one on the other end of communication, language itself begins to disintegrate. The sound of language spoken but not heard, of trees falling in lonely woods, the sound of one hand clapping. Yet Viñas continues to write.

Julio Cortázar's sense of exile, we recall, sprang from being unread by his "natural" audience. Russian poet Joseph Brodsky sees this as a useful

lesson in humility. Brodsky, who like Cortázar had an international readership (but who, unlike him, was forced into exile and suffered a period of
extreme dislocation and despair), writes of the egotism of the exile writer,
particularly of the one who was known in his own country (the masculine is Brodsky's): "And the reality of [exile] consists of an exiled writer
constantly fighting and conspiring to restore his significance, his poignant
role, his authority. His main consideration, of course, is the folks back
home; but he also wants to rule the roost in the malicious village of his
fellow émigrés."[21] José Donoso's dissection of the frustrated, failed, talent-
less writer in *El jardín de al lado* (*The Garden Next Door*) is of a piece with
Brodsky's gleefully unsympathetic observation.[22]

Addressing a conference on writers, like himself, in exile, Brodsky
linked space and language as key elements of exile, saying, "[I]n our profession, the condition we call exile is, first of all, a linguistic event."[23]
Language takes on particular resonance in exile. In the extreme case,
which was that of many Southern Cone exiles who landed in Holland or
Scandinavia, as opposed to France, Germany, or the United States (whose
languages may well have been studied in school), or Spain, Venezuela,
Cuba, or Mexico, where the language difference is palpable but does not
impede communication in any profound way (or maybe only in profound
ways, but not at the level of basic interaction), to be set down in a place
where the language is unfamiliar is to be returned to a state of dependency
and to be perceived as intellectually incompetent. This extreme shift in
social status occurs simultaneously with the sense of physical dislocation
to which it is connected, and it can make even apparently minor linguistic
differences resonate with major distinctions in prestige and power.

The difference in language for the Uruguayan exile in Spain is primarily
phonological, and, as Cristina Peri Rossi suggests, it is all the difference:

> His accent gives him away: he drags his esses a little and pronounces
> *b* and *v* the same. Then a kind of silence grows around him. It is not
> a big silence, but he perceives some curiosity in the looks on their
> faces and a small readjustment in their gestures, which become more
> emphatic. (Imperceptible changes to a casual observer, but exile is a
> magnifying glass.)[24]

Peri Rossi's exile is known by his accent, and what makes him recognizable
also makes him "other." Fernando Aínsa makes a similar point in titling
his novel about the generational repetition of exile from Spain in 1937
and Chile in 1973, *Con acento extranjero* (With a foreign accent).[25] Aínsa
and Peri Rossi both address the very particular relationship between Spain
and its former colonies in these narratives. Aínsa's father and son are
both Spanish, but thirty-nine years in Chile have made them foreign, a
foreignness that is marked primarily by their manner of speaking:

Nevertheless, these Spaniards have an air that is hard to define, a certain something that says they're foreigners. Details, gestures that people notice, especially when they speak. Words, sayings, turns of phrase, ways of understanding and of conjugating verbs, things an official stamp or an identity card can't hide.

Let's say it clearly, from the start: these Spaniards speak with a certain foreign accent.[26]

Father and son are almost completely accepted by their neighbors; the former was born nearby, and the latter "is someone 'who could have been born here, exactly the same,' as they tell him kindly."[27] The one element that continues to distinguish these two from the people they live among is the way they speak. The diminutive *igualico* that marks the son's similarity is one he, raised in Chile, would not naturally use himself.

Latin American varieties of Spanish are considered a fall from grace by peninsular Spaniards. As this colonial history shows, these linguistic relationships are culturally and historically specific. Language difference plays out in other ways in other cultures. Nadine Gordimer's novel *None to Accompany Me* describes, among other things, the return of South African exiles.[28] In that text, language difference within the country is negotiated within families, among friends, and across political divides, all established prior to exile. The white, English-speaking protagonist is unable to communicate with the wife of one of her coworkers, a woman who lives in one of the townships and speaks only her indigenous language; both women know a limited amount of Afrikaans, but their vocabularies — one from the courtroom and the other from the countryside — do not coincide. A husband and wife blend her Zulu with his Xhosa, one language or the other chosen to meet particular circumstances. Their daughter, born in exile, raised in London, is a cultural hybrid. Under these conditions, the need to accommodate to new languages in a series of countries of exile (Tanzania, Botswana, England, Sweden, and Russia are part of its trajectory) is not even remarked upon.

In the cases I am looking at, Spanish is the language of the characters, and of the text itself.[29] Although many of the exiled writers had studied other languages, the societies they came from were largely monolingual. In the United States, where Spanish is less prestigious precisely because it is spoken there by an already marginalized group, the situation is again different. The European countries of exile that elicit the greatest linguistic dislocation are those that are similarly monolingual, whose language is not Spanish, and who may well think of Spanish as a less prestigious language than their own, but also of lower status than other equally foreign languages.

On some days, the language of such cultures may seem like blunt instruments, hideously and brutally deforming thought and expression.

Sergio Badilla's poem at the beginning of his 1988 collection, *Terrenalis*, is a nightmare version of code-switching, apparently written on one of those days. The poem is a sort of signpost embodying and signaling a Spanish crippled by a too-long interference by Swedish:

> A estas luces imudias de unas horas
> traspondió dos vertiginosamente muyos
> los tacuales percotados cerca fi nuestros mismos
> aunque pauros unidos como piedras
> universales ero altid sama
> porque mus treco arisóbamos multum och myket
> repitiendo las tromeas casuas
> nu nar aluya vara fardiga
> nu nar yo ero contigo.
>
> Ronux Axel två
> Anno 2203

> [To these imudic lights of several hours
> two vertiginously walles transponded,
> the percotaded tacuals near weselves
> although paurs united like universal stones
> was altid sama
> because very treckly we arised multum och myket
> repeating the chancy tromes
> nu nar aluya var fardiga
> nu nar I are with you.
>
> Ronux Axel II
> Anno 2203][30]

What is left of Spanish here, in the year 2203, is nearly unrecognizable. The Swedish is similarly deteriorated. Language evolves naturally, but here it has apparently been assaulted, reduced to the simplest syntax, and bludgeoned into something nearly unrecognizable as human speech, much less poetry.

Luisa Valenzuela, living in New York during the time of the Argentine Proceso, spoke English as little as possible (although she speaks it, and French, fluently) and traveled to Mexico regularly in order to be in touch with the language she writes in.[31] In Marta Traba's posthumous novel, *En cualquier lugar*, the most militant of the exiles, who refuse to abandon the symbolically charged locale of the railroad station (that is, who refuse to arrive at the place of exile, insisting on preserving that first moment of being in transit), also refuse to learn the language of the unnamed European country they have (almost) come to.[32] Yet one of the means of survival in exile is learning the host language. José Leandro Urbina's *Cobro revertido* (Collect call), which takes place in Canada, offers a wonderful blend of languages — the protagonist's roommate speaks Portuguese, and they communicate in an amalgam of that language and Spanish.[33] French and English are required for negotiating Montreal. Megan, the protagonist's girlfriend, and later wife, speaks halting Spanish; theirs is a multilingual communication; his subsequent girlfriend speaks French. His Chilean friends discuss politics in *chileno* over countless bottles of beer. But this Babel seems to make it impossible for the protagonist to recognize the accent of his own country when one of its speakers is talking in another language. At the end of the novel, as noted earlier, he is badly beaten as an indirect result of not recognizing a woman's accent in English? French? as Chilean. That beating, in turn, is the definitive stroke in precluding his return to Chile, his goal throughout the novel.

Ana María Araujo's short story "Mercedes" also links language to body and geography, with the possibility of a real connection to home dashed at the end by the switch from Spanish to French.[34] The exiled protagonist, living in France, comes to know she is unable to intervene in the reality of the disappearance of her friend when her lover, speaking in French, tells her there is nothing she can do. Through this effortless code-switching she realizes that she is fundamentally changed:

> Mercedes, Mercedes disappeared.
>
> Je sais . . . Mais écoute, Isabelle, calme toi. Nous sommes ici; allez, de toutes façon [*sic*] tu peux rien faire. . . . On va appeller sa soeur; et aprés. . . .
>
> In that precise moment, Isabel understood that distances invade bodies, inexorably and for always.[35]

Language and distance effect change, change that is known and registered in the body. Even Isabel's name is altered, barely perceptibly, but, as Peri Rossi notes in another context, it is an alteration that, for the exile, is magnified.

Beatriz, a child of exile in Mario Benedetti's *Primavera con una esquina rota* (Springtime with a broken corner), whose separation from her country will, according to her grandfather, preclude forever her ability to return fully, acquires not a second language but her first language together with its variants.[36] Beatriz is sensitive to both phonological and semantic difference: *fresa* and *frutilla* are the same strawberry ice cream flavor. Her friend hears the word *sarcástico,* which she thinks is so pretty she makes it her new puppy's name. Beatriz gives us a sense of the newness and contingency of language. Words are in the process of becoming signifiers in her world, and on the way they can be waylaid.

Cristina Peri Rossi also takes advantage of the special relation children have to language in her short story "La índole del lenguaje" (The nature of language), in which language for the protagonist, a seven-year-old boy, has material substance.[37] Spelling, writing, and authority all come together in his battle with the presence and absence of the silent letter *h*. For him, on the one hand, eyes are naked, lashless, without the protection of an *h* at the beginning of the word *ojo;* on the other hand, leaves on the ground seem protected by the *h* in *hoja* that goes from the stem of the leaf to its edge. The letter has a function that goes beyond the purely orthographic. When the narrator realizes that the silent, protective *h* in *ojos* is wrong, he tries to erase it, an act prohibited by his teacher. When he makes a hole in the paper, he knows he will be punished; the hole is a mark of an absent presence — not just *ojo* without an *h*, but with an erased *h* that has made itself known by its very absence. The punishment, however, is worse than the failing grade he expected; the teacher tears up his paper and throws it away, stripping him of the product of his language labor.[38] This child, who defines himself as a poet and who wonders who was the first namer (that is, where the authority of language derives from), finally comes to the conclusion that language belongs to those in power. Since his school is a military academy and his uncle has been imprisoned for refusing to accede to the military government, a fact kept silent by his family, the question of the power over language as it relates to power in general is not incidental.

Peri Rossi's child, living under dictatorship, is defeated by those who police his use of language; Beatriz in exile lives language as adventure. For her, everything is filtered through language and its meanings, and it is she who notes the subtle differences between the Spanish of Uruguay and the Spanish of Mexico, which for her is a way of noting the differences between the two countries:

> This country is not mine, but I like it pretty much. I don't know if I like it more or less than my country. I came when I was very little and I don't remember what it was like. One of the differences is that in my country there are *cabayos* (horses) and here on the other hand there are *cabaios* (horses). But they all neigh.[39]

Like a Beatriz grown to young womanhood in exile, the protagonist of José da Cruz's short story "Noticias de papá" (News of dad) lives in an atmosphere (exile in Sweden) marked by a hybridization of a language that has taken on physical characteristics and that is, as well, her only link to a national identity:

> What was her land? Weren't Morocco, Portugal, or Colombia all about the same? The only thing that connected her to that country where her parents' imagination bloomed was a form of Spanish that was now surely antiquated: a fossil-dialect filled with Swedish, maybe even with English, with who knows what, mixed with the

Chileanisms and Uruguayanisms of her friends, with a melody of phrase now forever indefinable. She arrived "there" and someone commented:
"She talks like a Central American."
She didn't know what to say.
Maybe it was true.[40]

Similarly, novelist and psychologist Ana Vásquez notes distinctions between the Chilean Spanish she grew up with and the Continental Spanish that has begun to take it over after years of living outside her native country:

My language was Hispanicized, the typically Chilean characteristics were erased. I have spent a great deal of time in Spain and there [to say "money"] you don't say "la plata," you say "el dinero"; "la plata" means you're going around with a silver ingot.[41]

Unlike Benedetti's Beatriz, for whom *cabaio* and *cabayo* occupy similar registers of meanings (*todos relinchan*), Vásquez presents this distinction from the point of view of the Spanish (as opposed to Chilean) speaker; the peculiar image is the one evoked by the Chilean term. Vásquez is sensitive to both the enriching and debilitating aspects of bilingualism, annoyed when the *mot juste* is in French and she has to go to the dictionary to find a way to say it in Spanish. The child Beatriz also has adventures with the dictionary. When she tries to figure out the meaning of the word "pollution," she is sent down the semantic garden path by a dictionary that deals in euphemisms and connects pollution with ejaculation. Beatriz does not quite have language right yet, and when the words and the meanings do not, or cannot be made to, coincide, the words are still in the process of being created. Her notion of the seasons is that there are three: spring, summer, and winter, the seasons she knows. Her mother assures there is another: fall, which Beatriz renders as she hears it, one word, *elotoño* ("thautumn").

Lest we think the child's confusion about words is merely a charming way of displaying her innocence (which it also is), Benedetti's Beatriz struggles as well with words that have life-and-death meaning for her imprisoned father and, by extension, for Uruguay as a whole:

Amnesty is a hard word, or like my Grandpa Rafael says, it's prickly, because it has an *m* and an *n* that always go together. Amnesty is when they pardon you from a punishment.[42]

Beatriz learns a word that is crucial for her father, making it hers by thinking about the very letters that constitute it. She understands that "amnesty" is a word of great difficulty, but she transfers that difficulty from the semantic/political to the orthographic. Beatriz further incorporates the word by identifying herself with/as the recipient of amnesty, cued by the use of the feminine in the otherwise impersonal, but grammatically masculine, "one" ("cuando a *una* le perdonan"). Another way of making the word her own is by establishing herself as the one who is in a position to grant amnesty, mastering the spelling, and turning noun to verb, whose meaning she is also in a position to explain: "Teresita, I amnesty you" ("Teresita yo te amnistío"). When her friend takes this as an insult and begins to cry, Beatriz gives meaning to the word: "Teresita don't be dumb; I amnesty you means I forgive you."[43] Beatriz's adventure in language is about the struggle of the subject to make meaning. Her naive negotiation of words and meaning is part of the establishment of an active subjectivity. But it is also about the attempt at cooperation between the subject and the specific linguistic context. This latter is itself subject to degradation at the hands of dictators.

Beatriz's grandfather, Don Rafael, counts language as one of the victims of the military dictatorship in a passage that uses language as the objective correlative for the society rent by state violence. Uruguayan society is figured as a sentence, interrupted by the parenthesis of dictatorship; the orderly grammar of society is irrevocably destroyed:

> The implacable ones, the ones who won their epaulets in militant cruelty, those who began as puritans and ended corrupt, those people opened an enormous parenthesis in that society, a parenthesis that surely will close one day, when no one is able anymore to pick up the thread of the old sentence.[44]

Here language functions as metaphor, but in the next sentence language and society acquire a metonymic relationship. Language is one of the aspects of society that the dictatorship claims as victim:

> They will have to start weaving another [sentence]; arranging another, in which the words will not be the same (because there were also pretty words that they tortured or condemned or included in the rolls of the disappeared), in which the subjects and the prepositions and the transitive verbs and direct objects will no longer be the same. The syntax will have changed in this as-yet-unborn society which at that moment will seem sickly, anemic, vacillating, excessively cautious, but with time will begin to recover, inventing new rules and new exceptions, flaming words from the ashes of those that were prematurely calcified, coordinating conjunctions more adequate to serve as bridges between those who remained and those who left and will then return. But nothing could ever be the same as the prehistory of seventy-three.[45]

The syntax *of* society, the broken sentence in need of repair, is also syntax *in* this crippled culture. Language becomes coterminous with the nation.

The adjectives of weakness Benedetti invokes are ambiguously assigned, now to society, now to the sentence, further imbricating them. Benedetti's exploration of the link between language and society is echoed in an anecdote of Ariel Dorfman's in which Dorfman, making an all-but-clandestine visit to Pinochet's Chile, encounters an example of speech enfeebled by dictatorship. In an interview with Raquel Ángel, Dorfman recounts being told by a group of young Chileans that he does not speak Chilean. But, says Dorfman, what they do not understand is that it is they who have lost the loud and open voice that characterized Chilean discourse prior to the coup. What it means to speak Chilean is time-specific and historically determined.[46]

The powerful evocation of language in society and language as society, neither subsumed under the other, gives way to considerations of space. As Benedetti says, those who repair the Uruguayan sentence cannot be those whose experience was of non-Uruguayan geography and history:

> Perhaps the officiates, the makers of the pendulous and peculiar nation, will be those who are now children, but who remain in the country. Not the little boys and girls who bear on their retina the snows of Oslo or Mediterranean sunsets or the pyramids of Teotihuacán or the hills of the Appian Way or the black skies of Swedish winter.[47]

Sensory experience of the landscape is prerequisite to the ability to act with thorough knowledge. The primacy of the physical connection is tied to the (secondary) political connection, the expression of which was rendered not only in, but as, language. Yet Dorfman's experience suggests that the children of dictatorship cannot repair the national utterance alone. Even more bleak is Abril Trigo's reading of the children of the generation who remained, whose cynicism is, at least, an antidote to the false memory the exiles had of what he calls the Uruguayan "Model Republic":

> In contrast to the territorial exiles, who found refuge in the ineffable certainties of the imaginary of the Model Republic, the Dionysiacs [the generation that grew up under the dictatorship], cut off from it, suffered a double orphanhood that forced them to put into play the productivity of exile.... [I]nstead of de-exiling themselves, they radicalized their radical alterity, to break with Uruguayanness and deconstruct the nostalgic restoration of the homogenizing historical-pedagogical memory of the imaginary of the Model Republic, threatened by the proliferation of multiple and antagonistic cultural-performative memories.[48]

For Abril Trigo, the dictatorship and the questionable restored democracy that followed it did Uruguay the favor of "locating the question of memory at the center of the national problematic," so that the myth of the homogeneous Switzerland of South America could finally be called into question.[49] He rejects Benedetti's hope for rebuilding a shattered Uruguayan language/culture, preferring the radical cynicism of this generation. In the face of demands to forget, proposed by both the dictatorship and the democracy that followed it, he holds out the promise of "antimemory" and "negative memory," forgetting to forget.

Ricardo Piglia, too, is much less sanguine than Benedetti concerning postdictatorship, this time in Argentina. Even for those who did not leave and so did not have to come back and readjust, this is a hallucinatory place, and an uncannily corporeal language is at the center of the weirdness of his novel La ciudad ausente. Metaphor is made concrete in this novel — the woman-become-machine, the child for whom words and their referents are completely unhinged and who only comes back to a sort of language through a regimen of repetition of theme and variation.[50] The reproduction of experience as museum — deracinated, made unheimlich — is the same metaphor for death (with its overtones of aestheticization) that Peri Rossi uses in El museo de los esfuerzos inútiles (The museum of useless efforts) and Los museos abandonados (The abandoned museums).[51] There is an S F feel to this text, although the story is historically precise.[52] The woman who has been turned into a machine is not Donna Haraway's happy cyborg, tripping carefree across previously proscribed borders separating human from machine. She is, instead, trapped, hidden, imprisoned in a nightmare space that cannot be freed from its history. References to specific, key dates like 1973 and to such events as the discovery of bodies in wells in the countryside make the purely fictional (or what apparently is purely fictional, and even hallucinatory) take on a certain historical veracity.[53]

In the self-erasing place that is the absent city with its self-censoring newspaper, language stops absolutely being representational. It certainly cannot sustain a plot. Generically, La ciudad ausente is less a modern novel than a romance, a quest tale in which the object of desire is knowledge. Reminiscent of Enesco's Me llamaré Tadeusz Freyre (My name will be Tadeusz Freyre), whose object of desire is an official identity endlessly deferred, the search for knowledge in this novel is simply unachievable. Stories are placed within narrations in a seemingly endless regression. Like the child in this novel, for whom language has become unmoored, we are left with the sense of absolute contingency in reading La ciudad ausente.[54] The protagonist is called by a name, Junior, that is not a name, but a reference to an empty genealogy. He is progeny without provenance. When Junior finally, after a series of adventures, finds the technologue of language who can unlock its secrets and make it work (Russo is, after all, the engineer, not the pure scientist), what he learns about, surprisingly, is the human body. Russo, who knows the secret of the mysterious machine that wrings life from events, tells Junior:

A story is nothing other than the reproduction of the order of the world on a purely verbal scale. A replicate of life, if life were made only of words. But life is not made only of words; it is unfortunately made of bodies, that is, as Macedonio [Fernández, Argentine writer] said, of sickness, of pain, of death. Physics develops so rapidly, he interjected, that in six months all knowledge has grown old.[55]

Like her countryman Ricardo Piglia, Luisa Valenzuela interrogates language, pushing it to the extremes of representation and representability.[56] *Simetrías* (Symmetries) was published in 1993, after the writer's return to Argentina. In one of its stories, Valenzuela experiments with the word under erasure. The protagonist in "Viaje" (Journey) writes down her thoughts as she is traveling so she can dispel them. She writes in order to erase:

I'm taking a notebook in case I decide to write down any ideas about Carlos or any of the things he says, which I will carefully erase to get them out of my head. I'm taking about five pencils from the office, the kind with erasers on the other end. I'm also taking a soft eraser, since that's what it's about. I'm going to write down stuff about Carlos and erase it. When I get back this will be like a blank notebook again, but all erased. I like it already.[57]

The erasures are successful and satisfying. Moreover, the protagonist discovers much later that there is writing in the book in her own hand that she does not remember putting there, writing about herself as Kali, the creative and destructive goddess. The purposeful erasure of Carlos makes the emergence of self-as-Kali possible. The power to erase written language — actively to forget — emerges in this story as more potent even than the authority to command remembrance. It is usually forgetting that is unconscious and the production of language, of text (which is also a kind of memory), that is conscious. Here Valenzuela authoritatively inverts these processes for the woman writer, for whom writing itself depends on the power to choose what to forget, as opposed to being told what is appropriate to remember and what, therefore, must be forgotten. Doing so, she reiterates and significantly modifies a dominant theme in the political debates that followed redemocratization in Argentina, as well as in Chile and Uruguay, in which amnesty for the military was legislated.

The woman who writes and erases traverses space without its making even the mark that she obliterates from the page. She wishes to be absent from her work, from her relationship with Carlos, but not be present anywhere else. She is in transit, but only away from, not to, anywhere. In another of the *Simetrías* stories, "El café quieto" (The still café), space is more circumspectly drawn, and spatial differentiation is founded on the venerable binary of gender. With the men along the wall and women next to the windows, Valenzuela draws the distinction with irony, invoking a diminished male valor that attempts to attract the attention of the waiters. Even within this impoverished sphere, spoken language has its material consequences. The sound of the men calling "mozo," with its sound of *o*'s, produces a physical reaction in some of the women. What it does *not* produce is a waiter (that is, to signify as intended) — *they* circle the room on their own terms:

> Sometimes, in a burst of what we might call bravery, [the men] raise their heads and with a determined voice emit the word *mozo* (waiter) as if they were calling.
>
> When this word sounds I think I note the acceleration of hormones in the nape of the neck of some of the women. I think that word, *mozo*, said like that in such a serious voice, so laden with *ooo*'s, also makes my hair stand on end.
>
> I realize that some of the women, like the one who is sitting right in front of me, allow nothing to disturb them. It must be that they've been here longer — years maybe — in this café that is so still and that they know, among a thousand other things, how useless that call is. The waiter will come when it's time, without any fixed or predictable rhythm, or he'll come when he feels like it or when he gets more coffee.[58]

Spoken language has lost its power to summon even a waiter, and the written language, the language of the story, also stops — when the paper and ink run out. The narrator is writing on paper napkins and is aware that they are diminishing. The end of the paper and ink is connected to the end of all the necessary items here — coffee, and the world itself: "The problem will occur when my ink runs out and the last paper napkin is used up and the coffee is gone and the world dissolves."[59] The end of the physical means of producing language — ink and paper napkins here, no less the coffee that fuels the writer and legitimizes her occupying a table in the café — means the end of the world, which is perhaps the world of this story, writing about writing.

Yet this diminishing space for language recalls a referent beyond this text, that is, prison writing, and the whole question of language in prison, where the written word was prohibited and therefore virtually impossible to produce, no less distribute, and the spoken word could result in torture.[60] The content of the language, from the jailers' point of view, could be anything: it was the sounds of language that alerted them and that constituted the transgression. The precious object — the manuscript produced in prison, the banned book, the single poem — is truly a part that is taken from the whole and invested with great meaning. The prison text is all that is available from the whole person who produced it. That text represents her or him; and if it is fetish, it is fetish with the negative connotations, the connotations of neurosis, removed.

I began this chapter with a reference to "La densidad de las palabras," in which Valenzuela rewrites a European folktale about two sisters, one good and beautiful, rewarded for her forbearance with the gift of producing jewels and flowers as she spoke, the other spoiled and nasty, whose punishment was that snakes and frogs would come from her mouth whenever she tried to talk. In her retelling, Valenzuela stresses the physical nature of words — their viscosity and the very horror they elicit when they come from a woman's mouth. The speaker in the tale is the wicked sister, cast off into the forest (which she twice calls her exile), who finds that she is not altogether displeased with her fate. Just as Benedetti's Don Rafael makes his punishment, his exile, his own,[61] this sister makes her words her own:

> And that is why
>   now
>   I am alone in the woods and from my mouth
> c o m e   f r o g s   a n d   s n a k e s.
> I am not entirely sorry: now I am a writer.
>
> The words are mine, I am their mistress, I say them clearly, I let out all the words that were prohibited to me; I yell them, scatter them through the forest, for they leave me, hopping or slithering, all with lives of their own.[62]

How different the ecstatic emission of living language for the able writer from the frustration experienced by José Donoso's writer-protagonist in *El jardín de al lado*. If language is a bodily product, the failed writer can gag on it. "Why do I have to live my whole life choked by these metaphors, instead of metabolizing them to reanimate my work?"[63] Julio Méndez's metaphors never get beyond the unassimilated state. They are unmalleable as stones; he is incapable of turning them into something that is suggestive beyond themselves, or even of evoking the reality he experienced.

At the end of "La densidad de las palabras," the forest-dwelling writer rescues her bored good sister, who is stuck in the castle, married to the handsome prince, a husband only interested in her words for what wealth they bring him. The two sisters, created in the folk tradition to be eternal rivals, effect their own reunion. Together, they produce words that are both frightening and beautiful, alive and sensual, powerful and fanciful:

> My sister comes toward me, running across the bridge, and when we embrace and burst out in voices of recognition, I perceive on her shoulder that a diadem of gems glitters on one of my snakes, a ruby appears on the forehead of my cobra, a certain great carnivorous flower is digesting one of my poor frogs, a toad chews a red jasmine

and begins to blush, there is another flesh-eating plant like an oily trumpet digesting a snake, a very open and red bromeliad catches a tadpole and offers it its heart as a nest. And while my sister and I tell each other everything we could not say ever before, a thousand bejeweled frogs are born in the bromeliad, and they serenade us with their, let's say, polyphonous chorus.[64]

It is the mother who sends the girls to the well and another mother figure who turns their language into matter. It is no surprise that the title of the original story given in collections of European tales is "Mother Holle." The mother tongue is the visceral language, the one that inexorably ties the body to language: mother tongue, lengua materna. But there is another side to the mother's tongue: it can be subverted by the daughter who, in defiance of the mother, but even more of the unseen father, becomes a gender outlaw. The two sisters whose reconciliation Valenzuela effects had been written not only as an object lesson in appropriate femininity, now to be deconstructed, but also as ever-sundered opposites whom Valenzuela reunites. In passing, she also reconciles the geographical binary between forest and civilization (here enclosed in the castle) that, as Robert Pogue Harrison has so elegantly argued, underlies Western culture.[65]

The reconciliation of binary opposites in Valenzuela's story occurs in material(ized) spaces in language that has fully recovered its origin in the body and manifests itself exuberantly and excessively on the bridge linking the castle of one sister's civilized confinement to the barbarous forest of the other's exile. The originary home has dissolved in this tale. It was an unpleasant little cottage, marked by an overdetermined but under-theorized rivalry among women, and within the individual woman. The mother in the story reproduces herself in the form of two girls, both of whom she ultimately repudiates. The daughter she first embraced and then rejected was the one most like herself. The other, who was rewarded with the best situation in the land of monarchical patriarchy — queen of the realm — was the father's likeness, the obedient and long-suffering daughter. Marriage merely returned her, as a virtual prisoner, to the site where, according to the old script, she belonged. Furthermore, if the evil daughter is the one most like her mother, and she has become the hero of the story who rescues her bored (and boring) good sister, what might that tell us about the mother, who produced both these girls? Valenzuela's return to the source of this story in language makes its rewriting possible, both in the obvious sense of her commandeering the old tale and retelling it and in the more subtle sense of her examination of language itself as a product of an already gendered body.

Chapter Five

BETWEEN EXILE AND RETURN

Exile covers, at best, the very moment of departure, of expulsion;
what follows is both too comfortable and too autonomous
to be called by this name, which so strongly suggests a
comprehensible grief.

— JOSEPH BRODSKY

The focus on spatial relations in this study does not preclude my tracing a temporal, almost orderly, trajectory, beginning with the rootedness
of home and the development of a national identity, followed by the displacement of exile and the processes of acculturation and alienation, to
this chapter's investigation of relative emplacement in the new country
and the transition toward one form of *desexilio* or another.

Still, this imposed orderliness should not obscure the very messy
overlappings of the affective states of exile. In an article on Latin American exile literature in Sweden, critic, poet, and fiction writer Leonardo
Rossiello states, "[F]or us exile has ended; its literature has not."[1] This is
a way of saying that the processes of exile are not definitive, that the subject produced in and by exile continues to experience the world through
the circumstances of exile, even after many years, and even after return
home has become juridically possible. Rossiello's own writing seems to
have avoided the issue of exile, at least thematically. The short stories of
Solos en la fuente (Alone at the fountain), *La horrorosa historia de Reinaldo*
(The horrifying story of Reinaldo), and *La sombra y su guerrero* (The shade
and its warrior) are marked by a formal purity and, with rare exceptions,
avoid direct expressions of the conditions or the spaces of exile, the nostalgia for home, or the denunciation of repression.[2] Yet Rossiello's very
formalism, his visceral love of the shape of words and sentences, is an
expression of the desire to keep alive and nourished the fragile orchid
of the Spanish of exile, vulnerable because its leaves and flowers — the
linguistic artifacts he and other exile writers produce — are rooted not
in the self-renewing soil of everyday speech, but in the air of a foreign
country. It is in that part of his critical work that concerns itself with
contemporary writing that Rossiello speaks overtly to the issues of exile
and in which he permits us to see that the unending literature of exile is
as much a function of its reading as of its writing. Commenting on Car-

los Liscano's one-act play, *Retrato de pareja* (Portrait of a couple), about a carping, demanding wife (played by a man) who interrogates and ex-coriates her husband (played by a sports bag wearing a baseball cap) as an allegory of torture, Rossiello joins others for whom the literature of exile is, thematically, less about the experience of exile than about the repression left behind.[3] Whether or not Liscano's play is about anything more than its manifest, if parodic, content of a very troubled marriage, Rossiello's reading directs us to the overwhelming number of exile texts that, by telling the story of political repression and state terror through poetry, fiction, testimonio, and journalism, denounce them to the world. Certainly, exile criticism has focused on these texts and may well be just another genre in which such storytelling takes place. As Juan Armando Epple points out about Chilean critics in exile, this scholarship "tend[s] to reaffirm...the legacy of a historical memory and to value, often to overvalue, those works centered on the experiences of the coup or that convey a critical vision of the dictatorship."[4]

This is precisely the form of exile writing José Donoso disdains in *El jardín de al lado* (*The Garden Next Door*), a novel about life changes undergone in exile that complicate the possibilities of either remaining or returning, a novel in which Donoso counsels the writer in exile to quit nursing old political wounds.[5] Under this novel's terms, it is far better to write attending to aesthetics, not politics. One critic, apparently in agree-ment with the novel's depoliticizing project, claims that "*El jardín de al lado* is a successful exploration of the contradictory ground that separates politics from the autonomous work of art, an exploration carried out by the transference of the notion of crisis from the political realm to the aes-thetic."[6] But what does it mean to transfer the notion of crisis from the political realm, where crisis is a matter of state terror — the disappearance, torture, and murder carried out on thousands and threatening any oppo-sition — to the aesthetic realm? What can "aesthetic crisis" possibly mean in this context? Under what circumstances and by what means can the notion of crisis be "transferred"? In whose interest is such a transference carried out?

Donoso's text makes an ultimately self-canceling argument against art getting mixed up with politics. His protagonist, a failed writer named Julio Méndez, has written a rather bad testimonial novel based on his six days under arrest, which has been rejected for publication. In his desire to write the definitive political novel, Julio is slightly ridiculous and more than a little pathetic. He is somewhat sheepish about the easy time he had of it in prison and the short time he spent there; in fact writing his account is a way of claiming his place in the political struggle. But Donoso will not allow his protagonist any such heroism; he is not going to dwell on the political aspects of exile in this novel, except to show how empty they are. Julio is a lukewarm revolutionary at best, a man whose contribution to anti-Pinochet activity is only to rewrite his hopeless novel, a man whose political ineffectiveness is inherited from a father who had been a middle-of-the-road, do-nothing liberal member of the government. Moreover, Julio does not even manage to write. Instead he moons over the beautiful young baroness who occupies the house, and the garden, next door.

Donoso's successful artist-character, Pancho Salvatierra, cares nothing about politics and even tends to be benevolent toward aspects of the military dictatorship. Written as an extraordinarily generous and sympathetic figure, Salvatierra is a relentlessly apolitical man whose pro-Pinochet speech is made with his tongue only part way in his cheek. He is also kind and forgiving, clearly a model human being and very likely Donoso's alter ego. Although not a superstar of the brilliance of Salvatierra (whose name exalts him as the savior of the earth), Donoso, as *his* name suggests, is unquestionably a gifted writer. Unlike Salvatierra, he has been controversial, for not using his influence as Chile's most internationally recognized contemporary novelist in order to take a public stand against the dictatorship.[7] In the novel Donoso displaces the controversy surrounding the apolitical artist onto his foil, excoriating instead the opportunistic "committed" one. Donoso is most savage toward politically engaged art and literature in his depiction of the fat, buffoonish painter Adriazola who makes his hypocritical living off political murals and sententious pronouncements. The visual artists, Salvatierra and Adriazola, reflect and exaggerate the distinction that is ultimately drawn in the realm of literature between the merely untalented and misguided Julio and the character who emerges as a successful, unpretentious writer, his wife Gloria. She turns out to have been the author in the text — the writer of the novel we have been reading all along.

Yet this novel is also a testimony to the destruction wreaked by the dictatorship. Donoso does not caricature political engagement per se. It is, rather, its exploitation by (inevitably) untalented artists and the bad writing it encourages that are the targets of his wrath. Donoso leaves no room in the text for genuinely talented artists or writers whose work is politically motivated. Only hypocrites like Adriazola, who claim a kind of postfacto exile and enjoy thinking they would be targeted by the government if they went home, and the hopelessly untalented, like Donoso's protagonist, Julio, make political commitment the center of their art. Whereas exile writing, particularly in the testimonial vein that Julio mines, has relied on claims of authenticity, Donoso suggests that it is precisely the inauthentic nature of much of this writing that is contemptible: both Julio and Adriazola make false claims of political engagement in their work. Genuine political struggle is its own product, and, even in this novel, it can be admirable. Julio's friend Carlos Minelbaum, whose clandestine oppositional activities in Argentina have made him a true political exile, unable to return, is second only to Salvatierra in garnering his author's admiration for his qualities of compassion and loyalty to his friends.[8]

The cultural conservatism subtending Donoso's desire for purity, which he exhibits in his insistence on maintaining the sharp distinction between literature and politics, is also expressed in his condemnation of other forms of impurity and inappropriate mixings. Donoso marks his unsavory characters by giving them traits that transgress the conventional boundaries of identity that allow us to tell male from female, animal from human, Indian from white, upper class from lower, and European from Latin American. The outlandish Adriazola is physically repulsive; his key characteristic is his fat, which gives him breasts. These, moreover, are hairy; he is described as looking like a Diane Arbus hermaphrodite, that is, brutish, pathetic, and somewhat frightening. In addition, the narrator says his face is *aindiado* — "with . . . marked Indian features."[9] Hybridity of gender and race, tinged with class meaning, makes Adriazola both monstrous and ridiculous. The racially marked *aindiado* is typically assigned by an upper-middle-class speaker to someone whose physical characteristics and behavior are considered a mark of (a multivalenced) "ill-breeding." The unnaturally powerful literary agent, Núria Monclús, who makes and breaks Latin American writers wanting to make it big in Spain, is a masculinized, but also bestialized, devouring female. She is described as a spider — all webs and seductive, voracious power. Bijou, the beautiful young man whom Julio comes to suspect of being his son's lover, is, we are told, angelic looking, childlike and feminine in his nudity.[10] He violates boundaries of gender and age-appropriate sexuality as well as national and ethnic divides. More French than Chilean, he speaks French, not Spanish, when he is awakened from sleep, and his Spanish, when he uses it, is French-accented. Such crossings are a threat to the precarious stability Julio has managed to achieve. Bijou not only violates boundaries himself; he elicits transgressive desires in Julio, who both admits and denies his own homosexual attraction to Bijou, significantly in the phone booth where Bijou takes him to call his mother in Chile. They cross the tracks, cross into the homosexual and youth subcultures, and cross as well into petty criminality, a miniature trip to the Inferno with Bijou as the unlikely Virgil to Julio's Dante. Happily, for Julio, they cross back again. For Donoso boundaries of gender-appropriate behavior, race, and nationality need to be maintained to preserve the social order and Julio's precarious sense of well-being, always threatened by the upheaval in class status that exile has imposed on him.

The transgression of intrapsychically experienced boundaries such as race, age, sexuality, nationality, gender, class, and even species in *El jardín de al lado* have the emotional and aesthetic currency of geophysical border-crossings that I have been associating with territorial exile. Nevertheless, since exile and failure have already deadened these characters,

the present site of their lives — Spain — has become less significant to
them as their place of exile than as the country where Latin American
novelists go to be published if they are to achieve success. In this reduc-
tive atmosphere, great writers and artists may care about their craft and
dedicate themselves to art for art's sake, but they also have an eye to the
big, prestigious European market.

Although we know there is an authorial hand in this novel, up until
the last chapter we accept that the narrative's true teller is Julio, recount-
ing his own story. It is not until the very end that it becomes clear that
there has been a level inserted between author and narrator, in the person
of Julio's wife, Gloria, a character in what we now learn is her own novel,
written by her and in which she has made her husband both protagonist and speaker. Now we look back and see where the fissures were —
that Julio's novel always sounded trivial and slightly foolish, and it was
she who ridiculed his literary efforts, that Núria was too much the phallic
mother, all-powerful and castrating in the eyes of the male child, refusing
him the satisfaction of desires she is perfectly able, in fact designed, to
satisfy. Julio's portrayal of her is a caricature; now we see that it is Gloria's
version of Julio's version: the feminist account of a failed male writer's
view of the woman who has his professional destiny in her hands. Gloria's
Julio hates and fears Núria; he projects his feelings onto the Gloria that
Gloria has him narrate. The "real" Gloria, the Gloria of the last chapter,
is quite charmed by Núria.

Almost from the moment of the novel's publication, this narrative
sleight of hand has caught the attention of critics. What has not been
widely acknowledged is the apparent clumsiness of the appended chapter
and the interpolated author.[11] For Rosemary Geisdorfer Feal, the multiple displacement of narrative voice rightly suggests Donoso's ambivalence
toward complicity in his own text, a text of exile: "In telling the story
of exile, Donoso ... takes flight from his own *I* — always a potential empty
shifter in literature."[12] Nevertheless, Donoso *is* complicit; in fact he is fully
responsible. Moreover, by exposing Gloria as the narrative's "real" author,
he has tipped his hand. Once readers begin to think about who is really
telling this story, it is not long before they must come to the realization
that if Gloria lies behind Julio, presenting his version of the story, then
behind Gloria is José, pulling her strings. This female author is a fiction
who does the bidding of *her* author.

Donoso's exile book wants to be about not the political but rather the
psychological and social aspects of exile, but it is questionable whether
the two can be separated. Gloria's text (which is Donoso's) is presumably devoid of political content and is instead about the inner life of
the characters. Inevitably, however, it is about exile, since the alienation
of exile *is* the intimate reality of their lives. Speaking through Gloria's
narrative, Donoso depicts those who remain inside the community of

exiles as hopelessly stuck. Her friend Katy is an aging hippie, exempli-
fying the community's inability to let go of the past. The exile community
is claustrophobic, tedious, predictable — but it is these characters' only
community.

Donoso's focus on the daily reality of a long-lived exile and the crisis
of individual personalities (which is, of course, the mark of the traditional
psychological novel) makes this text an ideal ground for looking at representations of diaspora and return. Donoso's pathetic characters remain the
alienated exiles described in chapter 2 of this study. Living in Sitges, they
presumably speak their foreign Spanish to the Catalans, for whom Spanish
is, one supposes, not the primary language of daily interaction. In Madrid,
Julio rather desultorily reminds himself that Pancho Salvatierra lives in a
piso, not a *departamento*. That is the extent of attention to language differences among the novel's characters. Gloria and Julio use alcohol and
barbiturates to anesthetize themselves against the pain of their own alienation, to which Gloria's nervous breakdown and Julio's sense of economic,
political, parental, and artistic impotence are vivid testaments. They feed
on their sense of outsiderness; it enervates and comes close to destroying
them. Spanish society is enemy territory, but the characters also feel the
need to succeed by its terms. Going back to Chile is impossible for reasons
having little to do with politics. Julio is unwilling to return as a failure who
has neither a job nor a published novel to his credit.[13] Moreover, he has
been afraid of being engulfed by his mother and the childhood home she
inhabits:

> Now that my mother is dead I can return without fear of being
> trapped by my feelings, and I can live in the real garden next door —
> not the reflection in the rich artificial water. Patrick, then, would
> be Pato once more, and Gloria would be able to drink her pisco
> sours and chat with her friends, giving herself up to a contemporary
> and, if possible, political version of my mother's work among "her
> women." No, she'll have to do work that will bring in money, be-
> cause I've got nothing and the inheritance from my mother will be
> insignificant.
>
> I can't go back. How? Without a single book published in Spain,
> with my tail between my legs, without work, unable to get back into
> the university I was fired from? At least in Spain I can hang around
> publishing houses begging for work..., writing jacket blurbs...,
> translating from English, correcting proofs, barely enough to make
> ends meet. But over there? Nothing.[14]

The option of return has long remained open for Julio and Gloria in *El
jardín de al lado*, inasmuch as they are more or less voluntary exiles. Although Julio was arrested and spent the six days in jail that would qualify
him to write the great testimonial novel that he is less and less sure will

make his reputation, he was not thrown out of Chile on his release, and he does not face sure prison or deportation if he returns. Nevertheless, his terror of being trapped by his dying mother keeps him from making a return visit. When she finally passes away, Julio realizes that he can return without danger of being swallowed up by her need. Yet he is still trapped by his attachment to the house she inhabited, and that holds a similar, ambivalent, attraction to him. It is the site of the originary garden next door, the lost paradise only partly recompensed by the visual (but no other) access to the Spanish garden and its inhabitant: the idealized woman who is both lovingly maternal and sexually desirable. The garden in Spain, despite being the most beautiful garden in Madrid, is only a simulacrum of the real garden, the mother's garden, left behind.

After his mother's death Julio is reluctant to sell the family home, but he is in no position to maintain it. Once it is sold, Julio is both free of it so he can return and freed from it so that ultimately he will not. The selling of the house is the symbolic rupture of all ties with Chile, despite the presence of his brother there. Moreover, not even the end of the dictatorship, which can only be hoped for, not foreseen, holds the possibility of return; Gloria and Julio's son keeps them in Spain.[15]

Now an adolescent, Pato has grown up in Spain. He is not Chilean anymore and has no interest in the most crucial events in his parents' lives, events that they have made the foundation of their existence but that he must go beyond, that are someone else's history for him. The second generation as represented in the novel is a disaster — they do drugs; their parents worry about their sexuality; they drop out of school; they want nothing to do with their elders' memories or politics. Gloria and Julio's son is an alienated, drug-besotted seventeen-year-old who is literally and figuratively lost to them. An object of conversation and concern who never appears in the novel, he does not even have a stable name. His parents want to continue thinking of him as Pato, the childhood nickname that marks him as a Chilean; he calls himself Patrick. His given name, Patricio, is all but lost in the text.[16] The absent Pato is a figure very much taken from reality, if we are to believe a recent study by Mauricio Rojas. Rojas, a Chilean living in Sweden, has written about the lost children of exile, so many of whom feel they belong nowhere, not fully welcome in the only society they know, dependent on parents who themselves have been made powerless and dependent.[17]

There is a certain psychological realism in this tale of personal frustration and failure, but Donoso undoes it at the end with the resolution of the (aesthetic?) crisis. Embraced by a top literary agent, Gloria, not Julio, publishes her secretly written novel. The publication of this work, rather than the prison novel, signals healing and the acceptance of exile. *El jardín de al lado* concludes with a grand reconciliation, not only between Julio and Gloria, whose marriage has been disintegrating since before the novel's beginning, but also between the two and Spain. In the last chapter we learn that Gloria, surreptitiously collaborating with Julio's far more successful brother, who remained in Chile, has contrived to sell the parental home that had kept Julio in thrall to his childhood. Julio, who for years has been trying to get a position at the university in Barcelona, suddenly has one and finds his true vocation as a teacher of English literature. This man, for whom translating was a distasteful chore, produces a translation that is a work of art. His magnanimous buddy Pancho Salvatierra has forgiven him for the theft and vandalism of one of his paintings. Pato, whose sexuality his father had worried about at the beginning of the novel, is safely ensconced in a heterosexual relationship and has liberated his parents by no longer needing them; he is being taken care of by his girlfriend. This sudden reconciliation with the world is simply not justified in terms of the psychological-realist novel we have been led to believe this is. The text has been rather hastily, and with no discernible irony, turned into romance, in a last chapter whose ultimate (fictional) authorship remains ambiguous. Is it Gloria's or Núria's?[18] The romance ending transforms the story of alienation into a tale of successful diasporic *desexilio*. All the unhappiness is taken care of, and the story is recontained in a happily apolitical, heterosexual world, wrapped up in the unmotivated final chapter. But the strain of tying it all together with a ribbon shows.

In contrast, Leonardo Rossiello's short story "Paparamborda a bordo" (Paparamborda aboard) takes us along a trajectory in which the acclimated exile, from all indications living a normal family life in northern Europe, is hounded by the absurd cosmic forces that sent him from his country in the first place.[19] The protagonist is an apparently well-adjusted Latin American father with a charming, high-spirited little son, the two of them on a day trip to an island off the west coast of Sweden. The geography is precise; the new territory has become familiar enough so that it can be a place of pleasure and recreation for them, as it is for the natives. This now familiar place, however, becomes the space in which progressively more bizarre events occur, experienced and witnessed not only by natives and this father and son pair, but by other foreigners, who are perhaps even more strange to the narrator than they are to the Swedes. The inordinate number of immigrants and refugees who intrude on this simple Scandinavian ferry ride occur in various startling blendings of acculturation and ethnic difference and stereotype. They range from the Feyadin who shoots the head off a bothersome dog in the habit of eating people's ice cream cones, to a group of twenty or so Africans (identified as Watusi by an annoyingly knowledgeable Swede) in full tribal regalia who speak perfect west-coast Swedish and argue with authority about the best way to eat herring, to the whale-hunting Eskimos who trade some fine harpoons for an aging Swedish woman. Paparamborda, the imaginary trickster character invoked by the protagonist, is the sign that things are going to go ironically, darkly, bizarrely wrong. The protagonist himself, who just wants to spend a day on an island with a beloved child, cannot stop being a foreigner. His stance is ever ironic; he is the outsider within, the bearer of the consciousness of the trickster. In this tale, exile is never fully resolved into acculturation; diaspora is the dance of not belonging. The narrator's catastrophic fate shadows him on board the boat with the unpronounceable, irredeemably foreign name of Styrsö. Paparamborda "solemnly shits on tourists, on voyages, and on all the archipelagos in the world."[20] That is to say, Paparamborda despises the people (tourists), places (archipelagos — intermediate sites of land and sea), and processes (voyages) of travel, international movement, the stuff of border transgression and exile. The day trip ends with an explosion that sinks the ferry; reconciliation among all these disparate elements is unthinkable.

José Donoso's *El jardín de al lado* gives us resolution with a vengeance: Gloria's young and beautiful rival is dead, killed off by the writer/wife who placed her before her protagonist/husband's gaze in the first place. The unhappy couple is reconciled, and the son has made the dangerous transition to an appropriately heterosexual object who will, conveniently, take him off his parents' hands. This type of neat but ultimately unconvincing resolution in heterosexual containment is to be found in other texts as well. The sanctified heterosexual reunion with which Mario Benedetti concludes *Primavera con una esquina rota* (Springtime with a broken corner), published a year after *El jardín de al lado*, also bodes ill, not because it is unmotivated, but because Benedetti has undermined it with its ultimately reinforcing myth of the love triangle in which one heterosexual coupling is displaced by another.[21]

Like Donoso, Benedetti has written a novel of the process of *desexilio*. These two men belong to the same generation of writers, yet they have followed very different paths. Donoso is a recognized member of the boom, internationally acclaimed and widely translated. Benedetti, also widely translated, is known as much for his poetry and journalism as for his fiction. Donoso has attracted a certain notoriety for his nonpolitical stance; Benedetti is very much a politically engaged writer.

Benedetti published *Primavera con una esquina rota* in 1982. Despite some similarities to *El jardín de al lado*, Benedetti's narrative deals in a very different way with the same period of exile. Both novels play with levels of narrative reality, although Donoso, who conceals his narrator's identity until the end, is considerably more manipulative than Benedetti, whose story of Uruguayan exiles in Mexico is periodically interrupted by apparently autobiographical or reportorial chapters. Benedetti's more straightforward mixture of levels of reality is, in its way, more demanding of the reader, who is periodically shuttled from one narrative level of reality to another. This abrupt Brechtian switch between registers allows Benedetti to trade on the emotional capital he has elicited in the fictional chapters to impel a transference onto the political, calling on the reader's agency beyond her or his involvement as a reader of a text.

Benedetti marks his autobiographical/reportorial vignettes by setting them in italics and invoking in one of them his own, full name: Mario Orlando Benedetti. The use of the middle name creates a sense of hyper-reality; Benedetti does not commonly use it, so when he does, it appears to proffer even more intimacy than does his familiar public name. Set off visually by the use of italics, the chapters that Mario Orlando Benedetti narrates make no pretense to weaving themselves into the story on the level of interaction with the lives of the fictional characters. Still, their presence as interruptions in the story line draws attention to the convention of a mutually exclusionary distinction between fictionality and truth. The same situations of political repression, the same emotions, are represented in both parts of the text. Furthermore, Benedetti does not immediately identify the italicized interruptions as nonfiction. The first interruption is a third-person account that could just as well be fictional as journalistic or autobiographical. Its protagonist is never named; it could as well be the character Santiago as the projection *Benedetti,* or some other person, fictional or real. *Benedetti* appears, named, for the first time in the second italicized chapter. This deliberate slippage between fiction and reportage, engendering a potent encounter between aesthetic and moral imperatives, recalls Alicia Partnoy's *The Little School,* also a tale of repression and dictatorship, written by a political prisoner who survived. In that text, the slippage takes the first italicized vignette and links it to both levels of narrative reality, in a text in which the fiction is also narrated by several narrators, in first and third person, and from different points of view. The testimonial vignettes, as a result, draw the fiction into history: the story is based on real events. At the same time, the testimonios' truth value is compromised, since the stories they contain have been narrativized, too.[22]

The end of exile and the stories it engenders occupy very precise moments in national and personal history. Benedetti's *Primavera con una esquina rota* was written between October 1980 and October 1981, just when the first signs appeared that the Uruguayan dictatorship would eventually fall. On November 20, 1980, the vote-of-confidence referendum, called for by the junta itself, resulted in a resounding "no." Benedetti began the novel approximately one month before the referendum, shortly after it had been announced. The novel is concerned precisely with the transitional moment that will make exile obsolete. The vote of no confidence, recollected more than once in Benedetti's novel, is the historical fulcrum of the text. From that moment exile (and prison, which is also a space of this novel) becomes contingent. The possibility of an end to exile grows visible, even though exile itself continues.

The plebiscite is a moment recalled in other Uruguayan exile texts as well. In María Gianelli's "Aquí no pasó nada" (Nothing happened here), written in Stockholm in 1983, the narrator first makes reference to it by tying it to the prisons, which were still very much filled with dissidents for whom the referendum was crucial. The reference is fleeting, buried in midsentence: "...Muñeco fixed it so the triumph of the No in the plebiscite would be broadcast, over the loudspeaker no less, in Libertad Prison."[23] The narrator immediately demeans this triumphant act by likening it to the broadcasting of soccer scores and then weakens it even further by questioning whether the announcement ever took place. The plebiscite, here, is a historical marker of the text, but it is also an ambiguous sign of change. Muñeco dies in prison before the plebiscite does him any good.

Gianelli's chronicling of the change that is not to be trusted, that is not perhaps quite a change, is not unique among writers in exile. Ricardo Pérez Miranda's novel *En esa copia feliz del Edén* (In that happy copy of Eden) is a dystopic vision of Chile in the mid-1980s.[24] One of its main characters, an army captain named José Manuel Levián, is presciently aware that the military has "lost the war."[25] For Levián, any government harbors its own opposition and its own undoing. He points out, cynically, that the left came to power under conditions of free elections, only to see itself crushed by a military regime that will have to devise a way to keep itself alive under conditions of democracy: "Ironies of fate, my little rat: Those who built your party under a democracy had to act and defend themselves in a military setting, and the leaders who emerged when the military was running things will have to act and defend themselves in a public, civilian, setting."[26] With this deterministic political deconstruction in mind, Levián fashions an operation involving kidnapping, sexual humiliation, and torture, in order to infiltrate the left and keep a foothold for the next round of political change.

The novel's title is bitterly ironic. It is a line taken from the Chilean national anthem, and its claim that Chile is a copy of paradise is so blatantly contrary to reality that it requires no editorializing on the part of the author. Unlike José da Cruz, who alters the words of the Uruguayan national anthem in titling his novel *Sin patria ni tumba* (Without homeland or grave), Pérez Miranda does not need to do anything more than copy down the words as they are sung to point out the lie they represent.

On one level, *En esa copia feliz del Edén* returns to the familiar trope of woman-as-nation, an absolutely passive body, the ground on which competing elements play for power. Tellingly, the woman's name is Patricia, with its reminiscence of *patria*. But this is a homeland that, brutalized at the hands of the military, is rendered incapable of even the smallest measure of opposition or resistance. In the end, she is the conduit between her military captor and the head of a movement to resuscitate the fragmented left, with the ordinary citizen — the narrator/boyfriend who has lived with her — remaining willingly, if not willfully, ignorant of the un-speakable truth of her history. Patricia as a character is even less than the Lévi-Straussian token of exchange among these men, because one of them, her torturer, holds tight to his ownership of her.

Patricia's military captor refers to her, in English, as "the Hamster" and addresses her as *ratita* (little rat). He and his subordinates systematically rape and torture Patricia, and he forbids her speech. Unfortunately, so do the other narrators of this text: Patricia's in-the-dark boyfriend, José Luis Esprella, the stand-in for a kind of credulous Chilean, whose first name links him, however tenuously, with the captain; and the third-person nar-rator, who is closest to the authorial voice. Like Donoso, Pérez Miranda inserts another authorial level in his novel by invoking the fiction of the discovered text, Esprella's letter/manuscript, which the narrator brings to light in these pages. Unlike Alicia Partnoy's prison tales in *The Little School,* where the protagonist struggles to survive and resist, wresting the power of narration from her captors, the distance between author and narrator is widened in Pérez Miranda's text, and his Patricia is mute in the telling of her own story. Furthermore, in *En esa copia feliz del Edén* the reader is forced into complicity with the torturers. Approximately one-third of this short novel is filled with detailed descriptions of sex-ual torture, which cross well over the border from mere literary voyeurism into pornography. Captain Levián films the sessions of sexual torture for sale to foreign buyers of hard-core sadism, a practice that has its basis in historical fact and that Pérez Miranda reproduces in this fiction. The reader of this purportedly oppositional text becomes a consumer of sadis-tic pornography, treated to page upon page of a sexual torture that ends with the victim's abject, orgasmic response to the most brutal of practices. These are always and only narrated from the point of view of Patricia's captor, who, when he is not actually present at the sessions, demands that he be provided with detailed accounts of her torture in the form of official reports, which eventually make their way into Esprella's hands and which in turn become the content of the text we are reading. Aside from a brief glimpse of Levián's wife, the only other women in this novel are another victim of this treatment, who dies early, but only after the reader is presented with scenes of her torture as a kind of taste of what is to come, and Birgitta, a Scandinavian nurse/psychologist who helps de-sign, and also participates in, the sex-torture sessions. Birgitta is a peculiar character, an odd rent in the fabric of the text that connects it with the geographical indeterminacy of the author. Despite the fact that Birgitta's nationality is clearly stated — she is Norwegian — Pérez Miranda links her to Sweden, the country of his own exile. In a drunken session with Levián, Birgitta tells him that she is a disciple of Wilhelm Reich, a Jew who was denied permission to remain in nominally neutral Sweden during World War II. There is a curious identification here between the Nazi-like

Birgitta, Aryan in her large, athletically sensual body, and the Jew, Reich. The locus of this connection is Malmö, the port city where Pérez Miranda lives and where Reich sought asylum from the Nazis. The presence of Birgitta in this text snares it between a home whose leaders cannot be trusted, the site of pure debasement, and an exile that is, in its othering of the Chilean self, on some level complicit with the abjection of the nation.

In the novel's last chapter Patricia has disappeared, only to be discovered and lost again by the erstwhile boyfriend, who has come into possession of the papers describing the experiment Levián performed on her. (These documents come to him from his grandfather, a former military man unhappy with the way that institution behaved. Thus, even Esprella, the apparently neutral man in the street, is linked by blood to the military.) It is at this point in the text that the readers are explicitly instructed to repudiate the pornographic text to which they have just been subjected, and where claims of serious critique are made. The question Esprella is left with is the crucial question of memory, though its connection to justice and survival is oddly submerged. "Is forgetting the price of happiness?" he asks. Given the brutality of this novel, the idea that happiness might be possible, or even an objective, seems insensitive at least; and forgetting, for Patricia, is impossible. The brutality has been inscribed on and in her body and psyche. She carries it with her, with no option of forgetting.

If forgetting is the price of happiness (and let us keep in mind that Esprella never states this, always questioning it), then all concerned must forget. The happiness that the ordinary citizen derives from forgetting is the placid contentment that comes with disowning knowledge once held. Ignorance is bliss, and forgetting is willed ignorance. But this willed disavowal of knowledge leaves open the possibility that the ones who performed such evil will do so again. Indeed, *En esa copia feliz del Edén* is the story of the military man who does not forget, but rather goes underground with his ever-more-cruel actions in anticipation of the military's reinstatement as the controlling factor in the government of the state. Not only indirectly, through the story he tells, but overtly in his introduction to the novel, Pérez Miranda proclaims himself clearly in favor of remembering: "[T]his novel is an argument for not confining evil and fear to the territory of forgetting, so that, capable of assuming our defects and memories, we might struggle to overcome them."[27] Moreover, in the jacket copy, which he wrote, Pérez Miranda declares his commitment, with only partial irony, to use the inevitable fame this book will bring him to "fight for a change in power relations."[28] The text he has produced, however, calls these laudable intentions into question.

En esa copia feliz del Edén is an extreme example of the narrative of mistrust. In anticipation of redemocratization (the novel takes place around

1986), the military begins its low-intensity dirty warfare: the same tactics, performed on a targeted few, in order to maintain its position even when it has been relegated to the political background. The people are dupes, and any resistance is doomed from the beginning. Writer and reader, in whom some hope might have resided, are both complicit with the sexist and explicitly homophobic pornographic text of domination.

Read one way, these narratives of disbelief in the return to democracy may well be the product of an exile that, however closely connected to home by phone and mail, was still lived at great physical remove. Growth and change elsewhere cannot be identical to growth and change at home. The exile's inevitable mistrust and fear of the state power that ejected him or her have little opportunity for the sort of modification brought about by the dailiness of living at home. Survival under dictatorship requires some adjustment and accommodation — which is not the same as collaboration. It breeds a familiarity that makes it possible to go on living a life, developing strategies that make such living possible. I do not mean to suggest that those who remained were unanimous in their trust that the plebiscites voting no confidence in the dictatorships were going to lead easily to democratic change. This is the transitional moment in which, to take Chinua Achebe only superficially out of context, things fall apart. What Benedetti sees in this moment is hardly a utopic future, but rather an opening that makes a space for the transformation, growth, and repair on both a national and individual level, and that had been put on hold during the years of the military dictatorship.

In Benedetti's *Primavera con una esquina rota*, time slows down for Santiago, the political prisoner who is one of the novel's narrators, while in exile his father, Don Rafael, grows old and his wife, Graciela, grows from youth to responsible adulthood and motherhood. Benedetti's story pays attention to generational issues and differences. The child exile Beatriz wonders what her homeland is, since she remembers virtually nothing of Uruguay and knows, she says, a great deal about her adopted country. Don Rafael, who lived the bulk of his life at home, sees his role as supporting the very young who will take on the future. Graciela lives four crucial years of her young adulthood in exile, keeping on with her life and the responsibilities of being a mother, her boring job, her freedom. She slowly realizes that she has changed, that she has become different, and that she has grown away from her husband, whom she continues to respect and admire. Nor, when Graciela falls in love with one of Santiago's best friends, also an exile, can it be a matter of acculturation to the new country. The mere fact of separation and growth, rather than the particular circumstance of exile, is responsible for these changes. For her husband in prison, change has to do with shedding the hatred he has for his captors, who do not deserve his attention, and learning to order his memories so that he can control them and invoke them.

During this time Graciela has struggled just to keep herself and her daughter housed and fed, and to survive in exile. The promise of change brought by the plebiscite means an open horizon to possibility, to her husband's release from prison. It also means an opening to think of a future over which she has some control, to see her life not just as a matter of daily survival, but as something she can decide upon. The plebiscite returns the sense of possibility and the sense of power to individuals and creates the conditions for change. In Graciela's case, the change involves the recognition that she no longer loves her husband. On one level, this sounds banal, and it is. Benedetti has devised a perfectly predictable heterosexual plot, perfectly credible in its very banality.

Like *El jardín de al lado, Primavera con una esquina rota* is a novel of the dailiness of exile, interrupted by the awareness of inevitable change. On the political level, this change is cataclysmic — it will release Don Rafael's son Santiago from prison — but on the level of daily life in exile, it involves the emergence of changes that had, imperceptibly, been occurring. Don Rafael's insight that everyone must live his or her own exile, that there is no single story of exile, tells us that to live one's exile is to live one's life. He makes it clear that the idea of exile imposed from the outside, the idea of a single exile that is the punishment meted out by dictators, is another form of oppression.

In *Primavera con una esquina rota,* the story of transition is one of change, of looking toward the future. Ana Pizarro uses the transitional moment, the trip home, to reflect on exile in *La luna, el viento, el año, el día* (The moon, the wind, the year, the day).[29] In this text, the entire memory of exile is contained in the time and space of the plane trip home. If the ocean voyage, with its rich symbolism of shipwreck, is the densely mythic and chaotic figuration of first exile in Peri Rossi and Moyano, the sleek, rapid, modern airplane in all its no-nonsense immediacy is the preferred mode of the return trip for Pizarro. Pizarro's autobiographical novel deliberately and completely takes the opportunity to reflect on the whole experience of exile. Like other exile tales, this one explicitly includes testimony and denunciation of the repression at home, telling the story of the narrator's sister, involved in the opposition and kidnapped and killed by the regime. *La luna, el viento, el año, el día,* told from the space of the airplane bringing the narrator home from exile, brings Rossiello's observation on exile and its literature to mind. For Pizarro, the end of exile is the occasion for producing the literature of exile.

Silvia Larrañaga writes another version of the transitional story in *La fusión de las siluetas* (The fusion of silhouettes).[30] This is a novel of vicarious return, in which it is not the exile who goes home to Uruguay but her lover, who goes there for a visit and re-creates a version of her life. His knowledge of the place has been entirely verbal — her stories of her house, the parks, the streets of Montevideo, her mother, and her friends.

As a photographer, his primary mode of apprehension is visual; we must assume that the narrative version of this place is particularly insufficient for him. The return effected by the narrator/lover is further distanced by the insertion of another layer of narrative: that of a man in a similar relationship with a woman, who has left him this story to read and edit. The silhouettes fuse only partially in this ever-receding reach for return, for identity, and even for the possibility of maintaining sexual relationships, which are threatened by physical separation and the appearance of other women, who themselves are versions of the primary, absent women. This novel, written and distributed in France, published in Uruguay, enacts its own rootlessness. There is no stable center in Larrañaga's novel, only the ever-receding, redoubling figures, reminiscent of the weightless figures in Peri Rossi's "Los desarraigados" (The uprooted), who seem hardly human, "men and women who float in the air, in a suspended time and space."[31] These are wanderers who inhabit the transnational spaces of McDonald's, whose trespass against purity is to eat the noncuisine of fast food or to mix dishes from one country with those of another:

> They eat Mac Donald's [*sic*] hamburgers or Pokins chicken sandwiches, whether in Berlin, Barcelona, or Montevideo. And what is much worse still: they order an outrageous dinner, composed of gazpacho, puchero, and creme anglaise.[32]

Or perhaps empanadas filled with duck ceviche. Unlike other immigrants and refugees, one of whose first gestures is to reproduce the food of home, Peri Rossi's rootless ones are gustatorily disconnected. In the 1970s, as we saw in chapter 1, Latin American restaurants in Queens opened up to serve the exile and expatriate communities there. The deterritorialized cooking of Patria (which can be anyone's homeland, as long as that homeland is Spanish-speaking), in contrast, is the sort of cooking that Cristina Peri Rossi's rootless ones would be likely to eat if they had the money. As it is they consume transnational, cheap fast food, choosing menus that are an international hodgepodge: the nightmare version of the postnational food stylings of Douglas Rodriguez. Among the many border transgressions taken up by Peri Rossi — transgression of national frontiers, gender boundaries, racial distinction, conventional sexuality — there is another: the hybridization of menus. The same writer who encourages sexual transgression and looks benevolently on child-man love in *La nave de los locos* (*The Ship of Fools*) finds the mixture of national cuisines reprehensible. There is something powerful in the meanings attached to food.

In Luisa Valenzuela's *Como en la guerra* (*He Who Searches*) a mysterious woman makes Argentine food appear, stunning the protagonist and propelling his mythic journey home.[33] On the list of things that keep Vlady Kociancich's Renata in *Últimos días de William Shakespeare* (*The Last Days of William Shakespeare*) from going into exile in the first place is the familiar food of home, which she links to other visceral needs, including language as sound and conversation.[34] The *parrillada* that does not get made is a sign of the dysfunction of the exile community in Donoso's *El jardín de al lado*. Larrañaga's recipes for traditional Christmas food in *La fusión de las siluetas*, the turkey and nut cake made in Paris and repeated in Montevideo, are detailed enough so the reader can re-create the dishes. Ana Vásquez's protagonist creates a feast of Chilean food in France for the exiled narrator and her family in a pivotal scene in *Mi amiga Chantal* (My friend Chantal). Food is such an important signifier of home that when one character in Juan Miranda's play *Regreso sin causa* (Return without reason) wants to emphasize the importance of the people he left behind, he does it by counterexample, comparing it to the importance of the food and to the land itself:

> MARIO: Of course, it's fine...the truth is...you...I don't know, you want to go back, not...not because of the empanadas, not because of the red wine either, not for any of these things,...not even for the land itself....You go back above all for the people, for your people, for all of you.[35]

In Peri Rossi's version, the consumption of deterritorialized food (produced by a *patria* without a referent and that therefore can mix cuisines with impunity) constitutes irrefutable proof that her rootless ones are profoundly transient. Waking at night not knowing where they are, what day it is, the name of the city they live in, they are disconnected in time as well as space. Significantly, what they lack is a connection to both a past and a place:

> Lacking roots gives them a characteristic look in their eye: a light blue, watery tone, the look of a person who instead of being firmly held by roots sunk into the past and into the land, floats in a vague and imprecise space.[36]

This vision of exile is finally despairing. Those uprooted ones who proffer an optimistic version of their state, lauding freedom and independence, are interrupted and dispersed: "In the middle of their speech, a strong wind comes along, and they disappear, swallowed up by the air."[37]

Chapter Six

MAKING MEANING
Gender, History, and Agency

Los antepasados hablan de una época donde las palabras se
extendían con la serenidad de la llanura. Era posible seguir el
rumbo y vagar durante horas sin perder el sentido, porque el
lenguaje no se bifurcaba y se expandía y se ramificaba, hasta
convertirse en este río donde están todos los cauces y donde
nadie puede vivir, porque nadie tiene patria.

[The ancestors speak of an era when words spread out with the
serenity of the plains. It was possible to follow its course and
wander for hours without losing the meaning, because language
did not diverge, and it spread and branched out, until it turned
into this river where all the channels come together, and where
no one can live, because no one has a homeland.]
— RICARDO PIGLIA

The deracination that exile produces in Cristina Peri Rossi's "Los desarraigados" (The uprooted) is not limited to those who left; it may also
be shared by those who have remained at home but who refuse to partake of the official version of reality. They too struggle to make sense
of what is going on around them; but there the possession of knowledge
might be deadly, and the voicing of oppositional positions is proscribed.
When meaning is caught between exile and repression, it can only be contingent, determined by ideological positioning and geographical/cultural
(dis)location. Making meaning is a form of naming reality and one's place
in it and is for that reason the exercise of a kind of power. It is a means
of taking action, a way to stamp a difference on what has been the same.
In this chapter I look at different meanings of gender and history as they
have developed in exile and at home. Gender, understood in terms of the
relations of power between men and women, and history, defined here
as the nation's representation of itself, come together obliquely as the
meaning of each is made. Gendered sexuality and the violence of history
intersect in the naming and therefore in the making of the nation as well
as of the individual who identifies with that nation.

The meanings attached to gender difference and to historical events are not just a matter of interpretation (although they are also that). Under Pinochet, Videla, and the Uruguayan junta, the conscious manipulation of meaning and the imposition of official meanings had the force of the military apparatus behind them, however brittle and easily cracked the language of dictatorship may be. Action and agency, not mere pronouncement, always underlie the making of meaning. Nevertheless, the most powerful agent may well have a stake in falsification; thus the disjunction between perceived and enforced truths. Renata, Vlady Kociancich's protagonist in *Últimos días de William Shakespeare* (*The Last Days of William Shakespeare*), discovers that meaning in an oppressive and capricious state has become utterly unstable.[1] In this novel, the by-now-familiar narrative technique of alternating narrators takes on a new urgency as a manifestation of the unsteady ground on which reality rests. An aspiring writer, Renata keeps a diary and sends letters to her friend Emilio, who has fled the country. Renata's intimate writing, which constitutes the most reliable account of what is going on in Argentina, alternates with a third-person narrative by Santiago Bonday, a publicly acclaimed but arrogant and egotistical novelist whose accommodation to the state assures his survival and success. *Últimos días de William Shakespeare* is a contemporary allegory of the Argentine military dictatorship, in which the contested discourse of nation vies with the presumably concrete and unchanging place where the nation resides (in microcosm at least: the space of the national theater and the space of a public park in the center of the capital) as both disintegrate. Like the nation itself, which it purports to represent, the national theater is there, but it is invisible. It occupies an entire city block in the middle of the city, but no one seems to know where it is. The park is a mirror image of the theater. It appears open and seems wholly visible, but it contains a dark and hidden passageway that is both secret and treacherous. What is there cannot be seen, and what can be seen is not all that is there.

Beset by bureaucracy, flood, inefficiency, shabbiness, and its endless performances of *Hamlet*, the decrepit theater/nation has been virtually forgotten. It is only when the government decides that *Hamlet* is an artifact of cultural imperialism that the meaning of the place is brought into play. In an attempt to foment nationalism, the government elevates the performance of Shakespeare that nobody attends to the level of a threat to cultural sovereignty and allows an inconsequential theater worker who has developed a cult to the fleur-de-lis to become head of the theater, encouraging him to establish the cult broadly. The irony of substituting a French symbol for a British one is lost on the repressive government, whose sense of history we might charitably characterize as deficient. In its attempt to establish sovereignty, dictatorship, in its ignorance, is capable of creating only a paste and cardboard mock-up of nation. It has, nonetheless, worked diligently to make a reality out of a discourse. Renata's writing in the minor, personal form of letters and diary constitutes a counter-discourse, but one that cannot, despite its privileged access to truth, make itself heard. Unlike the extravagantly celebrated, self-important Bonday, who is either appallingly hypocritical or completely blind to what is going on around him, and therefore guaranteed an audience and success, Renata cannot communicate her knowledge. Even her letters are confiscated before they leave the country. Renata's integrity makes it impossible for her to sign her name to what amounts to a loyalty oath to the fleur-de-lis, just as her sense of identity, tied to her need to remain in place, makes it impossible for her to save herself by going into exile. In contrast to Don Rafael in *Primavera con una esquina rota* (Springtime with a broken corner), she cannot imagine being able to create her own exile.[2] Renata believes that she would necessarily be living out a predetermined role:

> What keeps me here? Perhaps it's my imagination that makes a coward of me and shows me another possible side to Paris: being a nobody except within the safe walls of a colony of exiles; becoming a caricature of that tangle of virtues, defects and habits that I have been and am without realizing it; losing the language it took me so long to acquire only to plunge into another; embracing a nostalgia for something I never much loved.[3]

To Renata, as a writer, the threat of the loss of her language is particularly significant; the rest is a twice-useless nostalgia. Beyond that, she finds exile's interruption of a life intolerable, even though she realizes that remaining might be fatal.

As in Valenzuela's *Como en la guerra* (He Who Searches), in which a vast locked house impedes communication between inside and outside, those at home and those in exile cannot communicate in *Últimos días de William Shakespeare*.[4] Similarly, in Piglia's *Respiración artificial* (Artificial Respiration), those who are exiled or missing — Maggi, Tardewski — cannot make themselves heard.[5] The tension between within and without, the impossibility of making coherent meaning between one place and the other, is also apparent in *Primavera con una esquina rota*. There the difference between prison and exile and the ways each can be survived make it impossible to reconcile them. Experiencing one seems to preclude comprehension of the other, and indeed the marriage between the exile Graciela and the political prisoner Santiago unravels as a result. Meaning in all these cases requires communication and material consequences. Renata's sense of being ineffectual and the uprooted ones' lack of weight are functions of having no bearing on the social systems that ultimately destroy them. To make meaning is to have an effect on the world.

For some of those for whom lightness of being is a product of exile, deracination can be remedied by the radical therapy of clandestine return that connects outside and in. If Peri Rossi's rootless transients have neither the heft nor the roughened surface that might hold them by gravity or friction to a place that would enable them to leave their own mark in their comings and goings, those who risk going back to their country illegally are weighted by history, and they experience their refusal to obey the sentence of exile as the sort of defiant act that will ultimately precipitate political change. Peri Rossi's transients seem bereft of meaning, unweighted by the ballast of significance or even the hope of signifying. To undertake return, particularly the defiant return of clandestinity, indicates a powerful intent to signify. Moreover, the deliberate creation of political change, of making a difference by engaging in oppositional action, is a form of production and alteration of meaning, not least around the discourses of gender and the writing of history.

The lifting of restrictions on most Chilean exiles in the 1980s that eased movement between home and exile for some was not extended to such active members of the opposition as Clodomiro Almeyda, Mireya Baltra, and Julieta Campusano. After surreptitiously entering the country through the Andes, Almeyda, leader of the democratic left's radical social wing, turned himself in to the courts, which promptly jailed him. He then worked and spoke from prison for the no-vote in the plebiscite on whether the then-current government should remain in power. At approximately the same time that Almeyda was incarcerated, Baltra, who had been Salvador Allende's secretary of labor, together with Campusano, her colleague in the Central Committee of the Communist Party, went back to Chile illegally.[6] They too were arrested. Former Communist senator Volodia Teitelboim also returned to Chile clandestinely, but he remained underground in his determination to travel widely and report on Chile upon his return to exile in France. A journalist, and editor of the exile review *Araucaria de Chile,* Teitelboim wrote a memoir of his visit home. Its title, *En el país prohibido: Sin el permiso de Pinochet* (In the forbidden country: Without Pinochet's permission), was an overt challenge to the dictatorship.[7] Teitelboim's accounts of covert return are memoirs and journalism, not fiction. Yet the grounding tropes of memory and landscape we have seen in fictional narratives recur in his writing.

Teitelboim's geographical reveries more than once interrupt a narrative of brave people confronting Pinochet's dictatorship and of his own adventures in clandestinity. "It is nature," he writes in one of them, "that gives me the most genuine sensation that I have returned to a very personal country."[8] Return to the physical territory gives rise to the sense of returning to an emotional place where he also, rightly, resides:

> The vision of the countryside in which I had lived until a mature age was making the submerged land, which abroad had become more and more shadowy as the years passed, reappear, emerge once again, above sea level. Now I was getting it back as a moral, af-

fective territory. I was recapturing the emotional history that each person possesses by the mere act of living the greater part of one's life in a particular country.[9]

This sense of territorial belonging is the stuff of memory: "Almost everything I saw brought me memories, returned pieces of life to me."[10] It is a corporeal sense of pertaining to a place. This embodied relationship to the land finds its way to gendered metaphor. On more than one occasion Teitelboim is unable to resist comparing Chile to a woman: "Nature appeared to me naked, like a solid and beautiful woman. I breathed in her fragrance. Her beauty struck me."[11] And later:

> At times the landscape gets sullen. It is a mountain cave. And by intervals it is one of the most welcoming lands of the world, like a bony, skinny woman whose flesh, nevertheless, is warm and savory and replete with curves. Slim, she offers herself like a panoramic view, an extended body where all climates can be found. She is a female with deep gorges, her thighs; breasts whose rich nipples provide every nourishing milk, the sweet fruit of her temperate zone. Her hips are good valleys, quiet backwaters, a warm lap. She is a fruited and mineraled woman. Cold in the north, until her treasures are discovered. Warm in the center, hot if her depths are penetrated. Cold in the snows of Magellan; but warm and sheltering with her merino wool.[12]

Teitelboim's musings on Chile's sexy curves and motherly bosom bring Mary Ellman's words to mind: "At the present time . . . a person who points out breasts, thighs et al. in the contours of a landscape, is asked to leave the average car."[13] Yet Teitelboim is a sophisticated political thinker, well aware of women's role in the opposition, respectful of women novelists, journalists, and political actors. His no doubt sincere sexualization of the landscape is an unintentional parody that, in the end, deconstructs itself. Julieta Campusano and Mireya Baltra, about whom Teitelboim writes with respect, presumably did not respond to the Chilean landscape in quite the same way as he. To take another example, the relationship between women and the political and geophysical landscape that Miguel Littín captures in *Acta general de Chile* (1986), the documentary film he made during his similarly heroic clandestine return to his homeland, depicts both women and terrain whose depth and character go far beyond the merely sexual and merely maternal.[14]

Teitelboim himself has written movingly about women's courage in their participation in the struggle against Pinochet's dictatorship. One 1987 issue of *Araucaria de Chile*, which Teitelboim dedicates largely to articles about women, includes interviews with political activists Carmen Rojas and Julia Monasterio, recently returned from exile.[15] These interviews depict the vitality of women's political agency, and they make space for Rojas and Monasterio to talk about their work in women's groups as well as within traditional party structures. Exile in these interviews has been relegated to the past. Rojas and Monasterio make fleeting reference to time spent away, but in these interviews they concentrate on the political work under way: demonstrations, the communal soup kitchens, the daily challenges of life under siege. The women themselves speak, and they focus on the political work in front of them.

In contrast, Teitelboim's article "El retorno de dos mujeres" (Two women's return), on the clandestine return to Chile of Mireya Baltra and Julieta Campusano, is a study in the dissonances of conflicting discourses, in which the concept of the woman militant is not intelligible.[16] After several failed attempts, Baltra and Campusano broke their exile and returned to their homeland covertly. Campusano, sixty-nine years old, had been prepared to commit suicide at the Chilean embassy in Argentina in protest against the Pinochet government. Sneaking back into the country was her alternative. Baltra, who had been in exile with Campusano in Holland, and who, like her, was a grandmother, went back as well. Their prison sentences separated them: one was sent to the north, fourteen hundred kilometers from Santiago, the other, eighteen hundred kilometers to the south of the capital.

Teitelboim uses the vocabulary of gallantry to recall Campusano's beauty as a young woman, and the language of sentimentality to write about her as a grandmother. He employs the lexicon of political hardheadedness when he reports on her courage, and Baltra's, in the public sphere. The complex identities that these women claim — woman, grandmother, political actor — are, for Teitelboim, quite literally incoherent. The elements that constitute them, that are thought to adhere to one or another of their constitutive aspects, do not hold together in any single discursive field Teitelboim can find. The elements "woman" and "grandmother," associated with tenderness and inspiring sentimentality and courtliness, have no purchase in an identity that also includes "minister of labor" and "communist activist," which call forth a vocabulary of public responsibility, valor, defiance, and even possibly despair. The cracks are evident in Teitelboim's text, where the discourses of grandmaternity and political opposition come up against each other with such dissonance.

Teitelboim notes that the Pinochet regime, lacking a firm base of support, still holds sufficient power to arrest Campusano and Baltra. In the context of the military dictatorship, the moth-eaten discourse of gender, which underlies the incongruity in Teitelboim's own approach to these women, similarly hangs by the fingernails onto a power it can no longer assert, and to which it never had a legitimate claim in the first place. The repressive government, however, finds it necessary, in ways Teitelboim obviously does not, to supersede its own dependence on this rhetoric. Campusano and Baltra behaved sufficiently unintelligibly for grandmothers so that the dictatorship, intolerant of any ambiguity, stopped regarding them as women or grandmothers at all. They were, therefore, not to be treated with the questionable deference one affords elderly ladies. They would simply be arrested as would any other clandestinely returned dissidents. Teitelboim, better able than Pinochet to tolerate the apparent ambiguities of the grandmother militant, still cannot reconcile them. The subjects themselves are silent in Teitelboim's article, since, unlike Monasterio and Rojas, Campusano and Baltra are in prison. Teitelboim has no access to them; he must rely on secondhand accounts and his own prior knowledge of their lives and work. Yet despite Teitelboim's difficulty in making sense of Campusano and Baltra, they go ahead and live lives that weave together a militancy that does not preclude the family and familial relations that well may have served as one of the incentives for their militancy in the first place.

The discourse of gendered domesticity, as it relates to the public, political sphere, is a complicated pattern governed by time, place, and generation. It is by now a commonplace to note that the Mothers of the Plaza de Mayo animated traditional notions of maternity in staging their very political, very public, demands on the military regime. Jean Franco is among those who have written with most complexity about this phenomenon, focusing on the war for legitimation in which the military Proceso took hold of meanings of gender and family, even as the Mothers of the Plaza de Mayo used traditional notions of motherhood to make a space for political intervention.[17] And not only used them — lived them, which is part of what made them so powerful. The Mothers' redeployment of the meanings of maternity took place at a time when, as anthropologist Estela Grassi notes, the state was making ever more traditionalist claims on the meaning of the relationship between family, state, and individual. Using its own rhetoric of maternal responsibility against the regime itself, the Mothers embodied an idealized, traditional notion of motherhood that was also oppositional. Grassi's work, tracing the "familialist discourse" (discurso familiarista) of the past four decades, links shifts in that discourse to economic and political changes from the 1930s on, always in relation to an unstable political situation.[18] She goes on to show how gender is pivotal in this redefinition; femininity and masculinity are both at stake.

Grassi demonstrates how moments of political and economic openness, in which the rights of citizens included not just access to a political process but also the right to work, to health, to education, and to consumption, have coincided with notions of freedom that make it possible to wrest women from their traditional position in the family, and that make the historical nature of that position visible. She elides, however, the problem that these moments have not been entirely liberating for women; in this century, for example, they are marked by a psychoanalytic understanding of the function of the family and the individual that does not hesitate to blame the mother for the personal problems of the child.

Grassi argues that the apparent shift of power from the state to the family during the Proceso is an attempt to retraditionalize the family and make it the responsibility of the family to produce the economic actors and "good citizens" the state requires and whose compliant conduct it enforces. This reassigning of responsibility relies on the naturalization of traditional gender roles within the family that had been under interrogation in the 1960s and early 1970s. Furthermore, she argues, this shift takes place in an unstable world economic environment and at a time when utopian systems such as Marxism, welfare state humanism, and feminism are going through a crisis marked by the so-called end of ideology.

Grassi links the techniques of familial discourse that serve to limit women's full societal participation to the oppression of the working class, arguing that the military government closed down the public space for workers' voices at the same time as it began its familialist campaign, and in part via its manipulation of notions of family. She writes:

> What I am suggesting is that a line of coherent argument exists among the different levels of familialist discourse that started to become hegemonic at the beginning of the 1970s, and that re-covers elements of traditionalist, basically Catholic, ideology rooted in the conservative sectors of Argentine society, of whose ideology the armed forces have considered themselves the guarantor. It is this "argumental coherence" that made it possible for the model of mental illness emerging from a pathogenic familial interaction to be used by the normativity established by the terrorist state to imbue values of social transformation with pathology, and thereby locate the family in a place of production and blame with respect to the disappearance or death of its members.[19]

The Proceso's pathologizing of the family, however, is enabled by psycho-analysis, one of the processes that Grassi sees as liberatory. The Freudian flotsam and jetsam bobbing around in the cultural sea of late-twentieth-century Argentina made it possible for the government's traditionalist notion of blaming the family to be dressed out in such modern terms as dysfunction and pathology.

In quoting from a wide range of sources — governmental, psychological, social service, religious — that sustain the ahistorical, gender-enforcing line that underlies family responsibility, Grassi, perhaps inadvertently, gives us a clue as to why these traditional notions of family are fairly quickly reinternalized, or why, deeply held and easily resuscitated, they have never been rooted out to begin with. Nevertheless, as Grassi argues, these shifts in meaning are linked to repressive political processes, the very ones that ejected the exile in the first place. Grassi's impulse is to attach traditionalist domestic discourse to the right wing, and she is convincing in her discussion of the ways in which the military government displaced its own responsibility for disappearance onto an imaginary dysfunctional family. But the fact that traditional notions of the family, and more specifically of motherhood, could be animated by the opposition suggests that they remained meaningful throughout society. Grassi is correct in her claim that the government closed down public spaces for workers' voices, but it is also the case that the power it gave over to the family made it possible for mothers, and only mothers, to claim a space in order to rescue their endangered children.

Marta Inostroza and Gustavo Ramírez similarly lay blame for the perpetuation of traditional gender roles fully in the lap of the dictatorships, and surely they are greatly responsible.[20] The left, however, has also maintained gender inequality and traditional domestic arrangements, for its own reasons. The reestablishment of traditional family, which military dictatorship fomented for its purpose, also serves to shore up very different leftist claims. Aidan Rankin sees this phenomenon occurring in the redemocratization process in Uruguay, where the left has been relying on traditional familialist discourses (to use Grassi's term), as well as on such utopian models as Marxism, in its efforts to combat the apparently new, or at least neo- (conservative, liberal), models the right has been proposing.[21] Rankin includes a note on the entrenchment of old gender norms in Uruguay, particularly in the left. "The feminist movement has yet to make significant inroads in Uruguayan culture," he says. "The left is in many ways the least feminist sector of all, associating feminism with the neoliberal wing of the Colorado party."[22] Similarly, Carmen Rojas elaborates on the frustration of women on the left in working in the traditional parties, where women's presence is forgotten, both in the present and in the past:

> The parties of the left, I think, have committed a great sin, and it is that they have not bothered to create a real politics with women, which is serious, because the right has done that, and that's the story of the saucepan [banging protests] and Pinochet's "women volunteers." . . . Women have never failed to be present, in one way or another, but history has always been written by men. Now, what happens is that in times of crisis we women appear more visibly.[23]

Unlike Grassi, for whom feminism is another of the (now discredited) utopian programs, like Marxism and welfare state humanism, lost to the left and reviled by the right, Rankin and Rojas perceive that, in Uruguay and Chile at least, the list of classic utopian models headed by Marxism quite determinedly excludes feminism.

For many exiles in northern Europe and the United States, where, after much struggle, the recognition of women's issues has become a part of a progressive political agenda, the association of feminism with bourgeois neoliberalism serves as a glaring emblem of the divergence of meaning at home and in exile, and among different sectors of the exile community itself. In an interview with anthropologist Jaime Vieyra-Poseck, one Chilean woman, whom he calls Teresa, outlines the interaction of political militancy, feminist awareness, and exile:

> I assumed a different role with respect to the relationship man/ woman when I began to take part in a political party (despite the fact that the positions of greatest responsibility are always occupied by men). But Sweden has helped me modify and adjust my ideas. These two factors (working in a political party and living in Sweden) have contributed to my thinking now that I, as a woman, have value, that a person can live part of her life crushed underfoot, and even ignorant, with no formal education, and nevertheless discover all of a sudden that despite that, you are worth something, that you have a capacity to do a variety of things that before you couldn't even imagine.[24]

She goes on to explain how, despite lip service to the contrary, women's issues have been excluded from the parties of the left in Chile and maintains that they must be included as part of a specifically political agenda in the future:

> The men, who are the ones in charge, say they understand these problems [matrimonial law, abortion, the single mother, etc.], but they argue that this change has to take place in the context of the global problem of Chilean society. But in this globality, up until now, the claims of women have not been included. From the moment we women begin being active in a political party together with men, it is because we accept political action together with them. Keeping in mind that women are a social group that is clearly discriminated against in society, objective claims need to be made for women, within the programs and the electoral platform of the parties.[25]

Teresa's understanding of the claims women have to make on society and on their own political structures, forged in her experience as a member of a party and as an exile in Sweden, is echoed by other women interviewed in Vieyra-Poseck's study. Women's greater participation in the public sphere is, within the exile community, generally understood to be a good thing, and not a symptom of either social disintegration or bourgeois individualism. In their handbook for Latin Americans considering return from exile, Marta Inostroza and Gustavo Ramírez have simply internalized the notion that women's full societal participation, practiced in exile, is to be desired: "The fact that sectors of Latin American women have found means of collective and individual development, different from those that exist in Latin America, can be interpreted as a benefit of exile."[26] They also recognize that this benefit can be threatened by return:

Previously we said that exile, despite its many painful aspects, had allowed Latin American women to occupy a more balanced and equal role in the family and in society. This situation is seen and felt to be threatened by the prospect of return. The evolution of women's social role in our countries is not comparable to that of Europe, more still in these years of dictatorship where conservative tendencies that pose the defense of discrimination against women and of the perpetuation of traditional roles have been reinforced.[27]

The shifting and competing meanings of family, sexuality, gender, and politics are indicative of the struggle over meaning under dictatorship and in exile. The traditional male-breadwinner/woman-at-home model is, for the right, the key to discipline and order. Its hierarchical authoritarian practice, once naturalized, serves as the justifying model for the workings of an authoritarian state, and in this model, the masculine is stressed. The left's version, although focused on the maternal function, is also, nonetheless, male-centered, with the son rather than the father as its focal point. This is the sentimental version of the traditional family, where the family is the locus of warmth and security rather than of order and discipline. In both versions, the emotional content of belief generated by personal memory of family emerges in ideological debates concerning the nature of the state.

This emotionally grounded memory plays out, then, not just in the struggle over meanings of the family, or personal history, but also in the renewed interest in national history among writers and critics as well as in official state discourse. Writing about Argentina, Santiago Colás notes that "[h]istory . . . became a fundamental site of military aggression in the early 1980s."[28] Ester Gimbernat González notes that for women this has been a double challenge: "First, they need to take on history in order to retell it from the private and measured space of women's gender; second, the hegemonic discourse, out of its repressive practices, imposes a syntax whose rules, in themselves, make a critical reading of official History difficult."[29]

For Colás, the struggle over historical meaning is grounded in upheavals best understood from a Marxist perspective. They are, he writes, "surely generated from within the cultural matrix of late capitalism."[30] Relations of power, understood from the perspective of class, as in Colás, or from the perspective of gender, as in Gimbernat, and which in fact can only be fully comprehended from a multiple perspective that includes but is not exhausted by these, determine the shape the newly revised history will take. Whatever its source, as Colás points out, "the problematization and rethinking of historical discourse ... surely function to destabilize the authority of the local structures through which it operates."[31]

In this vein, and adding race to the questions of class and gender already noted here, Hugo Achugar writes on the relationship between canon and nation as forms of regulation that carefully guard the gates against such undesirable intruders as Indians, women, and Blacks. He argues that the renewed interest in questions of Uruguayan identity and the increase in the publication of historical novels are intimately related to the aftermath of a dictatorship that called into question Uruguay's claims to a northern-European-style calm and stability: "I think that the turning of our gaze toward the nineteenth century at this turn of the century is no empty academic act; I think that the fracture of memory put into operation by the dictatorships of the Southern Cone has a great deal to do with this looking backward."[32]

Achugar reads two nineteenth-century poetry anthologies, one from Argentina and one from Uruguay, as deliberate attempts to establish nation via claims to an independent literature. He shows how the anthologies constitute an attempt to establish a body of texts that proclaim freedom as the greatest good, but that institutionalize that freedom only for literate, moneyed, white adult males. For Achugar, claims of a literature for nation in the nineteenth century are linked to the attempt to regain cultural and therefore political primacy in the late twentieth century.

As Achugar says of his own scholarship in this article, his discussion of nineteenth-century anthologies of poetry is "in a way a mere pretext" for dealing with some pressing extraliterary issues regarding a crisis in the legitimacy of the nation during a time when the concept of nation is being questioned in Europe and the United States and is being relegated to the so-called third world. At a moment when transnational postliterary culture is purported to be ascending, a new, critically analytical way of addressing national literary culture has become a central issue for Uruguay, Argentina, and Chile. It is a question of confronting

some preoccupations/obsessions: a connection to the problematic existence of Uruguay in a postdictatorial time that tries to reanimate the project of a country that in the past decades saw the agony and violent death of another project, in which Uruguay aspired to be the "Switzerland of America." A second one, related to the supposed feebleness or obsolescence of the category nation in cultural and literary studies. Even more, it is related to the affirmation that had its origin in a certain sector of first-world academia according to which the national variable belongs to the "third world." And finally, a third preoccupation or obsession that is connected to the exercise of literary criticism.[33]

The anthology in which this essay appears, whose title, *Las otras le-tras* (The other letters), implies an alternative literary history, is a case in point. Achugar is particularly interested in showing how the original intent of establishing a canon, and thereby a nation, was to define who would be in and who would be out of both. The texts canonized in the anthologies were clearly not the only ones produced. Indeed, as Achugar shows, it was necessary to create the apparatus of the canon to exclude the others. Virginia Cánovas's iconoclastic discovery of Uruguayan women novelists in the nineteenth century, including Marcelina Almeida, who wrote the country's first feminist novel, *Por una fortuna y una cruz* (For a fortune and a cross [1860]), which had been utterly erased from the official history, constitutes data that contest the received wisdom on the nature, content, chronology, and production of Uruguayan narrative in the nineteenth century. If Achugar and others are right about the de-liberate establishment of state via literature, the loss of these texts was not an unfortunate accident, but rather a deliberate exclusion that rele-gated women, as well as Blacks and Indians, outside the patrolled border of literary and political participation. These marginal groups, who could be represented in hegemonic texts, but always in a degraded form, could never be allowed to represent themselves.

The new interest in history and literary history, then, is a matter not of shoring up old ideas of Uruguayan (or Chilean or Argentine) identity, but rather of deconstructing received history, searching out the silences and exclusions. This process has two aspects. One is the search in the monu-ments of history for an acceptable way to understand the present moment. For Tulio Halperín Donghi, the recourse to history may simply "provide metaphors that make tolerable the evocation of a terror that is still too close," without being able to say very much about that terror.[34] Other ob-servers are more sanguine about the possibilities of the recourse to the more distant past for the purpose of coming to some understanding of the present, especially as such recourse approaches the other aspect of this interest, to wit, the contestation of official accounts. Blanca de Arancibia notes the urge on the part of "the continent's authors . . . to question offi-cial history and their own resulting identity. Their objective is to 'deflect' (or at least to decenter) historical, paternalistic, or totalitarian discourse, and the immediate result is the problematization of the legitimacy of this discourse and its ability to explain the present."[35] Although Arancibia may agree that official history offers little hope for explanatory power over the present, she nevertheless indicates a direction in the decentering of that history that will make way for other stories that might in fact give some clues, however indirect, to an understanding of the immediate past. As we have already seen, memory and forgetting are major themes for the post-dictatorship Southern Cone because they encompass the struggle over the meaning of the years of political repression. If it is true that the victor gets to write the history of the battle, then the present moment's discursive struggles are deciding just who won this war. The texts that engage with the history of the past century indicate that it is not just the recent past that is at stake, or rather that in order to make sense of the recent past it is necessary to set it in the context of the entire national story in all its racial, class, political, and gendered complexity.

Rereadings of national history in poetry, song, film, and theater, as well as in narrative fiction, resonate powerfully with the present. The stories of national consolidation and the lives of historical figures echo with the power of myth and have proved to be a sturdy base for allegories of the present. Like the nineteenth-century narratives they recall, these texts often use the material of the tragic love story as an allegory for the contemporary moment. However, whereas the texts studied by Doris Sommer in *Foundational Fictions* used fictional characters to tell contemporaneous stories of national consolidation in the popular form of the novel, such texts as Griselda Gámbaro's play *La mala sangre* (Bad blood) and María Luisa Bemberg's movie *Camila* recall historical figures from that very past to tell a tale of our present. *La mala sangre* takes place in an unnamed country and is about a dictator who refuses to allow his daughter to choose the man she loves.[36] The reference to the nineteenth-century populist Juan Manuel de Rosas and his daughter Manuelita is readily apparent to the Argentine viewer. The play between past and present, near and far (setting the play in the present, but in a distant country, basing it on a story of Argentina's own past), works out in a complex symmetry in which distances in space and time are interchanged so that the reference to the Argentina (not named in the play) of the present is unmistakable.

Camila also refers back to the same earlier dictatorship, finding a feminist tale in the struggle between the Unitarists, who wanted a centralized, liberal, urban-based government, and the Federalists, who fought for a loose confederacy that would give more power to the rural elites. As in Gámbaro's play, the oppression by the patriarchal family in *Camila* is a microcosmic version of the tyranny of the (also) patriarchal state.[37] These performative works of theater and film link the domestic with the state, just as surely as they link past with present. Gámbaro and Bemberg, however despairing in their depiction of tyranny, are optimistic in their belief that history can be known, reread, and drawn upon for the present.

Young writers, including the generation of Chilean poets who began publishing in the 1990s, are simply turning their backs on the politically engaged, historically marked writing of the generations that immediately preceded them.[38] Abril Trigo writes about the same generation in Uruguay, arguing that the cynicism of the *rockeros* and *grafiteros*, who grew up under dictatorship, is a reply to that of the dictatorships that fostered them. Ironically, it is their lack of memory of the discourse of prejunta Uruguay that makes them question radically the meaning of nation. The slash-and-burn tactics of the junta created an open, if bleak, field for them. With no memory (however false) of the dream of a Uruguayan Model Republic, they rebel against the ban on memory that is an insistence on amnesty. Arguing along with Kristeva and Said that exile encourages the individual to hang on to a past that never was, Abril Trigo notes that the *rockeros* and *grafiteros*, whom he calls "Dionysiacs," "instead of de-exiling themselves, they radicalized their radical alterity, to break with Uruguayanness and deconstruct the nostalgic restoration of the homogenizing historical-pedagogical memory of the imaginary of the Model Republic, threatened by the proliferation of multiple and antagonistic cultural-performative memories."[39] His notion of "antimemory" as a kind of negative memory, a willful forgetting of the prohibition on memory deployed by a cynical generation, ultimately makes a new kind of re-membering possible. These are, as Benedetti's Don Rafael hoped, the children who would undertake the reconstruction of Uruguay in unforeseen ways. This new inverted, if not perverted, means to memory is not unrelated to the recent re-visions of history emerging from the Southern Cone, both in scholarship and in literary texts and film.

Ricardo Piglia's *Respiración artificial* depicts a history that is irretrievably lost and forever unknowable.[40] The historian is gone, and without him there is no chance for writing the contestatory history that will make sense of the present. Tardewski, the Polish philosopher in exile unable to write his ideas once he is severed from his linguistic community, is another version of the loss of intellection in the person of a writer who, more radically than Cortázar, has lost his interlocutors.[41] Even when the historian/writer is present, divergent accounts of the same events, discrepancies in language, and the relation of the speaker and the interlocutor to the event make any hope of perfect communication an impossible goal.

Stories of the past may not be as hopelessly lost or useless as Abril Trigo, Piglia, and Halperín Donghi would have it, but allegories of the past, like metaphor, are always excessive or incomplete. Perfect symmetry is unattainable, and Luisa Valenzuela's choice of that word for the title story in her 1993 collection of short stories is playfully and cruelly misleading. "Simetrías" (Symmetries) overtly equates the past with the present, telling two tales of love, thirty years apart, in which the signifier love itself comes to mean something like its own absence, "what we call love for lack of a better term."[42] That is, the self-sameness that underlies symmetry is not possible even within a single word. One of these intertwined stories takes place in 1947 and is about the emotional connection between an orangutan and the wife of a colonel. The other is a story of the late 1970s, about a colonel and the woman revolutionary he tortures and with whom he becomes emotionally and sexually obsessed.[43] "Simetrías" does not quite come together in its equation of the two unconventional love stories. There are too many disjunctures in the similarities, too many places where the beasts elide into the people, where innocence and violence come up against each other. The story suggests rather than delineates parallels, which keep skidding off track, threatening to meet in defiance of Euclid's laws. The orangutan is caged, like the woman prisoner. He is, however, also linked to the colonel through their respective association with the sign "gorilla," the orangutan by metonymy and the colonel by metaphor. (In Argentina it is the anti-Peronist military who are called gorillas.) But by the rhetorical gesture that makes the colonel-as-gorilla the enemy, the orangutan is, the narrator tells us, decidedly not-gorilla. On the contrary, he is the victim of a jealous military husband. The revolutionary and the colonel's wife are objects of desire; the revolutionary and the orangutan are also objects of obsession. Desire and obsession are love from the vantage point of the desiring and obsessed subject, but for the victim what the torturer enacts is not-love. In a further breakdown of dichotomies, the tortured are better soldiers than the torturers. Every division into opposites is confounded. Binaries tend to settle into hierarchy, but Valenzuela explodes the binaries, throws them into confusion. Division by two is only one mathematical formula scrutinized in this story. The orangutan/colonel's wife pair is really a triangle, as the figure of the colonel shows, and the torturer/victim duo is intercepted by the institution of the military. The two love triangles do not lie neatly on a single plane. They, too, are configured in hierarchical relationships that are threatened as the points resolve into the figure of the love triangle.

Hierarchy is what remains, killing whatever threatens it. One threat, of course, turns out to be the outsider who refuses to respect the logic of simple division by two: the orangutan who as beast is outside the human masculine/feminine binary, and the guerrillera who refuses her place in that same dichotomy by occupying the active, resistant, soldierly role. Because the beast enters, masculinity and femininity are not the ultimate signifiers of difference in Valenzuela's story. An even more disturbing threat to hierarchy occurs at the moment when the figures occupying the middle position (the wife between the orangutan and the colonel in one case and the colonel between the revolutionary and his superior officers in the other) turn their primary attention to the figure below instead of above them. They threaten the stability of the structure by directing the gaze downward — the wife to the orangutan and the torturer to his prisoner, instead of upward, to the husband in the first case and the army in the second. The women and the orangutan decline participation in the going hierarchical systems, because they refuse to remain objects of desire and dare to desire themselves — the orangutan by loving the colonel's wife, the wife by her fascination with the orangutan, and the prisoner by her political activity and her refusal to speak.

The instability that the triad brings to the binary is reinforced by the act of narration itself. "Simetrías" is not so much narrated as interrupted. There is no single stance from which to tell it. The apparently omniscient narrator, who knows both stories and links them to each other, is contradicted by the woman in the torture center, some of whose words are in quotation marks, as if they are being read out of some testimonial document, while others are subsumed into the third-person narration. No single teller can exhaust the possibilities of this narrative. The only named character in the story is not one of its protagonists, but is, rather, positioned as its reader and perhaps teller, Héctor Bravo. His obsession is with these stories themselves; he wants to make them fit together, to constitute a coherent history.

In geometry, there are various kinds of symmetries. Valenzuela's seems to be closest to symmetry around a point, the point of the absolute power of the military. The violence of the military men who torture and kill is an expression of the institution's own desire for absolute dominance, a dominance that necessarily destroys desire issuing from elsewhere and annihilates humanity, love, eros, tenderness, any desire that escapes itself. This violence creates the restrictions of symmetry, the unforgiving tenacious center, where the suggestive, promising freedom of analogy might have flourished. But the threat of violence of the caged orangutan and of the torturer in love is a kind of ambiguity that is also contained within, as part of the material of desire that Valenzuela evokes so fully.

At the moment of disintegration only imperfect symmetry can be imagined. The old stories told the old ways do not hold. They are the worn-out stories of neat systems of hierarchy, the regulated nation as anthology of which Achugar speaks. I am not arguing that the constructed nation is somehow a false nation, only that it has suppressed the buzzing and humming of the non-elites, who have now emerged not just as other but as envoiced self. Valenzuela's view may not be optimistic in "Simetrías," but the very refusal of the parts to stay put and tell a coherent story is an effect of an ultimately hopeful multiplicity of voices. The speech of women and even the howl of the orangutan negate nihilism, because the voices make themselves heard as more than buzz and hum. Moreover, what they refuse to say — in the case of the prisoner who refuses to give up the names of her comrades — is as important, or more, than what they do say. Meaning can be made by the refusal to speak. Where speech is achieved, as it is by the teller of these tales, the stories told may be terrible.

Chapter Seven

STORIES OF RETURN

Luisa Valenzuela and José Donoso

El desexilio no es una estruendosa y única representación, no es
un acto único y definitivo. Es una herida larga que puede o no,
curarse.

[Coming out of exile is not a thunderous and singular performance, it is not a singular and definitive act. It is a long wound
that might or might not heal.]

— HUGO ACHUGAR

A few days after Christmas in 1990, Luisa Valenzuela, freshly arrived from
Buenos Aires, spoke before a packed room of attentive scholars at the
Modern Language Association's annual convention. One of a small number of writers and critics invited to the MLA convention, she was to
address the relationship between literature and values, a topic designed
to bring some coherence to this notoriously fragmented conference. But
Valenzuela had not written on the assigned topic; her paper-writing had
been interrupted by a military uprising in the interior of Argentina. When
the small group of battle-ready soldiers began their revolt, no one knew
whether or not they would be joined by others; and for five days clichés
took on real currency: a fragile democracy hung in the balance. The
threat of a coup was very real. Valenzuela, ever the professional, wrote
her paper for the MLA convention, if not precisely the one that had been
assigned. Titled "Five Days That Changed My Paper," it told the story of
the attempted coup and called into question any universalizing notions of
the uses of literature that the panel organizers might have had in mind.

It was a highly politicized and very seductive talk, and in that it was
classic Luisa Valenzuela, for whom politics, narrative, and seduction are
never far apart. The audience was beguiled by her storytelling, and as a
result many learned for the first time of the *carapintada* rebellion. Valenzuela had obeyed the first law of testimonial writing: spread the story. As
a political act, the presentation went beyond the overt gesture of bringing recent Argentine history into the field of vision of literary scholars,
however: Valenzuela also laid bare the politics of language. For the first
time in my experience, a general MLA audience was addressed, in part,

in Spanish. In the United States, where Spanish is a low-status language associated with the underclass, to bring Spanish into academic discourse is a considerable achievement. In that room, if you didn't know Spanish, you didn't get it — at least not all of it.[1]

Valenzuela's second politico-linguistic gesture was to translate the assigned topic into Spanish and, finding a cognate for "value" in the multivalenced Spanish *valor*, to redefine the topic. She shifted the theme of her talk from "values," with its intimations of a sort of disembodied morality, to "courage" (another translation of *valor*) in the face of a very real and specific threat. Valenzuela's performance foregrounded the specificity of language, first in the relative prestige assigned to particular languages in a culture, and second on the ground of individual lexical items as they are translated from one of these languages into another.

The *carapintada* rebellion that Valenzuela made vivid for U.S. academics was a symptom of the delicate state of Argentine democracy after the fall of the dictatorship. Although the attempted coup was a shock to all Argentina, Valenzuela herself had already staged it in a fictional text. Several years before the uprising occurred in real life, a group of soldiers blackened their faces with burnt cork in preparation for a military takeover in a work of narrative fiction Valenzuela called *Realidad nacional desde la cama* (National reality from bed). Just as, many years before, Cristina Peri Rossi foresaw the Uruguayan auto-coup in her short story collection *Indicios pánicos* (Panic signs), Valenzuela, two years before the fact, wrote an uprising of the renegade soldiers whose camouflage-painted faces earned them the nickname *carapintadas*. Certainly less intentionally than the Inuit storyteller who made events occur by telling them as stories in Leslie Marmon Silko's *Almanac of the Dead*, Valenzuela told the story of the *carapintada* uprising before it came to pass.

In *Realidad nacional desde la cama* (translated as *Bedside Manners*), the protagonist, just back in her country after years abroad, borrows her friend's country-club bungalow in an attempt to ease the culture shock of return.[2] Trying to take refuge from the confusion that surrounds her, the protagonist instead becomes its prisoner, in an updated, historically specific version of the madness and rest-cure narrative.[3] As an observer, the Señora seems to stand in for the writer. Of all the characters, the Señora comes closest to Valenzuela: recently returned from the United States, faced with the need and desire to remember, fearful of an unquiet military. Yet the difference between them is crucial. The Señora observes but is unable to move from her bed. All she can do is insist on seeing as much of reality as is available to her directly, always fighting the demand to forget. The writer Valenzuela, on the other hand, not only remembers but is prescient, and her ability to remember is what endows her with the ability to predict. She is both returning Señora and shape-shifting knowledge-bearer. Written on her own return to Argentina after years of living abroad, *Realidad nacional desde la cama* appeared in 1990, the same year as *Novela negra con argentinos* (*Black Novel with Argentines*).[4] *Novela negra*, Valenzuela's New York novel of alienation and acculturation, is a rich and complex weave of space and history. It considers the nature of violence and the meaning of identity, and it develops two quite extraordinary characters in relation to each other and to others they encounter during their sojourn in New York. It is a novel of masquerade, drag, and disguise; of sexuality, gender, and transformation; a work of art and artifice. Valenzuela herself has referred to it as the novel she published in 1990, excluding from that category *Realidad nacional desde la cama*, which, at 120 pages, is a less dense, much shorter work. *Realidad nacional desde la cama* is characterized by the immediacy and the shimmering superficiality of a dream. In its hallucinatory simplicity, it is a grotesque primer of return to Argentina from exile that registers the dislocation of return as surely as the novels of first exile register the shock of that uprooting.

A remarkably visual text, *Realidad nacional desde la cama* in fact seems made to be performed on the stage, with its single set and small group of characters performing in and around a large, white bed.[5] The novella's unnamed protagonist is far from Everywoman. She has a very clearly defined class position and a specific place in a national culture: she is the Señora, recently returned home from ten years' sojourn in the United States, after the end of the military dictatorship. Yet, as I have already suggested, the narrative is hardly a study in realism. Hands creep up from under the protagonist's bed to steal the groceries the maid has piled there, or to eat her breakfast croissants. Soldiers with bayonets are sent leaping over that same bed, sending the Señora deep beneath the bedclothes. The doctor who comes to examine her takes on a series of disguises that on one level are perfectly transparent but on another mark major shifts in personality, class position, and behavior. These events, however, are not pure fantasy. Rather, they intensify the reality the protagonist encounters: the hunger that drives the poor to steal, the shifting identities of Argentines themselves as they are forced into disguise (or merely impoverished), the encroachment of the military on the everyday. The hyperinflation that causes prices to rise daily so that currency must be spent rapidly lest it devalue is already so grotesque that it requires just a little narrative nudge to push it over the top. Similarly, the huge television set dominating the room is both apparatus and emblem of the effort to indoctrinate the populace in order to create a nationalist consciousness that nurtures militarism and surveillance. The television set bears the propaganda that says everything is fine in the face of the reality of hunger, unrest, and profound and ever-deepening class divisions.

María, the maid who attends the Señora, enforces the hegemonic discourse, which needs her to shore it up precisely because it is under siege. She stands in for the class of people that implements and mystifies what otherwise would be seen as coercion — the schoolmasters and social workers whose job is ostensibly to help people who are not suffi-ciently integrated into the culture, but who ultimately see to it that any opposition is neutralized. María's tool is the television, which echoes her assurance that all is well and under control. The threat of force, in the person of soldiers under the bed, and then at its foot, lies just beneath the surface of María's efficiency. She is the velvet glove hiding the iron fist, but the velvet is worn through. María, literally in a service position as maid, derives her considerable power not only from her collaboration with the antidemocratic rebel military commander, Major Vento, but also from the fact that it is she who mediates between the Señora and the market, the major, and the country club.[6] The Señora, then, is dependent upon María for her interactions with three key sectors: the economy, the military, and the members of the ruling class who assimilate Argentine identity to themselves.

María, as conduit, regulates the interactions between the Señora and these sectors. She does the shopping, making decisions on how (fast) to spend the money that hyperinflation will soon render valueless; provides the Señora with the military instruction book, which she treats like a manual for everyday conduct; and controls the Señora's field of vision, re-fusing to open the curtains and insisting on keeping the television turned on. The Señora's resistance to María's coercive behavior, together with the instability of the situation that María is trying to depict as serene, as if each sector were operating independently from the others, ultimately fractures María's regulatory system, revealing the connections among the three apparently separate sectors.

In the end, the spillover is complete; it takes shape around the *carapin-tada* uprising, which the Señora witnesses both in her own room, where she watches the soldiers paint their faces in an act that she finds both theatrical and vain, and, made public as well as more literally theatrical, on the television screen. To get rid of the sight of the soldiers in her room, the Señora throws a shoe at the television screen. The two realities have melded into one.

There is, as I have suggested, a surrealistic quality to this text. Among the techniques of surrealism in literature and the plastic arts is the creation of alarming juxtapositions and ravaged perspective, effected by tampering with the shape and relative size of objects. Valenzuela makes use of deviant perspective, so that proximity becomes superimposition. Slums, barracks, and the playgrounds of the rich really do abut each other, but in Valenzuela's text the borders dissolve. They all converge in the one-room bungalow that serves as the meeting point of country club, military base, and shantytown. The bungalow is a kind of deracinated aleph, not all the world of all time and space and history in one point, but rather a concentration or contraction in time and space of a particular moment in contemporary Argentine history. The disruption of spatial expectations gives this text its scent of the uncanny. Its effect is heightened by the deployment of puns (willow/low will disease) and shape-shifting that are also characteristic of the dreams that underlie surrealism.

The bungalow, built safely within the protective borders of the exclusive country club, was meant to shield the protagonist, so vulnerable in her recent return from exile, from the realities of her own country. Nevertheless, the national reality of the Spanish title asserts itself and invades that safe space. The old borders do not hold; the military has occupied the territory of the club, performing maneuvers on the golf course, but also invading the private space of the bungalow. The encroachment is first symbolic, in the form of the U.S.-authored military manual the maid gives the Señora to read, and then becomes quite literal in the person of Lucho, the foot soldier who has burrowed his way into her room. In the end, a whole squadron of soldiers invades this small space.

The television, appropriately enough, serves as media(tor). Its large screen is invoked as the antonym of the window through which reality can be seen, when María can be persuaded to open the curtains. Repeatedly switched on by María and resisted by the Señora, the television, familiarly enough, invades the space of the room and reconstitutes national reality. Inside the room, it projects a happy representation of Argentina: the places — parks, streets, and thoroughfares of Buenos Aires — cleaned up, Disneyfied, clearly false but meant to be reassuring. Only at the end of the novella does the representation on the screen cross over into the reality that is taking place inside the Señora's room so that the screen characters respond to what is going on in and around the room, confounding even the recognizable boundary between television screen and concrete reality. It is at that point, when a now-fuzzy voice and image report on the events occurring in the real-time and real-space of the text, that the Señora is caught, and indeed fascinated, by the image the television projects. An angry soldier's swift kick at the screen puts an end to that.

By that time, however, we have become accustomed to the peculiar invasions and overlappings of spatial reality. The country club has been taken over by the military, which might explain the presence of soldiers just outside, but cannot quite make realistic the secret tunnel that leads to under the Señora's bed, making it possible for Lucho to steal her food and creep under the covers. The shantytown has also made its encroachment. It was the soldiers who defoliated the border of the club, making the poverty just beyond visible to those club residents who would open their curtains. But the inhabitants of the shantytown are able to break down the barrier even further and, in one dreamlike scene, strip a soldier on guard duty of all his clothing, through a chain-link fence.

The overlapping occurs on the symbolic/linguistic level as well. Lucho, the soldier, is also from the shantytown. His loyalties are apparently divided, then — between obedience to his superiors, who represent the nation, and responsibility to his family, who are going hungry. This apparent contradiction is resolved on the lexical level. The major demands Lucho's loyalty to la Patria; his sister, who represents the family, is named Patri, short for Patricia. Lucho, whose name translates literally as "I struggle," has no trouble being loyal to his Patri(ci)a. Patri elides into Patria, and not just for Lucho. In the end, the major is trapped in the television screen while his men desert, joining the shantytown in a celebratory barbecue/bonfire.

Throughout the narrative, the Señora's inability to get out of bed is figured as an illness of sorts, connected to memory and thought, and finally to speech as well. She describes her paralysis as a failure of moral fiber: "It's morally that I can't move. I have no will."[7] The shape-shifting Alfredi, in his guise as doctor, diagnoses her:

> "You're suffering from what we call 'willow sickness,' it's very common in this part of the world. Sufferers show no desire to move, only to look, to remember, to tie up loose ends."
>
> "Mustn't overdo it, though, doctor. I'm a prudent woman and I know that remembering can be unhealthy."
>
> "Not at all."
>
> But someone had told her so a little while ago, they'd told her it was better not to think or remember. They'd said it almost like a threat and now she can't even remember who it was. It's obviously easily learnt, this forgetting.
>
> "At the moment I feel as if someone was trying to wipe my memory clean, I don't know, obliterate it with new inscriptions. I don't understand it at all."
>
> "That happens a lot here. What else is worrying you?"[8]

Memory and morality go hand in hand, because if memory is lost, so is the opportunity to obtain justice. Even more basically, memory is needed to see that history does not repeat itself. The question is one of strategy. The Señora considers that immobility is a way of preserving memory and a sense of orientation in the face of deliberate obfuscation. Talking to Lucho, she remarks:

> That was my city, the one on the TV. This new city isn't the one I used to know, they've changed everything. Now I don't know who the enemy is, I don't know who to fight against. Before I went away I did, now the enemy's no longer there, or at least he says he isn't but he is and I just don't know where I stand....I came back to find *that* not *this*. I came back to recover my memory and they steal it from me, erase it. They sweep it away. And what if lying in a strange bed unable to move was my way of preserving my memory and everything else they're busy snatching away from us...?[9]

Yet memory's connection to repose and resistance, on the one hand, seems to contradict its link to active opposition, on the other. Passivity may be cowardly self-protection. María, on the telephone with her voice disguised, threatens the Señora with terminology reminiscent of Nazi propaganda: " 'We know what your mission is. You're after your memory, but we're gonna get you first. History begins with us.' "[10] María's own lack of historical imagination, to say nothing of historical information, allows her to believe that her slogan is new.

By this time the soldiers are doing maneuvers in the Señora's room, jumping over her bed, grazing it with bayonets and rifle butts, "and she knows the only way out of the situation is to recover her power of speech like someone recovering a lost memory."[11] So memory is linked to speech as well. Toward the end, the memories come back, drowning each other out; "she feels like an overloaded computer," and the remembering that is supposed to be fatal may also be what is needed to survive.[12]

The Señora's inability to move is directly related to her struggle to retain her memory in the face of threats to her life. Yet ultimately she must move, get out of bed, and reenter her country as a full participant. At the end of the narrative she is still reluctant to leave the bed, whose purported safety has already been violated by armed soldiers:

> "Come on, let's dance," insists her versatile lover.
> The Señora takes his hand, but that's all, and tries to pull him down towards the bed.
> "No," he says, "standing up."
> "Oh, not vertical yet, not yet," she pleads.
> "Yes, vertical. With your head held high."
> "I need a bit more time."
> "Now is the time."
> "Wait. I want to understand. I'm afraid."
> "Get up. Only death can cure your fear of death. It's not worth it. It's better to be alive and moving, while you can. We have to celebrate."[13]

The incapacitated Señora, who has become an observer and recorder of what is going on, contrasts with the hyperkinetic Alfredi, whose mobility consists in his ability to take on new personas that respond to his circumstances and that allow him access to different social sectors: the working class (as taxi-driver), the professional middle class (as physician), and the military (as colonel). These transformations, uncanny because they seem simultaneously transparent (the addition of a prop, like a cabbie's cap or a stethoscope) and profound (a change in demeanor, behavior, and language), correspond to the more reasonable mobility of Alfredi's literal comings and goings as a cab driver who commutes daily from the city to the country club.

The first-level function of Alfredi's shape-shifting is economic survival: he cannot earn enough money as a physician, so he moonlights driving a taxi. Although the incongruity of the physician/cabbie is fully understandable in the context of real economics, it remains incomprehensible in terms of traditional class structure, thereby functioning as one of the text's many lateral moves and uncensored associations. Hyperinflation is speeded up only minimally in the text. María reels off the ever-rising price of foodstuffs; the longer the Señora puts off paying her, the more she owes. The change in the value of money has its counterpart in the rapid movements in the text, the permeability of physical boundaries, and the transformations undergone by the characters. The doctor's cure becomes sexual; the transformation from physician to taxi-driver plays out in the personality and language of the individual: the sensitive doctor/lover of the night becomes the boorish, sexually demanding taxi-driver/rapist of the morning. A transitional persona, a silly joke, pops up as well: the psychoanalyst, halfway between cabbie and doctor. Dress and undress become marks of identity; Alfredi costumes himself for each of his roles. Clothes are superficial, but the surface is all; they turn performance into identity. Like Alfredi, the major transforms himself into a general, and María disguises her voice to threaten the Señora. None of these disguises is complete, and none is particularly credible. Only naked can a character approach authenticity: Lucho stripped of his uniform and thrown into the pit as punishment, Alfredi in bed with the Señora. Her location in bed confers the same promise of authenticity on the Señora herself. Authenticity, however, is a notion that does not lie easy with the primacy of surface and performance. In identifying Alfredi as the one person who really knows what is going on, Lucho points to the existence of a reality that is there to be known and to a real identity under the strategic disguises. The Señora is confused about what is happening around her, not about her own identity, and Alfredi and Lucho tell her that the rest of the country shares her confusion. National reality may not be fixed, but it is somehow there, being produced and challenged by subjects who themselves are subject to contradictory interpretations and threats.

The instability of identity in this text is a function of survival. With the nation at stake, and the threat of loss of one's own freedom, or even life, philosophical questions of subjectivity and identity get put on hold. One takes on different roles at different times; it is a matter of surviving. But there is some kind of truth at stake, a difference between the view through the window and the view on the television screen. The agents who mystify reality, filtering it through the constructed reality of television, are the same ones whose defoliants made poverty visible. In one interchange, Valenzuela lays bare the inadequacy of effecting change by means of legislating discourse: the major intends to get rid of poverty by stamping out the poor, and specifically by making it illegal to name the reality that more and more people are living. This act will, quite clearly, not make it go away.

Similarly, at the end of the story, the shantytown dwellers are jubilant because they have taken the club over from the military. But whereas the military, the country club, and the nation all were made to converge in the telling of this story, the fact remains that the deracinated aleph is a kind of nightmare, and when the country wakes from it, what is left is the need to see things for what they are. The sectors once again recede to their designated places, and the club reverts to its status as country club. It may have been a forceful metaphor for a country when it was the locus of two nodes of power — the bourgeoisie and the military — but once it is liberated by the residents of the shantytown, that is, the poor and dispossessed, it is reduced to its physical dimensions. It is the country club, not the country. The hugely symbolic acts of taking over the club, using the soldiers' weapons as tennis rackets and golf clubs, and finally as the centerpiece of a malevolent children's circle game, cannot sustain the transformation from metaphor into material reality. The club may be theirs, as Alfredi triumphally announces, but the future of the country is still at stake. The text ends not only with a deflating question, but with the return of and to the real:

"Now the club is ours!" he says, stamping on the weapons.
"And the country?" asks she, ever the realist.[14]

Up to this point "realist" (or "realism") was not an operative word in this text. Brought to the surface now, as the last word, it colors the rest of the narrative. It is powerfully ironic to contend, as the English translation does, that the Señora has ever been the realist; for what can that mean in a context where realism and surrealism converge, and where a capacity for accommodating to the monstrous is prerequisite to survival? In the Spanish version, she is "la muy realista" (very much the realist). And the fact that the protagonist has been caught between the will to survive and the unwillingness to accede to the savagery that sent her into exile in the first place suggests that she is indeed a realist. It is reality that is bizarre, even alarming, despite which her struggle throughout has been to recover that reality — to take hold of memory and to resist the official interpretation, heavy-handed as in the military version or sugarcoated as on the television. That is why she is surrounded by white, dressed in a white nightgown, in a white bed. There is no (false) image to be had in that blankness, unless it is the illusion of luxury and oblivion. The room's whiteness is equivalent to the nakedness of Alfredi (first as her lover and then as he wipes the camouflage paint off his face), of Lucho (who is stripped naked as punishment), and of the soldier (who is sent to guard Lucho and is denuded by the ravenous poor). The blank screen and the white room might not tell the truth, any more than the apparent authenticity of nakedness reveals identity:

> "No more cabbie, colonel, doctor, or madman, I can at last go back to being me."
> "And who are you?" asks the Señora, slightly alarmed.[15]

His answer is less than satisfying:

> "Me? Well, let's just say I'm the one who came to put an end to this whole farce. Or at least to the players in the farce. As far as possible."[16]

But unlike uniforms, disguises, masks, and palliative images on the television screen, the blankness does not actively lie or manipulate.

The absolute control of the media that is a feature of the nightmare version the newly returned exile has of Argentina is also a feature of the Chile of José Donoso's *La desesperanza* (Desperation; translated as *Curfew*).[17] In that novel, the returning celebrity who is the object of media attention will be completely censored, and, over and over again, the newspapers present a version of events that further the interests of the dictatorship. In these narratives, the media seem passive, if not foolish, in their apparent acquiescence to power. In Valenzuela, the television screen projects images as if by its own accord; in Donoso, reporters ask pointed questions and receive powerful answers that will never find their way into print. Former Chilean senator Volodia Teitelboim, in contrast, reports on journalists who resist the censors, of a demonstration where newspaper reporters with gags in their mouths stage a silent march, led by their editors, and specifically of women journalists who write about the abuses of the government.[18] Teitelboim's stories of journalistic defiance reflect his objective: to tell the story of brave resistance in Chile, still under dictatorship. Valenzuela and Donoso record the censorship and official manipulation of the media that made such heroic acts necessary.

The long, slow transition to democracy in Chile is a function of the relative longevity of the country's dictatorship. The return of its exiles began years before Pinochet officially left power, and the military has retained a hold on power even after the installation of a civilian government. As late as April 1996, the Gothenburg newspaper carried a story verifying the slow and ambiguous transition, still taking place six years after the elections: a group of soldiers sent out to dig a foundation for a new building came upon a mass grave. Despite apparent efforts that had been made to mutilate the bodies beyond recognition, the bones were identified as those of leaders of a communist youth group, kidnapped and killed over twenty years ago. This was the first mass grave uncovered on military property and the first time the civil authorities were permitted to undertake their own investigation within a military base. Despite this major shift, the writer of the article points out that the Chilean military, unlike the Argentine, was never constrained to express any contrition for its acts and still maintains that, thus unreconstructed, it is the backbone of the nation.[19]

Chile's novels of transition and return are marked by ambiguity and mistrust, as we have seen in Pérez Miranda's *En esa copia feliz de Edén* (In that happy copy of Eden). The return in 1981 of Chile's most famous expatriate novelist, José Donoso, finds expression in *La desesperanza*. Like his protagonist, Mañungo Vera, Donoso was not barred from his home- land, and, like him, he came back right in the middle of the repression. Donoso anchors his novel in the historical reality of contemporary Chile. Mañungo returns to a Chile still in the thrall of dictatorship, on the day Matilde Urrutia, the widow of Pablo Neruda, has died. His is a tentative return, and until the end of the novel he is determined to go back to the comfort and relative peace of his exile in Paris.[20] Mañungo is in the company of other exile artists in Donoso's fictional world. Like Pancho Salvatierra in *El jardín de al lado* (*The Garden Next Door*), he is wildly suc- cessful; unlike Pancho, his success is directly related to his connection to the opposition. In a way he is a tempered version of the excoriated Adria- zola, whose fame is inexorably linked to his political presence. Mañungo, however, cannot sustain the pressure of his image, particularly as he grows less and less sure that the politically stirring songs he sings coincide with his own beliefs concerning the possibility of revolutionary change in Chile. All the revolutionaries in this novel are broken: Don César is literally cut off at the legs. A thief and a scavenger, he transverses Santiago on four wheels attached to a board. Lopito is a drunkard who inspires a mixture of disgust and pity in his friends. Judit is forever expiating the sin of her privilege. Ada Luz is paralyzed by her desire for the ideologue Lisboa, who himself is so caught up in the master narrative of Marxism that he cannot see his, or its, limitations in changing the direction of the country. Still, with the exception of Lisboa, who is depicted as the worst kind of ego- centric, coercive cad, Donoso is more generous toward these characters than he is to most of the politically inclined in *El jardín de al lado*. Donoso achieves this empathy without sacrificing a critical view of the charac- ters. Using a third-person narration that has no fixed point from which it is spoken, he moves from one character to another in free indirect dis- course. He wheels from one point of view to another with the dexterity of the ambiguously (un)trustworthy Don César on his board, so that we learn of each character from the perspective of the others.

In *Foundational Fictions*, Doris Sommer demonstrates how the hetero- sexual dyad, nuanced for class and race, comes to figure the reconciliation of differences in the imagining of the newly independent nation-states of Latin America.[21] Donoso's *La desesperanza* also relies on the heterosexual couple as a structuring device: with the exception of the underclass, all the characters are presented within the framework of heterosexual pairings. Here, however, the dyad is irrevocably wounded, and the promise of the next generation that motivates the trope in nineteenth-century narrative is sadly fulfilled only to mark itself as a failure in Donoso's narrative. The primary pair, Matilde and Pablo Neruda, whose joyous relationship is consigned definitively to the past with the death and funeral of Matilde that is the catalyzing event of the story, marks the end of the era of love. Ada Luz is (somewhat unconvincingly) in sexual thrall to the unpleasant Lisboa; the decision she must make concerning Matilde's last, personal wish to have a Mass said at her funeral becomes a political issue and the occasion of Lisboa's sexual coercion. Donoso piles up the couples: the aging Celedonio and Fausta; Judit and Farias, her would-be torturer; Farias and his mistress Liliana. All in some way fail the promise of heterosexual pairing. Mañungo's psychological return to Chile, which follows his physical return, is effected in his experience with Judit, whose birth into the oligarchy continues to protect her as she becomes ever more deeply involved with the opposition. Their growing desire and need for each other are repeatedly named as not-love. Their connection has to do with their shared history and with their imbrication in political struggle. Judit and Mañungo doubt the depth of their own commitment, but they are emblems of opposition. They fear being discovered, want to escape into a private life that is impeded, and ultimately cannot evade their commitment to the resistance. But love, like art, is evacuated from this complicated set of impulses, pushed aside by a situation in which the political displaces the personal.

The next generation, products of relationships that have been marked more by politics than by the already banished "love," offers no hope, certainly not the promise of a unified, happy nation. Judit's daughter lives with her paternal grandparents and has adopted their apolitical lower-middle-class values and, what is worse, their bad taste. Mañungo's seven-year-old son is quite simply not Chilean. Retroactively foreshadowing the problematic adolescents of *El jardín de al lado*, he speaks only French and wants only to return to his apartment in Paris. Lopito's daughter, as ugly and graceless as he, merely reinforces the hopelessness of this man and of his generation. All hopes of creating a better future are dashed in this little girl, who, as far as her father is concerned, is a grotesque repetition of himself.

The novel takes place in Santiago, but there are two other sites that play an important role in the text. The first is Paris, the location of a comfortable exile. The second is Chiloé, the island of Mañungo's childhood. Mañungo is connected to Chiloé less by memories of its actual geography, which in any case is utterly unstable, than by the magic that has held him there even during his exile. An island, Chiloé is not quite land and not quite sea. Tidal waves periodically reclaim it as ocean; the dead mother in this text in fact died as a result of one of these sea storms when Mañungo was a child. The tidal wave that killed her also rearranged the topography of the island, *madre tierra* as *madre mar*. The instability of the very place extends to its dead, that is, its history and memory. The cemetery, as well as the houses of the living, is periodically taken off to sea. The magic of Chiloé is a magic of transformation, associated with witchcraft, which throughout the novel is referred to as art and its practitioners as artists. This is quite alien to the definition of art as neurosis that Mañungo's Parisian/Russian ex-wife, Nadja, maintains. Mañungo suffers from tinnitus, a syndrome that serves as a fulcrum of these two worldviews. Nadja attributes the sounds he hears in his head to mental and emotional instability; Mañungo himself believes they are the sounds of the Pacific Ocean and of Carlitos, the lion in the Santiago zoo, whom he hears even when he is in Paris, thanks to the magic arts of Chiloé.

In Valenzuela's *Realidad nacional desde la cama*, the protagonist takes refuge from the incomprehensible modifications in the social, political, and economic structure of her country in a space that should be safe and protected but that obeys no laws of boundaries. The walls and floors of the bungalow are penetrated; the fences and shrubbery demarcating the country club from the military base are transgressed. Still, the general contours of the country remain. The Señora watches the parading soldiers in Buenos Aires, and although she says the city has changed, she is referring not to the topography but to the meanings attached to the spaces. In *La desesperanza*, in contrast, the very territory that is Chiloé is unstable. When natural disaster is not changing the land and seascape of Chiloé, the persistent drizzle makes its forms hazy and mutable. Santiago and its surroundings undergo transformation as well. Once-elegant neighborhoods now are abandoned by the rich and taken over by beggars. A perfectly ordinary section of town is given new meaning when Pablo Neruda and Matilde Urrutia take up residence there. In another instance, Judit compares present-day Santiago, with its imported garden plants and its built-up neighborhoods, with engravings of the same landscape two hundred years ago. Lopito, furthermore, says that Santiago has so changed in the past decade that Mañungo will not be able to find the cemetery without his help. Finally, the novel comes to an end at the exhibit *Chile in Miniature*, where the companies that sponsor the exhibit, which delights the children, create a landscape that emphasizes the places in which they have some economic interest. The miniature Chile has none of the soul or spirit of the real country. It is a simulacrum, very much like the parody of a nation, created by the military government, that makes it impossible for people to live private lives. The overriding sense of the instability of Chile's very geography in *La desesperanza* is echoed in Volodia Teitelboim's memoir, *En el país prohibido: Sin el permiso de Pinochet* (In the forbidden country: Without Pinochet's permission).[22] Although he

locates the seismic eruptions that settled as the Chilean landscape in geo-
logic history ("those mountains seem like petrified masses, dinosaurs that
were extinguished, according to rumor, sixty-five million years ago and
turned to stone"),[23] Teitelboim repeatedly leaves the impression that those
prehistoric changes continue to occur, linking the earthquakes and tidal
waves that Donoso's characters experience to the more subtle, continuous
changes the landscape has undergone in his absence:

> I do not know why I have the feeling, surely imaginary, that in
> my absence, time, the eruption of ash, has continued to model the
> topography.[24]

The most permanent feature of this landscape is its variety, which gives it
an air of constant metamorphosis:

> Nothing is more alien to this landscape than monotony. Its law is
> contrast. Its principle, rupture.[25]

What is more, Chile's geography serves as a metaphor for its politics in
the moment the book was written:

> Perhaps Chile is a drastic example of the traumatic evolution of the
> universe, which would explain its rent nature. As part of a unique
> system, I think that Chile's nature, like the Chilean himself, victim
> on the one hand of the violence of History, obeys, nevertheless, life's
> imperative.[26]

Mañungo's first impulse in obeying life's imperative is to plan a trajectory that will take him out of Santiago, first to Chiloé, the island of
drastic changes, and then back to Paris, which holds the promise of some
kind of normality and respite. A return to the past will make him whole
and allow him to escape the horror of the present in Chile. The political
reality of the country, centered in the capital, however, prevents him from
undertaking this journey of recovery. Much in the same way that events
in Santiago hold Mañungo in thrall, the political reality of Chile eclipses
all else for Donoso. In an interview with Amalia Pereira, he complains
of feeling compelled to write about that reality even though he would,
artistically, rather be elsewhere:

> Q. How does the turbulence that Chile is now experiencing affect
> the process of writing?

> A. It is impossible to write about anything else. We are all con-
> demned to this. I cannot stand writing about it, but nonetheless I
> cannot write about anything else. I find myself so completely ob-
> sessed by this problem that I have no other option. May it be
> damned! But what other option is there?[27]

Donoso's *El jardín de al lado* argues for an art that is above politics, be-cause the thematic of politics, of rancor, and of denunciation enmires the creative spirit. *La desesperanza* demonstrates that the inner life that is the prerequisite of such art is precluded in the extreme circumstances of Chile under dictatorship. If the exile has some choice, some possibility for dis-tancing himself emotionally, as he is distanced physically, the artist under dictatorship, like everyone else in that extreme circumstance, has no such choice. Moreover, Mañungo, the returning exile, who has believed that he can make the choice to escape once again, learns that he cannot, any more than those who stayed can now make that choice. It takes Donoso's protagonist a mere (if intense) twenty hours to go from a determination to return to the safety of Paris to a commitment to remain in Chile, from a sense of bewilderment and incomprehension to a full understanding of what is going on in his country, from the Holiday Inn to a downwardly mobile apartment in a Santiago neighborhood:

"Why did you come back to Chile at this particular time?" the reporters asked.

"To stay here."

"For how long?"

"Forever."

"Didn't you say last night in Neruda's house that your visit would be short because you didn't understand the situation your country was in?"

"Now I understand it." He thought for an instant and then went on. "I've changed my plans. In any case, after twenty hours in my country, I can assure you that I have never been clearer on any subject than I am on this matter of staying."

"In order to define your political action?"

"Could be."

"Armed struggle?"

"No, except in self-defense or to defend someone else."

"Songs?"

"I'd like that. But who knows if bombs won't turn out to be the only alternative? It's their fault. But what can we do when they force us into violence by taking away all our hope? I'm not justifying bombs, but I do understand them."[28]

Under these circumstances Mañungo can only *hope* to write songs. Armed struggle — from which he ambiguously distances himself — may be the only alternative. When asked directly, he rejects violence but mod-ifies that to allow for self-defense or for the defense of someone else. But Mañungo has already come to understand that the possibility of a private life, in which this sort of defense makes sense, has been ruled out by the state violence that turns every private act into a public one. He leaves his answer uncompleted, to return to it indirectly in response to a question about his artistic plans. His music, he implies, would have to be about events going on in his country, and not about the now-impossible private and personal, which is what he had wanted to write about. Moreover, art's necessary engagement with political struggle within Chile may not be enough. The hopelessness conveyed by the original title may ultimately be less about being politically helpless against an all-powerful, ruthless state apparatus than about the realization that the political can come to take over the individual's emotional or inner life. Donoso's faith in the independence of art and the artist, so evident in *El jardín de al lado,* is severely shaken in *La desesperanza.*

Donoso's need to write about the political situation in Chile, despite the fact that he would prefer to be writing about just about anything else, corresponds to Luisa Valenzuela's impulse to write about the *carapintadas* when she returns home to Argentina. At that same MLA convention where Valenzuela told the real-life story of the Argentine response to the *carapintada* insurrection, she tried out three new fictional texts, which would all be published in the 1993 volume *Simetrías* (Symmetries).[29] One was a cautionary tale concerning the desire for transparency in language; one was a horrifying tale of sex and violence the night of the great flood in Venice; and the last was a Freudian/feminist revision of "Little Red Riding Hood." This last was one of what, in the book, would be a group of retold fairy tales from the European folk tradition. She calls these tales "Cuentos de Hades" (Stories from hell), a play on *cuentos de hadas* (fairy tales). "La llave" (The key), which retells the story of Bluebeard's castle, is another of these rewritten folk tales, all of which turn out to have been sort of hellish in their original version and are now much more happily transgressive. Whereas the other diabolical stories maintain the magic space of fairy tales — castles, woods, mythic kingdoms — "La llave" takes place in Buenos Aires. Published three years after *Realidad nacional desde la cama,* it is an alternative story of return. The narrator of "La llave" has been living in exile, apparently in California, where she has made her living by running self-improvement workshops for women. Valenzuela gently parodies the New Age overlay, but the underlying notion connecting the personal to the political, and therefore the political to the personal, is of value to her.

The narrator tells us how she structures her workshops, starting with introductory autobiographical material and proceeding over a period of a weekend to involve the participants in an exploration of their own lives. The key of the title is the key to the secret room in Bluebeard's castle. The protagonist is a returned Argentine exile, but she is also the character who has been written into text from Perrault on (and who has her roots in Western tradition as far back as Pandora and Eve) — the woman with a will to knowledge. Valenzuela's protagonist works to break down the resistance of the workshop participants. On one level, the story is about individual attempts to deal with violence, domestic violence in particular. The women resist such attempts, agreeing with the patriarchal interpretation (initiated by Perrault, who, as the original writer of the tale, stands in for the patriarchal interpretation) that women should not be inquisitive, that they will find what they do not want to know, and that they will be punished.[30]

The narrator talks about the pain of the process of bringing violence to light. Every time she does this workshop, women come back recognizing the violence in their lives. The key of the title is, at first, a metaphor. The narrator gives each woman a symbolic ring of keys and tells them all to go home and open doors. It is an exercise in imagination and memory, but when the discovery gets made, the key to the chamber of violence becomes real. The descriptions are not of the key as metaphor but rather of the key as concrete object that cannot be scrubbed clean of the blood the women get on it when they open the door to the death chamber and discover the violence of the men they live with, the violence of patriarchal society. The women try to wash away that blood, pretend they did not find it, go back to the slim band of safety on which obedient women may find purchase. This story up until now has been of individual discovery, and of the mixture of women's bravery and cowardice. The workshop uncovers the institutionalization of domestic violence — a culturally sanctioned, yet hidden, phenomenon that is played out in the private sphere. Valenzuela, however, shifts her emphasis from one sphere to the other, rendering visible the connection between state violence and private violence. The first act of complete bravery, of the public display of the bloody key, is made by a woman wearing a white kerchief. The symbol hits home hard, and the story comes together. The white kerchief is the visible symbol of resistance and reclamation — the woman who is willing to display the key and denounce the violence openly is one of the Mothers of the Plaza de Mayo, whose valor has been celebrated all over the world. What Valenzuela does that is new here is to connect the historically specific act of bravery to the taboo on women's speech and women's curiosity, to infuse the former with a universal meaning that feminist practice names and the latter with a historically grounded practice of courage. The Mothers did not act out of the familiar feminist motive of women's self-actualization, but their act completes the feminist impulse to know and name institutionalized violence. Not even the workshop leader/narrator had had the courage to wave the key around in public. She, too, tried to wash it clean. Her ongoing heroic act has been to survive and bring her story to other women. The woman in the white kerchief, in contrast, has made the story public, at a time when doing so meant to risk one's life. All the women have recognized the risk of returning the key with the blood on it. The secret must be kept, lest one become the monster's next victim, but keeping the secret means complicity in the violence.

In the end we learn that the story is dedicated to Renee Epplebaum, one of the leaders of the Mothers. The dedication's unusual placement after the story permits the reader to be lulled by the fairy tale, lulled even by the send-up of California feminism. Valenzuela then brings us back to contemporary reality — first with the physical labor of trying to wash the key (still in the realm of turning myth to reality, and that has the effect of returning to myth), and then with the very immediate issue of the Mothers, producing that shock of recognition.

The narrative's contemporaneity — its location in California and Argentina, as well as in the symbolic regions of fairy tale — and its attention to the violence of current politics and of age-old gender relations place it in the internationalized realm of exile and return. That the MLA convention was the site of reading and presentation of its sister stories is not unimportant. Valenzuela belongs to a rather small group of writers and intellectuals who have been able to return home while retaining international ties.[31] In these stories, the return home is compromised and enriched by the patina of the internationalism of the exile. The sense of being part of a national culture, language, and heritage is tempered by the experience of living in another place, and the returning exile, Bluebeard's wife, has, in that exile, found a way to tell the story of the women who stayed behind.

Chapter Eight

BEYOND EXILE
Stories from the Diaspora

Et un matin quelconque du mois d'octobre, au début du printemps (du sud), ceux qui ne seront toujours pas rentrés éprouveront un besoin irrésistible de sentir le parfum de nos fruits, d'admirer la cordillere majestueuse...alors que ceux que seront la-bas, ressentiront la nostalgie du petit cinéma des Ursulines, des odeurs de Paris et de la couleur plombée de la Seine.

[And some October morning, in the beginning of spring (in the South), those who will never return will feel an irresistible need to smell the perfume of our fruits, to admire the majestic cordillera...and those who are there will be nostalgic for the little movie house on the Ursulines, for the smells of Paris, and for the lead color of the Seine.]
— ANA VÁSQUEZ AND ANA MARÍA ARAUJO

Ana Martínez's picture is in the Gothenburg paper today, in the highlights of the radio listings. It is a portrait in cultural hybridity—she wears a luxurious wreath of flowers, Swedish symbol of summer, on her thick dark hair. (A commercial for shampoo on television last night claims the product is formulated for "Scandinavian hair." They don't specify, but it means hair that is thin, limp, with no body. Ana Martínez does not need that shampoo to make her hair look good.)

Ana Martínez talks on the radio, telling stories and playing music, a sort of Latin American Garrison Keillor in Sweden. Her radio show today is a study in life after exile. Her stories are about the ways Argentina meets Sweden, on Swedish territory, in a world in which both those countries are peripheral to the rest of Europe and the United States. Speaking, for example, of the failure of the album *ABBA en español* to sell in its intended Latin American market, she remarks, with a certain archness in her voice: "Colonized as we are in Latin America, when we listen to [Swedish pop groups] ABBA and Roxette, we *want* to hear them sing in English." Like her countrywoman and contemporary, philosopher María Lugones, Ana Martínez lives a life negotiated between two cultures.

133

In contrast to the writers I have been discussing throughout this book, Martínez and Lugones write and speak for public purposes not in Spanish but in the Swedish and English of the respective countries in which they now live.

One of my underlying premises is that despite geographical transplantation and the trauma of exile, there is a sense in which identity is coherent, able to incorporate the new into the old. I have also been working out of a disciplinary training in a literary culture whose unifying trait is a shared language. My implicit claim is that it is sensible to look at the geographical dispersion of exile from three different countries through literary texts produced by writers from those three places. This claim rests in part on the fact that the texts I have looked at here were written in Spanish, whether or not they were written in the writers' Spanish-speaking countries of origin. In fact, as I have argued here, Spanish for these writers is a touchstone of identity and a mark of the impossibility of complete assimilation. Beyond geographical proximity and a shared history of right-wing military dictatorships, what unites the countries of the Southern Cone is language. I, no less than the writers whose work appears in this study, have held fast to Spanish as a constant, if not as a lifeline. But as Isabel Álvarez-Borland and Eliana Rivero have pointed out in their studies of Cuban literature in the United States, the adoption of the language of the host country in one's public utterances is one of the ways exile becomes diaspora.[1] Both Rivero and Álvarez-Borland point to the switch from Spanish to English among Cuban writers living in the United States as determinant in demarcating exile writing from ethnic writing. In today's United States this embrace of ethnic identity does not mean a denial of origins, but rather a fuller participation in the cultural life of the new country. It signals a choice to take part in a cultural debate that goes beyond that in the exile community. It is, at this moment in history, certainly not a matter of uncritical acceptance of all the new society's values and norms. The use of English, rather, turns the writer into one who, as Sonia Saldívar-Hull and Gustavo Pérez Firmat say, lives on the hyphen.[2] The situation of Cubans in the United States is, to be sure, significantly different from that of transplanted Argentines, Chileans, and Uruguayans. Current and past U.S. relations with Cuba as distinct from the Southern Cone; the length of time there have been exile communities from these regions in the United States; the size of those communities and the extent to which they are dispersed; and the political tendencies of the different groups and their attitude toward U.S. policy — all these affect the nature of exile. Here, suffice it to say that while there is now a significant body of Cuban-American literary texts written in English, Southern Cone fiction and poetry in the United States (as in Europe) are still overwhelmingly written in Spanish. Other public texts, however, are more frequently written in the language of the new country, signaling an engagement with the political, social, and intellectual life of those places. Ana Martínez and María Lugones write in what for them was once an utterly foreign language.

Martínez's and Lugones's engagement with issues of cultural hybridity is deeply marked by their awareness of language and language difference. The former's newspaper columns, published regularly in *Dagens Nyheter*, a Stockholm-based daily with national circulation, like the latter's scholarly articles in philosophy, are hybrid texts, bordering on the literary, as essays do.[3] As a storyteller, Martínez certainly qualifies as an author of fiction. Both she and Lugones have a writerly concern for language, which marks their particular kind of code-switching, aimed at a monolingual audience. This is not the easy flow between two languages that constitutes the everyday talk of family and friends in a bilingual community. It is also different from the juxtaposition of English and Spanish in, for example, Chicano border writing, which creates a new, mestizo language that challenges the dominance and purity of Mexican Spanish as well as U.S. English even as it serves as a link between them in its demand for a certain competence in both. In Martínez and Lugones the practice of code-switching is, rather, a (mostly) friendly assertion of bilingualism and biculturalism in the face of the intransigent monoculture. More often than not, Martínez and Lugones temper the inclusion of Spanish in their texts by translating it into the Swedish or English of their host cultures.[4]

Martínez says that Swedish is a struggle for her, but it is one she willingly embraces. I use the metaphor deliberately, since one of her earliest written pieces is about her passion for the Swedish language, which she personifies as a lover. Martínez sexualizes language, giving it body, weight, and intention. She opens her first book with that essay, and this summer as I write the present work she includes a portion of it in her radio show as well:

> I have an inventive, playful lover whom I must conquer every day. (Lucky I didn't say canchre.) An inventive lover. The Swedish language. In my crazy love battle I sleep with the dictionary of the Swedish Academy under my pillow and I dream a mad Latin American dream of always being able to make that unsubduable language do my bidding, that language with its one thousand different authorized nuances and accentuations. But tell me, dear listener, how many bridges must I cross before I come to rest on the shores of Swedish grammar? How many sleepless nights before I drink the innermost liquor of the words of Swedish?[5]

This declaration of love and abnegation no doubt ingratiates Martínez to her audience, who enjoy hearing that the language they think of as small and isolated is seductive and complex. The language and those who speak it are not equally adored, however. In the next sentence Martínez mimics the shrill voice of an unpleasant Swedish woman hypocritically praising Martínez's command of the language. What remains clear from listening to Martínez is that she does love the feel, the sound, and even the abruptness of the Swedish language.

Lugones, whose attitude toward English is more utilitarian than loving or ludic, makes the language do her bidding. As a philosopher, she de- velops extended metaphors to name and analyze phenomena that have been insufficiently attended to. Her concept of "world"-traveling, for ex- ample, is a metaphor for a kind of empathy derived from an experience of transcontinental displacement. In the essay in which she develops the concept, "fluency" becomes a metonym for acculturation in what Lugones calls a "world." With a specific mention of language (fluency's primary referent), Lugones tropes linguistic competence as the shorthand for a broader cultural competence:

> The first way of being at ease in a particular "world" is by being a fluent speaker in that "world." I know all the norms that there are to be followed, I know all the words that there are to be spoken. I know all the moves. I am confident.[6]

Fluency as a linguistic term itself relies on a spatial metaphor having to do with a substance's ease of movement from one place to another, and from one shape to another. It suggests flexibility and motility. Fluency recalls its sister, fluidity, the act of shape-shifting itself, the process of movement from one container to another, one place to another, and of adapting one's contours to that new container, without changing one's substance. Wine is still wine as it is poured from cask to bottle to glass. As metaphor, of course, this is not a perfect description of an individual's becoming capable in a new country. Most importantly, it elides the demands for compromise and accommodation that are made on both the person and the culture.

Martínez takes the same metaphor of fluency and also shows how it goes beyond the mere knowledge of grammar, vocabulary, and syntax. On her radio show, as in her writing, Martínez traces the extent to which she has become fluent in Swedish culture, one part of which consists of her proficiency in the Swedish language. Trading on her lack of confi- dence, Martínez recognizes that speaking a language well enough to be understood does not necessarily mean one comprehends its complexi- ties as a system that includes norms and values as well as a distinctive syntax, vocabulary, and grammar. She tells a story that illustrates how much harder it is to learn what she jestingly calls the psycholinguistics of Swedish. For Martínez, psycholinguistics — the value of words, as op- posed to their simple manifest meaning — is determined from without. It is the outsider's successful interpretation of what underlies the mani- fest content of a newly encountered language. The story is, in itself, quite horrifying as the narrator tells about losing a job because she could not differentiate between a request and an order. The tale becomes funny only in the telling, in Martínez's intonation, her rhythms and speech patterns. Martínez's story of the linguistic warmth of Spanish in contrast to the cool distance of Swedish runs through Lugones's work as well, with English in the second-language slot. But whereas Martínez shows how Swedish reticence may encode deep feeling, and how the warmth and passion expressed by Spanish effusiveness may or may not be genuine, Lugones rather more simplistically sets formulaic English utterances used to evade intimacy against Spanish terms that invite it.[7] Lugones's purpose in juxtaposing snatches of conversation in English and Spanish is to reveal the very different emotional and practical valences of the two cultures they represent. She draws distinctions between English and Spanish, and by extension the United States and Latin America, that, to use a formulation she will develop later, separate into purity. Martínez's linguistic and cultural differences bleed into each other like a well-worn madras plaid.

Lugones's "Playfulness, 'World'-Travelling, and Loving Perception" first appeared in the feminist philosophy journal *Hypatia* and has since been anthologized by Gloria Anzaldúa in *Making Face/Making Soul: Haciendo Caras* along with "Hablando cara a cara/Speaking Face to Face." Lugones's "Purity, Impurity, and Separation" was published initially in the interdisciplinary feminist journal *Signs* and has since been included in an anthology of feminist philosophy. I am making a point of these publication venues because they say something about Lugones's readership, which is primarily academic, consisting in large measure of philosophers. But insofar as she speaks to women's studies scholars and students her readership is far from strictly disciplinary. Anzaldúa's anthology, moreover, contains articles, fiction, and poetry by feminists of color not affiliated with the world of academia, as well as by scholars like Lugones, and it is marketed largely to a readership interested in questions of race and gender. Lugones's articles, then, occupy the border space between academia and the general (mostly feminist) public, just as they occupy border spaces in language and subject matter. Her work is primarily about cultural encounters, about power relationships, gender, sexuality, and the political as well as theoretical meanings of difference. These topics resonate with those broached by the exile writers discussed in earlier chapters, although Lugones's focus is on different(ly) racialized ethnic communities within the United States, rather than on the question of international displacement and its consequences; and the grounding of her focus in the discipline of philosophy perhaps accounts for its utopian flavor. María Lugones, like Ana Martínez, has come to an international feminism that emerges from and celebrates an Argentine background, but whose primary space — where it is played out — is the diasporic territory, which inflects it unmistakably.

It does no great violence to Lugones's metaphor of "world"-traveling to return it to its origins in actual physical displacement. It is not inciden-

138 / *Beyond Exile*

tal that Lugones, whose peregrinations took her from Argentina to the
United States, develops the concept of "world"-traveling, the capacity to
enter into the way of being of another person or group. The title of the essay in which she elaborates this concept, "Playfulness, 'World'-Travelling,
and Loving Perception," names the connection between an empathic apprehension of the (not entirely different) other and playfulness as both
stance toward the world and means for achieving loving perception.[8]
"World"-traveling depends on a certain amount of (always imperfect and
incomplete) ease. If we understand the relative levels of ease and unease
in terms of the notions of identity, rootedness, and uprooting elaborated
in chapter 3, we can use Lugones's formulation to see how Martínez has
become ambiguously at ease in Sweden. Her ease-with-an-edge, derived
from neither absolute alienation nor complete assimilation, follows Lugones's formulation: it is full of promise, possibility, and playfulness. Like
Lugones, Martínez is not totally comfortable with her own Argentine culture, but what emerges as grist for the philosophical mill in Lugones is
material for play and humor in Martínez, even when the topic is serious.

In "Purity, Impurity, and Separation," Lugones continues her discussion
of cultural heterogeneity and of the need to be playfully and constructively
destructive of racism and the ethnocentrism that is racism's wellspring.
Striving to reconcile the appeal of lesbian feminist separatism in the face
of homophobic culture with a revulsion toward a priori notions of an irreducible racial separateness based on fear of contamination and desire
for purity, Lugones shows how "separation" can be understood in at least
two ways. One form of separation, which Lugones names "separation as
curdling," is precipitated by contact and influence.[9] The other is a sort of
sterile purity characterized by the establishment and maintenance of fixed,
impermeable borders. What Lugones calls separation as curdling is an act
of conscious and willful yielding — a kind of submission, without the passivity usually associated with that term. It includes bi- and multilingual
experimentation, caricaturing both self and other, being the trickster and
the fool. Although she delights in impurity, and in "a practice of festive
resistance," Lugones fears she cannot be playful in her current identity as
Argentine feminist philosopher living in the United States.[10] What she
can do is write a treatise on playfulness. It takes the performer Martínez
to enact playfulness, in her writing and on the radio. Martínez's stories are
indeed examples of festive resistance. She is playful in her humor and in
the way her critical eye is tempered by what Lugones, following Marilyn
Frye, calls loving perception. In Lugones's formulation, loving perception
includes an awareness of differences among women that, left unexamined,
might otherwise lead to a failure to love. Martínez, who perceives lovingly,
turns her analysis inward upon herself, outward toward Sweden, and backward to her own Argentine history, a perspective that is hardly nostalgic,
but is nevertheless affectionate.

Martínez's stories tell about cultural misapprehension, even among members of a single family. To her young nephew, Martínez on a visit home is "Ana de Suecia," Ana of (that is, from) Sweden: visiting royalty. She writes stories about Swedish racism, but more important about the possibility of overcoming racism. Like Lugones, Martínez recognizes iniquity; also like Lugones, she is not immobilized by it. She can imagine her way through to the other side without losing her critical or moral edge, and also without losing her sense of humor. The happy ending of her story of Dalmiro from Patagonia who meets and marries Birgitta from Grytnäs consists of his using the same songs that tamed the whales of the South Atlantic and the cows of the valleys of northwestern Sweden to calm the angry hordes of neo-Nazis who come after him for defiling pure Aryan womanhood. The pleasure of the music-hath-charms resolution derives not from sentimentality, but rather from the satisfying suggestion that the gang is subhuman, albeit not without the same hope for domestication as the (other) dumb animals our hero is accustomed to dealing with: "Who could have known that Patagonia's whales, Dalarna's cows, and Swedish skinheads would have the same taste in music?" the storyteller asks.

Other tales poke fun at love between Argentine men and Swedish women, but Martínez demonstrates affection for both, as in the story she tells of the speaker's city-bred Argentine cousin. Roberto nourishes his dream of sexually free Swedish women only to meet Inger, a lover of country life, who agrees to schedule him for sex "on Tuesday at 7:30, between [her] feminist network meeting and [her] tent project." From the interstices of gender and nationality, and with gentle good humor, Martínez happily caricatures the stereotypical passionate Argentine man and the equally stereotypical sexually liberated, but passionless and routine-bound, Swedish woman. Her humor seems easy, natural, part of a warm personality; and her palpable pleasure in language gives that impression as well. It is of course performance, but performance that engages through tone of voice, through the physical transmission of language in a medium that fosters play and diversion. Lugones, in contrast, struggles for her sense of play; she fears it has been a casualty of transplantation. The linguistic playfulness of *porteño* Spanish does not find its tenor in her public performance in English, and she does not choose to participate in the retelling of tales of heterosexuality that so easily connect Martínez to the majority of her Swedish listeners. Lugones is a philosopher and a political activist; she has not managed in her public writing to temper these serious occupations with a light touch or the ambiguity of humor.

The "world"-traveler and her mother have a complicated relationship in the work of both Lugones and Martínez. Lugones refuses to be the dutiful daughter who gives her mother the unquestioning filial love that is expected of her, since in her understanding love so defined depends on the reduction of the mother to a function for the child. It means diminishing "mother," making her into the "matter" to which she is etymologically tied, and of "grafting onto her substance."[11] This concept, which Lugones takes from Marilyn Frye, names precisely what we have seen in numerous exile novels protagonized by men, in which the body of the mother is the nourishing source the man ultimately, but ambivalently, leaves. As a child, the daughter might well take this sort of parasitic advantage of the mother; as a woman and potential mother she does so at her own peril. Out of both self-interest and what she characterizes as a kind of naturally occurring ethical stance, Lugones seeks another way to know her mother, one that exceeds Argentine patriarchal expectations and that will, not incidentally, free Lugones herself from that bondage.

Lugones's journey in "Playfulness, 'World'-Travelling, and Loving Perception" requires that the subject leave and subsequently return to her mother in order to learn how to perceive her lovingly. Lugones writes of having to go away from her mother, using vocabulary to which she will come back, apparently in another context:

[I]t is clear that part of the mechanism that permitted my not learning well [the lesson of love as abnegation and abuse] involved a separation from my mother: I saw us as beings of quite a different sort. It involved an abandoning of my mother, while I longed not to abandon her. I wanted to love my mother, though, given what I was taught, "love" could not be the right word for what I longed for. . . . I *saw myself as separate from her, a different sort of being, not quite of the same species. This separation, this lack of love, I saw, and I think that I saw correctly, as a lack in myself.*[12]

"Separation" is a key word here, although it is not until several years later, in 1994, that Lugones returns to it, in "Purity, Impurity, and Separation," in order to subject the term to intense scrutiny. There the notion of separation occupies center stage, connecting only fleetingly to the mother, but, significantly, making that connection in Spanish. Lugones's primary metaphor in the essay concerns separating eggs, and the subsequent relationship between oil and yolk, in the making of mayonnaise. She enlists this complex culinary trope to illustrate two different ways of thinking about separation. In household mayonnaise production, separation not only means what Lugones calls separation into purity (accomplished in completely removing the yolk from the white) but also, and contradictorily, can derive from the irreparable, failed mixing of ingredients in which each contains a residue of the other. Lugones's argument is related to issues of alienation and acculturation, to the kinds of interactions that are possible and necessary among heterogeneous groups. Significantly, the metaphor she finds to illuminate her discussion is derived from her knowledge of separation as curdling learned in her mother's kitchen. The phrase, suddenly in Spanish: "Mamá, la mayonesa se separó," returns us

to the place and language of her childhood, recalling the fraught relationship with her mother established in the earlier essay. The restless
child whose mayonnaise fails — that is, separates — is learning both impa-
tience with her mother's way of life and the skills that will link them in
a long line of mothers and daughters. The event is also peculiarly rooted
in Argentina, where the making of mayonnaise is a necessary domestic
skill, and where Juan Domingo Perón's love of the eggy sauce is still
legendary.[13]

Like Lugones, Martínez's discussion of her mother is connected to food.
Martínez's mother does not teach her daughter culinary skills, however.
Instead, she enlists the child Ana as part of a female line that is bodily
connected not by maternity, but by their tendency to gain weight and
therefore by their need to diet. The mother disciplines herself and her
daughter around the practice of eating, and the result for the storyteller is
a brush with bulimia that haunts her ever after.

Martínez tells a story of submitting to the allegorical figure she calls
"Dame Bulimia," who makes her feel all-powerful, like a God who can
defy the laws of nature. She can eat without getting fat. This mother
figure, however, fosters an obsession with food, thereby taking away the
speaker's power to control her own life, and ultimately taking power from
her. At the end, the speaker is no longer a false god unto herself; instead she turns outward to a mother god who is both loving and forgiving.
Martínez's speaker (who on the radio is given voice by Martínez herself,
telling an autobiographical tale) traces her flirtation with bulimia to her
mother's kitchen, a kitchen that both provided and denied that eternal
enemy, food.

Although most of Martínez's stories are about language and the meeting of individuals as a result of transnational movement, she also tells of
embodiment, specifically around the issue of beauty and its relationship
to body size. Still, her story of bulimia, told as an autobiographical tale,
seems unconnected to the other stories she tells, which are loosely tied
together by the theme of Argentina-meets-Sweden. By telling this story
here, and ending her program with a self-affirming prayer to a feminine
deity, and gesturing to men as well as women, Martínez urges all of her
listeners to accept the goodness of their physical selves. Moreover, she ani-
mates the refusal to separate the global from the individual, rejects taking
the body out of discourse, and reinforces the power of the mother and the
daughter, who come together in the kitchen.

The kitchen is one of the spaces the mother occupies — Lugones's
more than Martínez's, clearly. It is the ambivalent space of the education
for normative Argentine womanhood, of nourishment, and of danger —
danger of becoming fat, danger of becoming the mother herself — but also
of sensual delight and creativity. Ana Martínez and María Lugones, upon
entering the narrative space of the childhood kitchen, also return to the

history of the real, historically located mother. Like Ana Vásquez in *Mi amiga Chantal* (My friend Chantal), they overtly connect mother and food, the labor and knowledge required in producing a meal, the ambivalence of providing and denying food. Lugones's childhood kitchen dialogue with her mother represents, on one level, an unsuccessful attempt at the socialization of the girl child. Lugones remains too impatient to make a decent mayonnaise, and she is unwilling to imitate her mother's willing abjection. Still, the kitchen is a site of power, creativity, transformation, and production, and of culture. From Latin America's first feminist thinker, Sor Juana Inés de la Cruz, who noted in the seventeenth century that if Aristotle had spent any time in the kitchen he would have written more, to her heir, feminist philosopher Lugones, whose knowledge of the chemical traits of eggs as they mix with oil was learned in the kitchen and serves as an object lesson on definitions of separation, the kitchen has been a good place to come to knowledge.[14]

Lugones's riff on separation in "Purity, Impurity, and Separation" stops short at the psychoanalytic use of the term with reference to the child's separation from the mother, but separation from the mother is at the core of "Playfulness, 'World'-Travelling, and Loving Perception," written before Lugones came up with the stunning notion of separation as curdling that would have helped characterize the resolution of her fraught relationship with her mother. In "Playfulness, 'World'-Travelling, and Loving Perception," the daughter must eventually come to a recognition of the separateness of the (m)other, of her mother's selfhood as a precondition of her own. In the case she describes but does not analyze, the daughter, as an unavoidable part of her differentiation, that is, of her separation from the mother, carries a bit of her mother with and in her. Paradoxically, only by maintaining this residual connection can she truly recognize her mother's wholeness, and her own. Life beyond exile, beyond the sense of immobilizing estrangement, means coming to an acceptance of the adult self and to an equally adult understanding of the mother as separate from oneself. The maternal metaphor functions thus in the text of a woman's assimilation: Lugones learns to see her mother more fully in separation from her, and the relationship with the mother is a critical part of her philosophical thinking, particularly around ethical questions that are the foundation of Lugones's writing on difference and on questions of knowledge and language and the essence of a thing. Lugones learns "world"-traveling in part as a means to enter her mother's "world," that is, her way of being and knowing. In Lugones, the mother lives in process, never in the rigidity of completion. The language the mother speaks breaks down around nouns that signify and therefore limit the definition and function of otherwise multifarious things. You have to enter into the Mother's process to understand her, but if you do, you have no trouble. But in order to enter that process safely, to ensure that "world"-

traveling includes a return ticket, a level of psychological separation from the mother is also essential.

In Martínez the ambivalent relationship to the mother is resolved by means of the substitution of the mother by a series of powerful maternal figures, each of whom has the power to destroy but who are ultimately as life-affirming as they are demanding. There is a line of maternal powerhouses in Martínez's store of tales, beginning with her own mother, continuing through Moder Svea (Mother Sweden), and ending with Mother God. Moder Svea is an exigent, castrating matriarch, who cuts off Martínez's name. Where once the teller of these stories was Ana María Mercedes Martínez del Valle, she is now Swedishly simplified to Ana Martinez, "like Ulla Svensson, but in Spanish." Yet Martínez says that she submitted to this symbolic castration voluntarily: the price of acceptance and love is often the willing sacrifice of a piece of one's identity. Martínez argues here that only the most rigid, self-absorbed, and lonely of us insist on perfect boundaries and perfect integrity. Life demands trade-offs, particularly in questions of human interaction, and she refuses to accept the notion that it is only poor, weak immigrant women who allow themselves to be altered, or to concede that willing adaptation is a form of passive acceptance of castration. Martínez's assertion echoes Lugones's rejection of at least two Anglo-American feminist philosophers' affirmation of independence as the ultimate good for women.[15] Although Lugones is not as explicit (nor perhaps as extreme) as Martínez in her willingness to submit to a kind of mutilation in pursuit of love (and here love has a much wider meaning than the love of one's sexual partner), Lugones's concept of "world"-traveling implies a certain giving over of the perfectly bounded self in the enriching process of entering another's "world."

The "world"-traveling exile, whether she returns or remains in the diaspora, is founded on separation — the separation from the old place, the sense of profound difference from the new, and, in return, the sad knowledge that the first separation has become in a way irreparable. I know I am yanking Lugones's elegant and complex metaphor of separation back to its literal meaning, but I do that, I believe, in the spirit of her work. Literal separation in the historical and geographical processes of exile contains a psychic and ethical component best understood and, I would argue, best lived as Lugones's separation as curdling, a separation whose meaning depends on impurity, hybridization, compassion, and empathy. It speaks of a flexibility of the spirit, of the subject, and of the palate. It refuses the static perfection of purity and the dictatorial state that, by means of prisons and purges, expelled the oppositional other. It likewise denounces the practices of the nominally compassionate host country that, by means of exclusion of the foreign other, freezes that soul into the bloodless, colorless being of Cristina Peri Rossi's nightmare sketch of exile, "Las estatuas, o la condición del extranjero" (Statues, or the condition of the foreigner), in which the foreigner and the inhabitants of the place are purely separate from each other and thus mutually unreal.

This chapter began with an epigraph from *Exils Latino-Americains: La malédiction d'Ulysse* (Latin American exiles: The curse of Ulysses),[16] by Ana Vásquez and Ana María Araujo, who call the final chapter of their study of Southern Cone exiles in France "Retour... Retorno." The title suggests a double return, its ellipsis a bridge that marks the connection and separation between France and South America. The repetition of the word, first in French and then in Spanish, seems to indicate an emphasis on interlingual understanding, as well as an intensification of the desire to return and an emphasis on the process of return among the former exiles. Yet the chapter is replete with examples of exiles who have chosen to remain in France or who, after going back to Argentina or Chile or Uruguay, return to France. "Retour... retorno" marks the double return that both undoes and intensifies itself, the irreconcilability and mutual need of separation and connection. The ellipsis is the unsteady plank that will take Cortázar's Oliveira to the window across the courtyard, back to France from Argentina, or to his death. It is the plane ride home to an altered city. After years of exile, of alienation and acculturation, of adapting the palate and the ear and the line of vision, the exile — and the exile's palate, ear, and eye — is no longer fully at home anywhere. The end of exile is a richness that must always bear a sense of loss and a desire for what is elsewhere.

NOTES

Prologue

1. "Que lo sepan todos de una vez: / el exilio no puede ser más una retórica" (Cristina Peri Rossi, "Estado de exilio," in *Las voces distantes: Antología de los creadores uruguayos de la diáspora,* ed. Álvaro Barros-Lémez [Montevideo: Monte Sexto, 1985], 257).

2. "Las sociedades autoritarias se caracterizan por prohibir el diálogo en una comunidad" (Rodrigo Cánovas, *Lihn, Zurita, Ictus, Radrigán: Literatura chilena y experiencia autoritaria* [Santiago: FLACSO, 1986], 131).

3. "En Chile, la interrupción del diálogo genera, en los primeros años de la dictadura, una afasia colectiva. A nivel cultural, la afasia implica un habla que no dice nada, un tejido amorfo de significados que equivale a los que en lingüística se denomina simplemente 'ruido.' Además de constituir un síntoma de la pérdida de los referentes culturales (se cuenta con discursos ideológicos absolutamente ineficaces para explicar una situación histórica nueva), este lenguaje dislocado es el efecto de una censura disgregadora, que la comunidad ha internalizado" (ibid.).

4. See, for example, Susan Bordo, "The Cartesian Masculinization of Thought," *Signs* 11 (1986), and the issue of *Hypatia* (6, no. 3 [1991]) on feminism and the body edited by Elizabeth Grosz.

5. Still, there is a lot of resistance to the recuperation of the male body, except, perhaps, among male queer theorists. It seems much more congenial to valorize the female body because it is already there in the discourse and because, for feminists, part of what we take as our task is to pay (a new kind of) attention to women.

6. Gayle Rubin, "The Traffic in Women: Notes on the Political Economy of Sex," in *Toward an Anthropology of Women,* ed. Reina Rapp (New York: Monthly Review Press, 1975), has called this web of relations the sex/gender system. Judith Butler's term in *Gender Trouble: Feminism and the Subversion of Identity* (New York: Routledge, 1990) is the heterosexual matrix.

7. See, for example, Janet Biezer, *Ventriloquized Bodies: Narratives of Hysteria in Nineteenth-Century France* (Ithaca, N.Y.: Cornell University Press, 1994). For a useful overview of the geographical literature on the body, see Robyn Longhurst, "The Body and Geography," *Gender, Place and Culture: A Journal of Feminist Geography* 21 (March 1995): 97–105.

8. See Sue Best, "Sexualizing Space," in *Sexy Bodies: The Strange Carnalities of Feminism,* ed. Elizabeth Grosz and Elspeth Probyn (New York: Routledge, 1995), 181–94, for an illuminating discussion of body-text as space. Best ultimately argues that the body as space cannot be relied upon to be passive because it is always already imbricated in and as language. Although I agree with Best's argument, I am more interested here in the sentient body as actor. I am in full agreement with

145

Best when she states that "the body-model does not secure a clear boundary for notions of 'human' space; on the contrary, this 'comparison' of the female body and space profoundly complicates the identity of both terms" (191).

9. Myra Jehlen, "Archimedes and the Paradox of Feminist Criticism," *Signs* 6, no. 4 (1981): 575–601; reprinted in *Feminisms: An Anthology of Literary Theory and Criticism*, ed. Robin R. Warhol and Diane Price Herndl (New Brunswick, N.J.: Rutgers University Press, 1991), 75.

10. Bell hooks, *Feminist Theory from Margin to Center* (Boston: South End Press, 1984).

11. Nancy Hartsock, "The Feminist Standpoint: Developing the Ground for a Specifically Feminist Historical Materialism," in *Discovering Reality: Feminist Perspectives on Epistemology, Metaphysics, Methodology, and Philosophy of Science*, ed. Sandra Harding and Merrill B. Hitinkka (Dordrecht: Reidel, 1983), 283–310; Patricia Hill Collins, *Black Feminist Thought* (Boston: Unwin Hyman, 1990); Adrienne Rich, *Blood, Bread, and Poetry: Selected Prose, 1979–1985* (New York: W. W. Norton, 1986).

12. See, for example, Mary Lynne Broe and Angela Ingram, eds., *Women's Writing in Exile* (Chapel Hill: University of North Carolina Press, 1989), and Seyla Benhabib, *Situating the Self* (Cambridge: Polity Press, 1992).

13. Rosi Braidotti, *Nomadic Subjects: Embodiment and Sexual Difference in Contemporary Feminist Theory* (New York: Columbia University Press, 1994), 22.

14. Panivong Norindr, " 'Errances' and Memories in Marguerite Duras's Colonial Cities," *Differences: A Journal of Feminist Cultural Studies* 5, no. 5 (fall 1993): 52–79, esp. 54. The de Certeau quote is from *The Practice of Everyday Life*, vol. 1 (Berkeley: University of California Press, 1984), 93.

15. Gloria Anzaldúa, *Borderlands/La frontera: The New Mestiza* (San Francisco: Spinsters/Aunt Lute, 1987).

16. María Lugones, "Playfulness, 'World'-Travelling, and Loving Perception," in *Making Face/Making Soul: Haciendo Caras*, ed. Gloria Anzaldúa (San Francisco: Aunt Lute, 1990), 396; emphasis added. I will return to this essay in chapter 8.

17. Carmen J. Galarce, *La novela chilena del exilio (1973–1987): El caso de Isabel Allende* (Santiago: Universidad de Chile, 1994), discusses a wide range of Chilean exile texts, only a small number of which coincide with the ones I write on here. Furthermore, the work of even collecting the writing of Southern Cone exiles is still under way. The Chilean ministry of culture has undertaken a massive project of collecting and cataloging the writing of Chileans abroad during the years of Pinochet's dictatorship. A recent article by Uruguayan writer and critic Leonardo Rossiello, "La literatura del exilio latinoamericano en Suecia (1976–1990)," *Revista Iberoamericana* 164–65 (July–December 1993): 551–73, lists 157 works of Latin American exile writing, most by Southern Cone authors, between 1976 and 1990 in Sweden alone.

18. Emily Apter, "Comparative Exile: Competing Margins in the History of Comparative Literature," in *Comparative Literature in the Age of Multiculturalism*, ed. Charles Bernheimer (Baltimore: Johns Hopkins University Press, 1995), 86–96. I am grateful to Debra Castillo for this reference.

19. See Mabel Moraña, "(Im)pertinencia de la memoria histórica en América

Latina," paper presented at the Twenty-Eighth International Latin American Studies Association Convention, Atlanta, Georgia, March 10–12, 1994.

1. After Exile

1. Ruth Reichel, "Restaurants," *New York Times,* April 8, 1994.
2. Elaine Louie, "Take the No. 7 to the Andes (Come Hungry)," *New York Times,* August 14, 1996.
3. Paraguay, the fourth country in this region, also recently shook its own, much longer lived, dictatorship. The Stroessner regime effectively isolated Paraguay from the rest of the region for close to forty years, and its situation, though no less worthy of investigation, is beyond the scope of my study. For a short, trenchant meditation on the meanings of repression and exile in Paraguayan literature, see Augusto Roa Bastos, "La escritura: Metáfora del exilio," *Nuevo Texto Crítico* 1, no. 1 (1988): 3–6. See also Teresa Méndez Faith's more extensive study of Paraguay and the literature of exile, *Paraguay — novela y exilio* (Somerville, N.J.: SLUSA, 1985).
4. For an overview of Uruguayan politics since redemocratizaton, see Aidan Rankin, "Reflections on the Non-revolution in Uruguay," *New Left Review* 211 (May–June 1995): 131–43.
5. Many Chileans who could afford the trip went back to vote in the elections (absentee balloting was not an option) and then returned to what has since become home in the United States or elsewhere. According to Thomas C. Wright, "Legacy of Dictatorship: Works on the Chilean Diaspora," *Latin American Research Review* 30, no. 3 (1995): 198–209, "less than a quarter of the political exiles had returned by mid-1994" (199).
6. Apart from "former Yugoslavia" and "the former Soviet Union" as serious common locutions (that nevertheless recall "the artist formerly known as Prince"), we have Jorge Abril Trigo's wonderfully sardonic "post-Uruguay"; see "Fronterías: Liminaridad: Transculturación: Para una hermenéutica de la neo-modernidad posuruguaya," *Estudios de investigación literaria* 3, no. 5 (January–June 1995): 173–98 (special issue entitled *Cultura, Poder y Nación,* ed. Beatriz González Stephen [Caracas: Universidad Simón Bolívar]).
7. For an illuminating discussion of the problematic term "postcolonial," see Ella Shohat, "Notes on the Term 'Post-colonial,'" *Social Text* 31–32 (1992): 99–113.
8. Benedict Anderson, *Imagined Communities: Reflections on the Origins and Spread of Nationalism* (New York: Verso, 1991), has persuasively argued that nation is an imagined, and therefore affective, community.
9. José Donoso, *The Garden Next Door,* trans. Hardie St. Martin (New York: Grove Press, 1992), 152. "¿Adónde, si se vende la casa, quiere que vuelva? Uno no vuelve a un país, a una raza, a una idea, a un pueblo: uno — yo por lo pronto — vuelve a un lugar cerrado y limitado donde el corazón se siente seguro" (José Donoso, *El jardín de al lado* [Barcelona: Seix Barral, 1981], 169).
10. For an enlightening discussion of the space and gender in novels written by women of the Caribbean, Venezuela, and Nicaragua, see Ileana Rodríguez,

House/Garden/Nation: Space, Gender, and Ethnicity in Post-colonial Latin American Literatures by Women (Durham, N.C.: Duke University Press, 1994).

11. José da Cruz, *Sin patria ni tumba: Crónicas del exilio* (Lund: Grans Boktrykeri, 1988).

12. I am grateful to Edmé Domínguez and Román Soto for directing me to this iconography. According to Domínguez, the Mexican image is racially indeterminate. In some texts she is blonde; in others she is dark, and her features blend European and indigenous characteristics.

13. Patria, mi patria, vuelvo hacia ti la sangre.
Pero te pido, como a la madre el niño
lleno de llanto,
    Acoge
esta guitarra ciega
y esta frente perdida.

Salí a encontrarte hijos por la tierra,
salí a cuidar caídos con tu nombre de nieve,
salí a hacer una casa con tu madera pura,
salí a llevar tu estrella a los héroes heridos.

Ahora quiero dormir en tu substancia.
Dame tu clara noche de penetrantes cuerdas,
tu noche de navío, tu estatura estrellada.

Pablo Neruda, "Hymn and Return," in *Neruda and Vallejo, Selected Poems*, ed. Robert Bly (Boston: Beacon Press, 1971), 96, 97.

14. José Leandro Urbina, *Cobro revertido* (Santiago: Planeta Biblioteca del Sur, 1992).

15. Mary Layoun, "The Female Body and 'Transnational' Reproduction; or, Rape by Any Other Name?" in *Scattered Hegemonies*, ed. Inderpal Grewal and Caren Kaplan (Minneapolis: University of Minnesota Press, 1994), 63–75.

16. When, deep into Donoso's novel, Julio calls Chile to find that his mother has finally died, he triggers a series of telephone calls:

Later on the telephone wakes me and Gloria answers it:
"Chile, . . . " she says. "Collect. How strange." (*Garden*, 154)

[Más tarde me despierta el teléfono, que contesta Gloria:
— Chile . . . — dice — Cobro revertido. Que cosa más rara, ¿no?
— ¿Qué es cobro revertido? (*Jardín*, 172)]

17. Juan Rivano, *Época de descubrimientos* (Furulund, Sweden: Alhambra de Lund, 1991).

18. "Un nacimiento, una salida con forceps, pero salida al fin, parto inminente" (Daniel Moyano, *Libro de navíos y borrascas* [Buenos Aires: Editorial Legasa, 1983], 153–54). For a more complete discussion of Moyano's novel, see Linda L. Hollabaugh, "Daniel Moyano's *Libro de navíos y borrascas*: The Expression of Territorial Exile," in *The Literature of Emigration and Exile*, ed. James Whitlark and Wendell Aycock (Lubbock: Texas Tech University Press, 1992), 143–56.

19. "Argentino destetado que decide romper formalmente con la madre" (Moyano, *Libro*, 201).

20. Donoso, *Garden,* 154. "Es arraigo, historia, leyenda, metáfora, territorio propio, término en que habita el corazón" (*Jardín,* 171).

21. Carlos Cerda, *Una casa vacía* (Santiago: Alfaguara, 1996).

22. Gillian Rose, *Feminism and Geography: The Limits of Geographical Knowledge* (Minneapolis: University of Minnesota Press, 1993), 56.

23. Inger Agger, *La pieza azul: Testimonio femenino del exilio* (Santiago: Editorial Cuarto Propio, 1993); translation of *Det Blå Værelse: Kvindeligt vidnesbyrd fra exilet* (Copenhagen: Hans Reitzels Forlag, 1992). Agger's study suggests that the work she did with these women made an important difference in their lives and that she is a sensitive, successful feminist therapist. The fact that even she chooses this metaphor for women's psyches indicates its power.

24. Ana Vásquez, *Mi amiga Chantal* (Barcelona: Lumen, 1991).

25. Marta Traba, *Conversación al sur* (Mexico City: Siglo XXI, 1981), translated by Jo Labanyi as *Mothers and Shadows* (London: Readers International, 1986).

26. Marta Traba, *En cualquier lugar* (Mexico City: Siglo XXI, 1984).

27. Cristina Peri Rossi, "La influencia de Edgar Allan Poe en la poesía de Raimundo Arias," in *La tarde del dinosaurio* (Barcelona: Planeta, 1976), translated by Tona Wilson as "The Influence of Edgar Allan Poe in the Poetry of Raimundo Arias," in *Contemporary Women Authors of Latin America,* ed. Doris Meyer and Margarite Fernández Olmos (Brooklyn: Brooklyn College Press, 1983), 226–34.

28. Economist Ricardo Lagos, forced to leave Chile after the coup, writes in *Después de la transición* (Santiago: Grupo Editorial Zeta, 1993), 24–25, of moving the social science think tank FLACSO, of which he was then executive secretary, to Buenos Aires during this period. In fact, branches of FLACSO were established in Costa Rica, Mexico, Argentina, Bolivia, Ecuador, and Brazil during the dictatorship, and even managed to survive in Chile. In this brief discussion of movements between Southern Cone nations I am oversimplifying by omitting Brazil. I leave Brazil out because of my own linguistic inadequacy, but the very language difference that causes this omission makes me need to include the observation that Brazil was part of this interchange and that refuge in Brazil involved a more substantial barrier for Spanish speakers than going to another Spanish-speaking country. Furthermore, between 1974 and 1978, Brazil suffered the dictatorship of General Ernesto Geisel.

29. Volodia Teitelboim, *En el país prohibido: Sin el permiso de Pinochet* (Barcelona: Plaza y Janés, 1988), 15.

30. Yossi Shain, *The Frontier of Loyalty: Political Exiles in the Age of the Nation State* (Middletown, Conn.: Wesleyan University Press, 1989), comments on the way disciplinarity limits an understanding of exile by noting that insofar as the disciplines of law, political science, and sociology do not go beyond their traditional borders in attempting to deal with exile, they inevitably see it partially.

31. Sharon Magnarelli, *Reflections/Refractions: Reading Luisa Valenzuela* (New York: P. Lang, 1988), 211–12.

32. Julio Cortázar, "América Latina: exilio y literatura," *Argentina: años de alambradas culturales* (Barcelona: Muchnik, 1984). In this collection Cortázar also reflects on the positive aspects of exile for the writer.

33. Carina Perelli, *De mitos y memorias políticas: La represión, el miedo y después* (Montevideo: Ediciones de la Banda Oriental, 1986). To the extent that this

state of affairs was supported in material ways by an external power, the United States, the sense of being in exile at home was only amplified. Kathleen Newman, "Cultural Redemocratization: Argentina, 1978–89," in *On Edge: The Crisis of Contemporary Latin American Culture*, ed. George Yúdice et al. (Minneapolis: University of Minnesota Press, 1992), points to the "heightened... awareness of national boundaries and societal divisions, in particular the division between those who stayed and those who left. The two cultures of exile, internal and external, produced a geography that consisted of Buenos Aires and scattered places of exile at the far ends of the earth" (172–73). For a thorough theoretical discussion of inner exile, based on the Franco years in Spain, see Paul Illie, *Literature and Internal Exile* (Baltimore: Johns Hopkins University Press, 1980).

34. Yi-Fu Tuan, "Rootedness vs. Sense of Place," *Landscape* 25 (1980), 3–8, cited in Barbara McKean Parmeter, *Giving Voice to Stones: Place and Identity in Palestinian Literature* (Austin: University of Texas Press, 1994), 4–5.

35. País de la ausencia,
    extraño país,
    más ligero que ángel
    y seña sutil,
    color de alga muerta,
    color de neblí,
    con edad de siempre,
    sin edad feliz.

    . . . .

    Me nació de cosas
    que no son país;
    de patrias y patrias
    que tuve y perdí;
    de las criaturas
    que yo vi morir;
    de lo que era mío
    y se fue de mí.

Gabriela Mistral, "Land of Absence," in *Selected Poems of Gabriela Mistral: A Bilingual Edition*, trans. and ed. Doris Dana (Baltimore: Johns Hopkins University Press, 1971), 82–85.

36. Yi-Fu Tuan, *Space and Place: The Perspective of Experience* (London: Edward Arnold, 1977).

37. Mario Benedetti, *Primavera con una esquina rota* (Madrid: Ediciones Alfaguara, 1982), 21; all translations from this text are my own.

38. Rosi Braidotti, *Nomadic Subjects: Embodiment and Sexual Difference in Contemporary Feminist Theory* (New York: Columbia University Press, 1994), 21.

39. "Llorando de los ojos, que no vidiestes atal, / así se parten unos de otros como la uña de la carne" (*Cantar de mío Cid* 1.18).

40. Al grito de "Sálvese quien pueda"
    todo el mundo se echó a los botes,
    casi todos, menos yo.
    Oscurecía y la mar estaba picada,
    veíamos caer, como aves derrotadas,

los cuerpos, uno a uno,
rebotar contra los botes.
Mi mujer, de las primeras,
saltó ligero —luces de los faros,
ínclitas —
sus manos al viento, desplegadas como velas,
sus piernas en el aire,
pareja de pájaros hambrientos;
detrás, una multitud.
No miró una vez hacia atrás.
En cuanto a su cuerpo se posó sobre el bote
—gárrula ave, luchadora —
ella, magnífica,
        dominante,
               comenzó a remar.
. . . .
Los botes se alejaban
ella tenía los brazos hinchados como velas
y remaba segura y firmamente
con el tremendo instinto de las madres
y de los sobrevivientes.
        De las catástrofes perduran los más fuertes.

Cristina Peri Rossi, *Descripción de un naufragio* (Barcelona: Editorial Lumen S.A., 1975), 82, 83.

    41. Si fui amarga fue por la pena.
El capitán gritó "Sálvese quien pueda"
y yo, sin pensarlo más, me lancé al agua,
como si ávida nadadora
como si siempre hubiera estado esperando ese momento,
el momento supremo de soledad
en que nada pesa
nada queda ya
sino el deseo impostergable de vivir;
me lancé al agua, es cierto, sin mirar atrás.
De mirar quizás no me lanzara
habría vacilado mirando tus grandes ojos tristes
. . . .
"Sálvese quien pueda"
había gritado el capitán,
la vida era una hipótesis de salto,
quedarse, una muerte segura.

Ibid., 87, 88.

    42. Cristina Peri Rossi, *La nave de los locos* (Barcelona: Seix Barral, 1984), translated by Psiche Hughes as *The Ship of Fools* (London: Allison and Busby, 1989).

    43. Cristina Peri Rossi, *Solitario de amor* (Barcelona: Grijalbo, 1988); Cristina

Peri Rossi, *La última noche de Dostoiewski* (Madrid: Grijalbo, 1992); Marta Traba, *De la mañana a la noche (Cuentos norteamericanos)* (Montevideo: Monte Sexto, 1986); Manuel Puig, *Maldición eterna a quien lea estas páginas* (Barcelona: Seix Barral, 1980), translated as *Eternal Curse on the Reader of These Pages* (Minneapolis: University of Minnesota Press, 1999); Luisa Valenzuela, *Novela negra con argentinos* (Hanover, N.H.: Ediciones del Norte, 1990), translated by Tony Talbot as *Black Novel with Argentines* (New York: Simon and Schuster, 1992); Antonio Skármeta, *Match boll* (Buenos Aires: Sudamericana, 1989).

44. Alberto Madrid, "Antonio Skármeta, 'Match boll,'" *Araucaria de Chile* 47–48 (1990): 266–68.

45. Ana Vásquez, *Abel Rodríguez y sus hermanos* (Barcelona: Gaya Ciencia, 1981).

46. "Los días se desarticulaban, los niños volvieron del colegio hacia el final de una mañana, los militares se habían llevado todos los profesores. Vinieron a buscar a mi marido. Se salvó por milagro pero ésta es otra historia" (Vásquez, *Mi amiga Chantal*, 169).

47. Alicia Partnoy, *Revenge of the Apple* (Pittsburgh: Cleis Press, 1992), 16–17.

48. "Esa nueva raza de los 'yo-estuve-exiliado-y-por-lo-tanto-soy-mejor-que-ustedes,' investido con autoridad en el extranjero" (José Donoso, *La desesperanza* [Barcelona: Seix Barral, 1986], 28).

49. Breyten Bretenbach, "The Long March from Hearth to Heart," in *Home: A Place in the World*, ed. Arien Mack (New York: New York University Press, 1993), 67–68.

50. Isabel Allende, *El plan infinito* (Buenos Aires: Sudamericana, 1991), translated by Margaret Sayers Peden as *The Infinite Plan* (New York: HarperCollins, 1993); and Isabel Allende, *Eva Luna* (Barcelona: Plaza y Janés, 1987), translated by Margaret Sayers Peden as *Eva Luna* (New York: Knopf, 1988).

51. "Lo esencial es adaptarse. Ya sé que a esta edad es difícil. Casi imposible. Y sin embargo" (Benedetti, *Primavera*, 21).

52. "Y desde entonces regreso cada tarde por una ruta distinta. Por otra parte, ahora no vuelvo a una habitación. Tampoco a una casa. Es simplemente un apartamento, o sea, un simulacro de casa: una habitación con agregados. Pero la nueva ciudad me gusta, ¿por qué no?" (ibid., 23).

53. Bretenbach, "Long March," 77. For Bretenbach, interestingly, the transculturation that the process entails is a form of *métissage*, that is, *mestizaje*, that quintessentially Latin American notion of nation-formation.

54. "Cecilia," in María Angélica Celedón and Luz María Opazo, *Volver a empezar* (Santiago: Pehuén, 1987), reviewed by Wright, "Legacy of Dictatorship," 206.

55. "Para ella ese taller [denominado VECTOR] que sesionaba todos los lunes de seis a nueve de la noche era una actividad peligrosa. Allí comprendí que había una forma distinta de entender a Chile entre esos jóvenes que se habían formado en la dictadura y los que, algunos años mayores, no lograban adaptarse o no aceptaban una situación en la que había riesgos evidentes" (Ricardo Lagos, *Después de la transición* [Santiago: Ediciones B, Serie Reporter, Grupo Editorial Zeta, 1993], 26).

56. Lagos is an economist who was a member of Patricio Alwin's cabinet. He

left Chile after the coup, opened an office of FLACSO in Buenos Aires (ibid., 25), taught for a while in the United States at the University of North Carolina at Chapel Hill (ibid.), worked for UNESCO in Buenos Aires in 1975, and returned to Chile in 1978.

The fact of those discussions, in the belly of the beast, not in exile, meant that the participants must have made some accommodations to their situation, however minor. There was a sense of being able to survive there, and also the awareness that with so many other actors gone, there was a responsibility to engage in these workshops toward a new way of making Chile viable. The discussions themselves took place over a long period of time and reflect transition not only in Chile but in the world. Lagos's sense of a workable leftist politics and economics has changed over time to fit in with changes not only in Chile but in the world economic and political order — with less emphasis on state ownership and pure ideology. This probably seems to many like selling out to the right, but Lagos makes a convincing argument for it.

57. Poli Délano, *Como si no muriera nadie* (Santiago: Planeta/Biblioteca del Sur, 1987).

58. Mario Benedetti, *Andamios* (Mexico: Alfaguara, 1997).

59. Kathleen Newman, "Cultural Redemocratization: Argentina, 1978–89," in *On Edge: The Crisis of Contemporary Latin American Culture,* ed. George Yúdice et al. (Minneapolis: University of Minnesota Press, 1992). See Partnoy, *Revenge of the Apple.*

60. Rankin, "Reflections," 142.

61. Moraña made these comments at the Twenty-Eighth International Convention of the Latin American Studies Association, Atlanta, Georgia, March 10–12, 1994. See also her *Memorias de la generación fantasma: Crítica literaria 1973–1988* (Montevideo: Monte Sexto, 1988).

62. "[L]a seducción del no-decir en una sociedad que aceptó en el pasado inmediato un castigo feroz e indiscriminado, y que resiste en el presente a reconocerlo" (Andrés Avellaneda, "Hablar y callar: Construyendo sentido en la democracia," *Hispamérica* 24, no. 72 [1995]: 38).

63. Cristina Peri Rossi, "Lovelys," in *Cosmoagonías* (Barcelona: Laia, 1988), 127; my translation.

64. Ariel Dorfman, "Commentary on 'Interventions' in the Field of Dreams with Ariel Dorfman," in *Learning History in America: Schools, Cultures, and Politics,* ed. Lloyd Kramer, Donald Reid, and William L. Barney (Minneapolis: University of Minnesota Press, 1994), 181. In an interview with Georgianna M. M. Coleville, Antonio Skármeta maintains that in Chile there was no division after the restoration of democracy: "In Argentina the people who stayed and the others who went away became enemies. They would dislike each other and whenever they had a round table discussion they would argue and attack each other. In the Chilean case it was quite different because when the coup destroyed the national family, the ones who left only wanted one thing: to come back, and the ones who stayed in fact wanted those who went away to come back....I would not say there was a split between the two faces of our culture" (*Latin American Literary Review* 20, no. 39 [January–June 1992]: 29). See, however, the disagreements between Nelly Richard and Hernán Vidal in *boundary 2,* no. 20/3 (fall 1993): 203–31 (special

issue titled *The Postmodern Debate in Latin America*, ed. John Beverley and José Oviedo), for less than friendly interchange.

2. Subject of National Identity

1. Yossi Shain, *The Frontier of Loyalty: Political Exiles in the Age of the Nation State* (Middletown, Conn.: Wesleyan University Press, 1989).

2. Shain (ibid.) reminds us that exile far predates the age of the nation-state and therefore is anterior to any sense of national loyalty and, I would argue by extension, of national identity.

3. Political boundaries can be physical as well, of course. City walls are one form they have taken. The difference is that they are built by people to ratify and enforce the idea of borders, whereas the natural formations of physical geography preexist their textualization. Geographers read the writing-on-the-earth that is (physical) geography. I am provisionally assuming here that this "writing" is not of human doing. For a useful discussion of the charting of newly conquered and colonized territory by travel writers, mapmakers, scientists, and others, see Graciela Montaldo, "Espacio y nación," *Estudios de investigación literaria* 3, no. 5 (January–June 1995): 173–98 (special issue titled *Cultura, poder y nación*, ed. Beatriz González Stephen [Caracas: Universidad Simón Bolívar], 5–17).

4. Shain, *Frontier*, 4.

5. Ibid.

6. Ernest Renan, "What Is a Nation?" in *Nation and Narration*, ed. Homi K. Bhabha (New York: Routledge, 1990), 8–22. For a discussion of the materiality of language see chapter 4.

7. Fredric Jameson, "Third World Literature in the Era of Multinational Capitalism," *Social Text* (fall 1986); Doris Sommer, *Foundational Fictions: The National Romances of Latin America* (Berkeley: University of California Press, 1991); Mario Vargas Llosa, "La literatura es fuego," in *Homenaje a Mario Vargas Llosa*, ed. Helmy F. Giacoman and José Miguel Oviedo (New York: Las Américas, 1972); Francine Masiello, *Between Civilization and Barbarism: Women, Nation, and Literary Culture in Modern Argentina* (Lincoln: University of Nebraska Press, 1992); Homi K. Bhabha, ed., *Nation and Narration* (London: Routledge, 1990).

8. Homi K. Bhabha, "DissemiNation: Time, Narrative, and the Margins of the Modern Nation," in Bhabha, *Nation and Narration*, 292–303. Bhabha here refers to Kristeva's "Women's Time."

9. Annette Kolodny, *The Lay of the Land: Metaphor as Experience and History in American Life and Letters* (Chapel Hill: University of North Carolina Press, 1975); Joan Landes, *Women and the Public Sphere in the Age of the French Revolution* (Ithaca, N.Y.: Cornell University Press, 1988).

10. Masiello, *Between Civilization and Barbarism*, 140.

11. Ibid., 141.

12. Ibid., 143.

13. Ibid., 164.

14. Benedict Anderson, *Imagined Communities: Reflections on the Origins and Spread of Nationalism* (London: Verso, 1983).

15. Sergio Badilla, *Terrenalis* (Stockholm: Bikupa, 1988).

16. Vlady Kociancich, *Los bajos del temor* (Barcelona: Tusquets Editores, 1992).

17. Miguel Enesco, *Me llamaré Tadeusz Freyre* (Barcelona: Editorial Anagrama, 1985).

18. John Agnew and James Duncan, conclusion to *The Power of Place: Bringing Together Geographical and Sociological Imaginations,* ed. Agnew and Duncan (Boston: Unwin Hyman, 1989), 294.

19. Ibid. Race itself is certainly part of the equation. On the one hand, authoritarian regimes, such as those in the Southern Cone, simply banned indigenous cultural expressions, purging the national of any non-European contamination. On the other hand, the nonindigenous opposition tends to assimilate indigenous people to its own project via their purportedly primeval connection to the land, displacing the real lives of people. The contest thus staged between the appropriation of the Indian as a symbol of nation, or the erasure of the Indian as subversive to the nation as a modern entity, obliterates indigenous subjectivity from both ends.

20. Bhabha, "DissemiNation," 302.

21. León Grinberg and Rebeca Grinberg, *Psychoanalytic Perspectives of Migration and Exile,* trans. Nancy Festinger (New Haven: Yale University Press, 1989), translation of *Psicoanálisis de la migración y del exilio* (Alianza, 1984), 130.

22. — ... ¿Cuánto paga Martel? En dólares una miseria. En pesos, no sé. Calculo que te paga el mínimo. No es tonto ese Martel. Pero nació en el país equivocado y ya está viejo para cambiar de rumbo.
— Si es por ambición, todos nacemos en el país equivocado — dijo Coper, con un fastidio que lo sorprendió. La monja [americana] y Dickens conseguían encender una chispa de fuego nacionalista donde jamás había brotado alguna" (Kociancich, *Los bajos del temor,* 228; all translations from this text are my own).

23. In order to focus on the historical/geographical issues surrounding exile, I am leaving aside the very real issues of racial and class differences that play into who gets to name the nation and be the nation.

24. Jorge Abril Trigo, "Fronterías: Liminaridad: Transculturación: Para una hermenéutica de la neomodernidad posuruguaya," *Estudios de investigación literaria* 3, no. 5 (January–June 1995): 173–98 (special issue titled *Cultura, poder y nación,* ed. Beatriz González Stephen [Caracas: Universidad Simón Bolívar]).

25. Luisa Valenzuela, *Novela negra con argentinos* (Hanover, N.H.: Ediciones del Norte, 1990), translated by Tony Talbot as *Black Novel with Argentines* (New York: Simon and Schuster, 1992). For perceptive readings of this novel, see María Inés Lagos, "Displaced Subjects: Valenzuela and the Metropolis," *World Literature Today* 69, no. 4 (fall 1995): 726–32; and Sharon Magnarelli, "Luisa Valenzuela Writing Bodies (Metonymically Speaking) and the Dangerous Metaphor," *Journal of the Institute of Romance Studies* 4 (1966): 281–95.

26. Masiello, *Between Civilization and Barbarism.*

27. Ibid., 35.

28. Ibid., 36.

29. Ibid., 164.

30. Ibid., 173.

31. "Mi escenario no se restringe a ninguno de esos lugares geográficos que ellos llaman patria" (Lucía Guerra, *Más allá de las máscaras* [Puebla, Mexico: Premia

Editora, La Red de Jonas, 1984], 13). The narrator also says her story has no "cardboard heroes or plaster tyrants," and that it cannot be properly situated in time ("No sé cómo ni cuándo empezó verdaderamente mi historia..." [13]).

32. National identity is not the same as nationalism, though it can easily be conscripted to nationalist ends. See the Argentine, and indeed Latin American, response to the Malvinas war: even though the war was self-servingly initiated and manipulated by Videla, left and right wanted the islands back from Britain. Nationalism, a survival mechanism for subaltern and emerging countries, but a dangerous one, is linked to power and dominance, war or the sublimated war of international sports and economic competition. National identification — a sense of self, (be)longing, shared memory, history — is not necessarily about, or driven by, this.

33. Agnew and Duncan, *Power of Place*, 13.

34. Roberto González Echevarría, *The Voice of the Masters: Writing and Authority in Modern Latin American Literature* (Austin: University of Texas Press, 1985), 125, notes that "[t]he most poignant question raised by modernity in Latin America was that of national or cultural identity, as well as of the link between such identity and literary production. The major literary figures of the nineteenth century (the founders of Latin American literature), Bello, Sarmiento, and Martí, conceived the issue [of national identity] in a rich metaphoric system linking humanity and culture to the land, to geography. Metaphors, drawn from nineteenth-century natural science, were mostly botanical or geological. From the times of the cronistas de Indias, American nature appeared to be the key to American differences, but most early historians were so imbued with scholastic thought that they could hardly conceive such a notion."

35. Victoria Ocampo, "Mujeres en la academia," *Testimonios: Décima serie, 1975–1977* (Buenos Aires: Sur, 1977), 13–23. In *Orlando*, Virginia Woolf (whom Ocampo knew and admired) links language to property and landscape: the poem, "The Oak Tree," that Orlando wrote over the centuries is the living symbol of the home Vita Sackville-West, the model for Orlando, struggled to keep in the face of English law barring female inheritance.

36. Mary Louise Pratt, "Women, Literature, and National Brotherhood," in *Women, Culture, and Politics in Latin America*, ed. Seminar on Feminism and Culture in Latin America (Berkeley: University of California Press, 1990).

37. Eso que vuela bajito
es mi poesía.
Rastreadora de olores
dentro del pasto.
Yo no busco la altura.
Vértigo el vuelo.
Embisto la distancia
volando bajo.

Alicia Partnoy, *Revenge of the Apple/Venganza de la manzana* (Pittsburgh: Cleis Press, 1992), 68, 69.

38. Nicholas Entrikin, *The Betweenness of Place: Towards a Geography of Modernity* (London: Macmillan, 1991), 12.

39. "Así, tan pronto como se deja de lado la tradicional noción del sujeto

productor — unidad y centro de sentido, — el exilio de los intelectuales latino-americanos obliga a plantear la cuestión del proyecto amplio en que se inserta el trabajo cultural realizado. Entendida la persona intelectual como una entidad social, y el discurso cultural como un código producido en relación con otros discursos y códigos, se hace especialmente importante considerar el lugar desde donde se habla, los modos de articulación del discurso y del trabajo intelectual. La reubicación geográfica forzada produce en los proyectos literarios y críticos latino-americanos fracturas y deslizamientos que deben ser analizados en detalle para dar cuenta de la totalidad que se intenta aislar como 'caso nacional' " (Andrés Ave-llaneda, "Estado actual de los estudios literarios: El caso argentino," *Hispamérica* 19, nos. 56/57 [August/December 1990]: 11; my translation, emphasis added).

40. Marta Traba, *En cualquier lugar* (Bogotá: Siglo XXI, 1984); José Leandro Urbina, *Cobro revertido* (Santiago: Planeta, 1992); Cristina Peri Rossi, "Las estat-uas, o la condición del extranjero," in *El museo de los fuerzos inútiles* (Barcelona: Seix Barral, 1983); Cristina Peri Rossi, *La nave de los locos* (Barcelona: Seix Barral, 1984); Mario Vargas Llosa, *La casa verde* (Barcelona: Seix Barral, 1963); Gabriel García Márquez, *Cien años de soledad* (Buenos Aires: Sudamericana, 1967); Julio Cortázar, *Rayuela* (Buenos Aires: Sudamericana, 1963).

41. "Es esta situación sin precedentes en la historia argentina la que perpetúa la necesidad de una versión de la historia que cubra a casi todo el pasado bajo un espeso manto de silencio, ahora para mejor asegurar su compatibilidad con esas dos versiones, por su parte perfectamente incompatibles entre sí, atesoradas por las memorias facciosas de dos movimientos políticos cuya rivalidad, que se esfuerzan por olvidar, llena los últimos cuarenta años de nuestra historia, y que por añadidura definen de modo radicalmente diferente sus vínculos con la historia previa.

Pero esta misma mutación afecta quizá de modo menos negativo a los esfuer-zos que no se orientan a expurgar al pasado de memorias peligrosas para la frágil concordia que está naciendo, sino tratan de ver la historia desde un presente que ya no es el de 1976, pero tampoco podría ser el de 1973" (Tulio Halperín Donghi, "El presente transforma el pasado: El impacto del reciente terror en la imagen de la historia argentina," in *Ficción y política: La narrativa argentina durante el proceso militar,* ed. Daniel Balderston et al. [Buenos Aires: Alianza Editorial; Minneapolis: Institute for the Study of Ideologies and Literature, 1987], 91–92).

42. "[N]os hallamos ante el primer esbozo de una nueva imagen de la experiencia histórica argentina" (ibid., 94).

43. Here we see an extension of the doctrine of national security of the 1950s, developed to fight communism's purported attack on national identity, which gave the military in Chile an ideological basis for modernizing its claim to be the guardian of the nation. I am grateful to Román Soto for pointing this out to me.

3. From Space to Place

1. María Rosa Olivera Williams, "La literatura uruguaya del Proceso: Exilio e insilio, continuismo e invención," *Nuevo Texto Crítico* 3, no. 5 (1990): 67–83, charts three stages of exile literature: (1) leaving testimony; (2) creating a lit-erature of exile through the transformation of historical reality into metaphor, a

process characterized by the struggle between memory and forgetting; and (3) universalization. While not identical to the processes of exile I discuss in this chapter, Olivera's stages can be plotted onto the map of alienation and acculturation I draw here. In fact the author she chooses to illustrate her thesis is Cristina Peri Rossi, whose work I discuss as well.

2. José Leandro Urbina, *Cobro revertido* (Santiago: Planeta Biblioteca del Sur, 1992).

3. "¿Soy extranjero? Hay días en que estoy seguro de serlo; otros en que no le concedo la menor importancia; y por último otros más (mejor diría que son noches) en que de ningún modo admito ante mí mismo esa extranjería. ¿Será que la condición de extranjero es un estado de ánimo?" (Mario Benedetti, *Primavera con una esquina rota* [Madrid: Ediciones Alfaguara, 1982], 15; all translations from this text are my own). The geographical and linguistic continuities of Mexico and Uruguay also help Don Rafael's sense of not being entirely foreign. He goes on to say that he would probably feel like a stranger in Finland, but corrects that and says that Finland is simply a term that is used to indicate foreignness, and why should that be?

4. "La primera, ésa en que te negás a deshacer las maletas...porque tenés la ilusión de que el regreso será mañana. Todo te parece extraño, indiferente, ajeno....La segunda etapa es cuando empezás a interesarte en lo que sucede a tu alrededor....[P]or fin se borran las vedas políticas que te impedían el regreso. Sólo entonces se abre la tercera y definitiva etapa, y ahí sí comienza la comezón lujuriosa y casi absurda, el miedo a perder la bendita identidad....[L]a vuelta a casa se te va volviendo imprescindible" (Mario Benedetti, *Andamios* [Santiago: Alfaguara, 1997], 21–22; all translations from this text are my own).

5. Adrienne Rich, "Diving into the Wreck," in *Poems, Selected and New, 1950–1974* (New York: Norton, n.d.). Maurice Halbwachs writes on how spatial imagery functions in reciprocity with collective memory. As Panivong Norindr, " 'Errances' and Memories in Marguerite Duras's Colonial Cities," *Differences: A Journal of Feminist Cultural Studies* 5, no. 5 (fall 1993): 52–79, points out, Halbwachs "argues that personal and collective formations of memory take their 'anchoring point on spatial images' (136) and, more specifically, on the 'material environment,' 'the home,' and 'the material appearance of the city' " (56–57).

6. Yi-Fu Tuan, *Space and Place: The Perspective of Experience* (London: Edward Arnold, 1977). The distinction between place and space is a handy device, but it must be recognized that just as nature does not exist prior to culture but is rather a cultural construction that makes "culture" salient, space is the necessary "other" of place.

7. "En un espacio difícilmente ocupable en los años del proceso, la literatura intentó, más que proporcionar respuestas articuladas y completas, rodear ese núcleo resistente y terrible que podía denominarse lo real" (Beatriz Sarlo, "Política, ideología y figuración literaria," in *Represión y reconstrucción de una cultura: El caso argentino*, ed. Saúl Sosnowski [Buenos Aires: Editorial Universitaria de Buenos Aires, 1988], 35; all translations from this text are my own).

8. "La empresa puede definirse en las expansiones y contracciones de espacios públicos permisivos, un nuevo planeamiento topográfico de los campos de batalla en pro de una expresión y oposición culturales. Desgarrados entre el cen-

tro y la periferia, entre el discurso dominante y la posibilidad de algo distinto, los escritores y artistas argentinos cultivaron pues el espacio marginal, que ofrece una alternativa a la centralizadora inmovilidad del régimen" (Francine Masiello, "La Argentina durante el Proceso: Las múltiples resistencias de la cultura," in *Ficción y política: La narrativa argentina durante el proceso militar*, ed. Daniel Balderston et al. [Buenos Aires: Alianza Editorial; Minneapolis: Institute for the Study of Ideologies and Literature, 1987], 12–13; all translations from this text are my own).

9. "[U]na nación separada de sí misma," "un nuevo territorio se define," "los disidentes fueron vueltos invisibles, evacuados del lugar del diálogo humano" (ibid., 11, 13, 14).

10. "[C]ircuito internacional de intercambios" (ibid., 15).

11. "Hasta el mapa miente. Aprendemos la geografía del mundo en un mapa que no muestra al mundo tal cual es, sino tal como sus dueños mandan que sea" (Eduardo Galeano, "Estructura de la impotencia: Apuntes para un retrato," *Araucaria de Chile* 44 [1989]: 125–36). Galeano continues: "En el planisferio tradicional, el que se usa en las escuelas y en todas partes, el Ecuador no está en el centro: el norte ocupa dos tercios y el sur uno. . . . América Latina abarca en el mapamundi menos espacio que Europa y mucho menos que la suma de Estados Unidos y Canadá, cuando en realidad América Latina es dos veces más grande que Europa y bastante mayor que Estados Unidos y Canadá.

"*El mapa, que nos achica, simboliza todo lo demás.* Geografía robada, economía saqueada, historia falsificada, usurpción cotidiana de la realidad: el llamado Tercer Mundo habitado por gentes de tercera, abarca menos, come menos, recuerda menos, vive menos, dice menos" (128, original emphasis; all translations from this text are my own).

12. Maurice Halbwachs, *On Collective Memory* (Chicago: University of Chicago Press, 1992), 136, 133; translation of *La memoire collective* (Paris: PUF, 1968), cited in Norindr, "Errances."

13. "Pese a mi buena voluntad, no puedo ver aquel lado de mi vida sino como el perfil de la ciudad que uno aborda desde el Río de la Plata. En la cara empinada, soberbia y gris de Buenos Aires, su gente no es más que las sombras de unos pocos rasgos mudables. Yo mismo, aunque estaba demasiado atento a las minucias de mi juventud, fui víctima de esa alquimia porteña que funde historias personales en la retorta de su propia historia, calles y amores, barrios y enemistades, voces y ruidos, pasiones y café, una amalgama indestruible. Ni siquiera recuerdo en qué tramo de aquellos días de noviembre dejé de ser Teddy Coper para convertirme in Byrne. Pero recuerdo vivamente los detalles, que iban quedando atrás" (Vlady Kociancich, *Los bajos del temor* [Barcelona: Tusquets, 1992], 253; all translations from this text are my own).

14. "País en el espacio y en el tiempo destinado al olvido, que se teme olvidado al otro lado del océano, existente sólo en el recuerdo. No pude por mucho tiempo recordarte, la nostalgia temía fuera la muerte, enredándome como los hilos de una araña, como la tierra movediza del pantano" (Elsa Repetto, "Destierro," in *Las mujeres del Cono Sur escriben*, ed. Ana Vásquez, Ana Luisa Valdés, Ana María Araujo [Stockholm: Nordan, 1984], 79–82; all translations from this text are my own). For a discussion of the defamiliarization of the native land in exile texts by Cristina Peri Rossi and Luisa Valenzuela, see Amy K. Kaminsky, *Reading the*

Body Politic: Feminist Criticism and Latin American Women Writers (Minneapolis: University of Minnesota Press, 1993), 33–35.

15. "Fue así, simplemente, cuando te vi asomarte...que supe que podría por fin recordarte, que tu tiempo había llegado, y el mío también, en que podía convertirte en recuerdo" (Repetto, "Destierro," 82). It is crucial to stipulate that forgetting is also what the dictators mandated, though not as a precondition of healthy memory. Forgetting is born of fear in this culture. This "culture of fear" (*cultura del miedo*) was the topic of a conference held in Buenos Aires in March 1985 (see Sarlo, "Política," 32).

16. Frances Bartkowski, *Travelers, Migrants, Inmates* (Minneapolis: University of Minnesota Press, 1995), 21–22, writes of "forelonging," by which she means the delighted anticipation of travelers to new places, as antonym of nostalgia.

17. "No es igual este viaje que otros viajes. Estoy en la misma parte donde antes estuve y no es para nada igual. Londres no puede haber cambiado mucho, pero una sí... Londres es la prisión, el exilio, el lugar obligado donde NO se quiere estar, porque el regreso absoluto y rápido es como la única respuesta que tenemos, el único grito, la única forma de saber que fuimos destruidos pero no derrotados" (Poli Délano, *Como si no muriera nadie* [Santiago: Planeta/Biblioteca del Sur, 1987], 184–85; all translations from this text are my own). The novel takes its title from a poem by Pablo Neruda, which is used as an epigraph to the fourth and final part of the novel. The narrative follows the lives of characters in the English department at the school of education at the university. The first three parts suggest that nothing is more important than their sex lives and to a lesser extent their careers. The last part, narrated from prison in 1975, tells of the disruption and destruction of these lives under dictatorship.

18. Vlady Kociancich, *Últimos días de William Shakespeare* (Buenos Aires: Emecé, 1984), translated by Margaret Jull Costa as *The Last Days of William Shakespeare* (London: Heinemann, 1990).

19. Anthony Vidler, "Bodies in Space/Subjects in the City: Psychopathologies of Modern Urbanism," *Differences: A Journal of Feminist Cultural Studies* 5, no. 5 (fall 1993): 32.

20. "No soy capaz de expresar todo lo que siento, ni de comunicarte como quisiera las arrugas que ha sufrido mi alma desde que perdí la tierra, el centro, la base firme, todo el contorno. No las empanadas, viejo Armando, ni la chicha de septiembre, ni el pastel de choclo. Es otra cosa ¿cachai?" (Délano, *Como si no muriera nadie*).

21. Victor Burgin, "Geometry and Abjection," in *Psychoanalysis and Cultural Theory: Thresholds*, ed. James Donald (London: Macmillan, 1991), 25, reproduces the text. It is cited in Vidler, "Bodies in Space," 32.

22. Vidler, "Bodies in Space," 31, writes: "[W]hat I am calling 'space' is, of course, no more than a cultural and mental construction; for, in historical terms, like the body, or like sexuality, space is not a constant but rather, as Victor Burgin has asserted, space 'has a history.'" Vidler traces this history, from the concept of an a priori space, existing without reference to a subject, through the idea of different historical perspectives on space (pun intended), to the theory of space as a projection of the human psyche, with reference to Lefebvre, Panofsky, Freud, and Lacan.

23. Edward W. Soja, *Postmodern Geographics: The Reassertion of Space in Critical Theory* (London: Verso, 1989). Soja's project is to claim for geography the same importance as history in understanding social, cultural, and economic relations. That is, he wants as much to reanimate geography as a discipline that can claim its place in the prestigious discourse of postmodernity as to place space into discourse. His stated theme is "the reassertion of a critical spatial perspective in contemporary social theory and analysis" (1).

24. Vidler, "Bodies in Space," 32.

25. Mary Louise Pratt, "Women, Literature, and National Brotherhood," *Women, Culture, and Politics in Latin America*, ed. Seminar on Feminism and Culture in Latin America (Berkeley: University of California Press, 1990), 48–73.

26. Cristina Peri Rossi, "La ciudad de Luzbel," in *Cosmoagonías* (Barcelona: Laia, 1988), 37–49. This story was reprinted in 1993 by the Uruguayan publishing company Editorial Trilce in an edition consisting of part of *Cosmoagonías*, under the title *La ciudad de Luzbel*. The collection is registered with an ISBN number in both Uruguay and Sweden and is part of a series published by Editorial Trilce under the direction of Peri Rossi and Ana Luisa Valdés. All translations from this text are my own. The title is ambiguous; it can be translated both as "The City of Luzbel" and "Luzbel's City."

27. Daniel Balderston, in *Out of Context: Historical Reference and the Representation of Reality in Borges* (Durham, N.C.: Duke University Press, 1993), has gone to some pains to ground Borges in his particular history and geography.

28. Gillian Rose, *Feminism and Geography: The Limits of Geographical Knowledge* (Minneapolis: University of Minnesota Press, 1993), 87.

29. Nicholas Entrikin, *The Betweenness of Place: Towards a Geography of Modernity* (London: Macmillan, 1991), 12.

30. William Gibson, *Neuromancer* (New York: Ace Books, 1984), 6.

31. Jacques Derrida, introduction to *Speech and Phenomena, and Other Essays on Husserl's Theory of Signs*, translated by David B. Allison (Evanston, Ill.: Northwestern University Press, 1973), 3–5, 15–16. What Derrida objects to, in fact, is "presence" as a transcendental precondition of being. I understand presence differently. As I use the term, presence is achieved, performed, and claimed. It is a political and social phenomenon, whose precondition is space to occupy. The particular space (its history, its relationship with others) one occupies is of critical importance to the kind of presence one might achieve.

32. Mary Louise Pratt, *Imperial Eyes: Travel Writing and Transculturation* (New York: Routledge, 1992), is a key text in this field, as are Edward Said's *Orientalism* (London: Penguin, 1978), and the collections *Nationalisms and Sexualities*, ed. Andrew Parker et al. (New York: Routledge, 1992) and *Nation and Narration*, ed. Homi K. Bhabha (New York: Routledge, 1990).

33. "El partido se rehizo en un espacio logrado a sangre y fuego en la estación. ...Tenían casi todo; directivas, miembros, cuadros; todo menos país, pero la estación era la ficción del país" (Marta Traba, *En cualquier lugar* [Bogotá: Siglo XXI, 1984], 77).

34. In a recent interview with Gema Pérez-Sánchez (*Hispamérica* 24, no. 72 [1995]: 68), Peri Rossi explains her use of a male protagonist in this novel by

saying that although many women certainly went into exile, in the collective unconscious the paradigmatic exile is a man.

35. The play with place-names — real and nonsense cities at once — recalls Molloy's coyness in *En breve cárcel* concerning the cities of her protagonist's exile. In *The Ship of Fools*, "On the basis of the hints given in the course of the novel, the reader must guess the identity of those cities alluded to" (Cristina Peri Rossi, *The Ship of Fools*, trans. Psiche Hughes [London: Allison and Busby, 1989], 32; translation of *La nave de los locos* [Barcelona: Seix Barral, 1984]).

36. Peri Rossi, *Ship of Fools*, 1. "[L]a ciudad a que llegues, descríbela" (9).

37. Ibid., 14. "Lo que amamos en toda estructura es una composición del mundo, un significado que ordene el caos devorador, una hipótesis comprensible y por ende reparadora. Repara nuestro sentimiento de la fuga y de la dispersión, nuestra desolada experiencia del desorden" (21).

38. Ibid. "Equis lo consoló diciéndole que los lugares eran como los pianos: había que acostumbrarse a tocarlos suavemente, ensayando unos pocos arpegios al principio, hasta que los lugares hicieran sentir sus mejores notas" (43).

39. These ways of "doing" space come from Vidler, "Bodies in Space," 32.

40. Cristina Peri Rossi, "Las estatuas, o la condición del extranjero," in *El museo de los esfuerzos inútiles* (Barcelona: Seix Barral, 1983); and José da Cruz, *Sin patria ni tumba: Crónicas del exilio* (Lund: Grahns Boktrykeri, 1988).

41. Giorgio Agamben, *La comunità che viene* (Turin: Einaudi, 1990), translated by Michael Hardt as *The Coming Community* (Minneapolis: University of Minnesota Press, 1993).

42. "No sentía ninguna nostalgia, al revés de muchos otros compañeros, ni del barrio, ni del café aquel ni de la cancha de Velesárfield; para él la patria se transportaba con la gente y estaba ahí donde siguiera la discusión y se armaran líos entre grupos y personas" (Traba, *En cualquier lugar*, 63).

43. Luis's mother, a lifelong Marxist, sees him as something of a failure because he cares more about politics than labor, but she is also a key communicator: she has set up a press to disseminate information and analysis. In another bit of irony, this upholder of the purest of Marxist orthodoxy, who is furthermore an Indian woman, has created the first industry owned and operated by exiles. She is a successful businesswoman.

44. Peri Rossi, *Ship of Fools*, 1. "¿Cómo debo distinguir lo significante de lo insignificante?" (9).

45. Ibid., 33; emphasis notes altered translation, closer to the original. "La mejor manera que tiene un extranjero de conocer una ciudad es enamorándose de una de sus mujeres, muy dadas a la ternura que inspira un hombre sin patria, es decir, sin madre, y también a las diferencias de pigmentación de la piel de un continente a otro. Ella construirá una ruta que no figura en los mapas y nos hablará en una lengua que nunca olvidaremos" (38).

46. "De som klarade sig bäst är de som snabbt lärde sig svenska, gifte sig med en svensk tjej och flyttade från gruppen" (Eva Wrange, "Görans dåliga samvete" [Göran's bad conscience], *Göteborgs Posten*, February 25, 1996, sec. 2, p. 1; my translation). Note how political refugees — or at least those who need jobs — are necessarily gendered male here. Interestingly, Johansson notes that what are called "second generation refugees" — children born or at least raised in Sweden,

who speak perfect Swedish and are socialized into Swedish society — come up against the same discrimination when they look for work. Having "the wrong last name" can be enough, he says. Clearly, "marrying a Swedish girl" is not going to have much effect here.

47. Herbert C. Kelman, "A Social-Psychological Model of Political Legitimacy and Its Relevance to Black and White Student Protest Movements," *Psychiatry* 33 (1970), cited in Yossi Shain, *The Frontier of Loyalty: Political Exiles in the Age of the Nation State* (Middletown, Conn.: Wesleyan University Press, 1989), 13–14.

48. "[U]n país llamado Lydia" (Benedetti, *Primavera*, 170).

49. "Tiene su poco de sangre india, enhorabuena. O quizá la tenga de sangre negra, también enhorabuena. Digamos que su linda piel es más oscurecita que la de Graciela o la de Beatriz, y aún más oscurita (y mucho menos arrugadita) que la mía" (ibid.).

50. Conversations with Edmé Domínguez have been invaluable to me in this discussion of Southern Cone exiles in Mexico.

51. María Luján Leiva, "Migraciones en América Latina: Historias para pensar el presente," in *Language, Minority, Migration: Yearbook 1994/95* (from the Centre for Multiethnic Research), ed. Sven Gustavsson and Harald Runblom (Uppsala: Uppsala University Press, 1995), 185: "El exilio en México podría hasta caracterizarse de un brain-drain (repetición del modelo del exilio republicano español)."

52. Urbina, *Cobro revertido*, 165–66. In another example of this sort, Poli Délano's *En este lugar sagrado* (In this sacred place) (Mexico City: Grijalbo, 1977), the protagonist moves from the South to the city, learns the new geography, and finds out about political and social relationships through contact with women from different social sectors. The time period is from April 2, 1957, to the eve of the coup, September 1973. In a symbolic/grotesque representation of national space, the protagonist narrates the novel in a movie-house restroom on the night of the coup. The film is a World War II movie about Nazis.

53. The lover as bearer of home and safety is another variation on this theme. For (a) woman to be *el reposo del guerrero* — as in Belli's *La mujer habitada* — means not that she occupies the space of home and comfort but that in/by means of her body she is the space of home. She becomes the place of the man's repose.

54. Quoted in Vidler, "Bodies in Space," 48.

55. Sylvia Molloy, *En breve cárcel* (Barcelona: Seix Barral, 1981), translated by Daniel Balderston and Sylvia Molloy as *Certificate of Absence* (Austin: University of Texas Press, 1989).

56. The job as a bus driver for a business that brings women in from outside of England, like the story of Vercingetorix, locates this novel in a particular historical moment, the early 1970s, when England legalized abortion and women from as far away as the United States went there to take advantage of safe and legal abortion. Peri Rossi's political reference points are those of the left in the Southern Cone (and particularly in Uruguay) and gender politics around issues of a woman's right to control her reproductive capacity.

57. Vidler, "Bodies in Space," 48.

4. Exile and the Embodied Production of Language

1. Ricardo Piglia, *La ciudad ausente* (Buenos Aires: Sudamericana, 1992). The geographies of Piglia's island are a blend of the literary-textual and the real-world/ historical. The island is located in Tigre, a water-maze of a delta not far from Buenos Aires whose swampy backlands have provided hiding places for any number of people in politically precarious situations. Although in Piglia's novel the island's inhabitants come from all over the world to this most Argentine place of exile, most of them are from Ireland. Argentina has a distinguished Irish past, with its O'Gormans and O'Higginses and Lynches, and Piglia is clearly tapping into that piece of Argentine identity, but in populating his language-heavy island with Irishmen he is also making reference to the linguistic capers of James Joyce.

2. Luisa Valenzuela, "La densidad de las palabras," *Simetrías* (Buenos Aires: Sudamericana, 1993), 143–52; all translations from *Simetrías* are my own.

3. Because child-rearing is a cultural arrangement, caregivers are not necessarily female. Children will acquire language from brothers, fathers, uncles, grandfathers, and male childcare workers as well as from women. It is useful to remember that in actuality, language acquisition is a long and complicated process. It begins with the recognition, differentiation, and imitation of sounds — discarding those that have no part in the language the child is being initiated into, reinforcing those that make sense to the baby's interlocutors.

4. Rosi Braidotti, *Nomadic Subjects: Embodiment and Sexual Difference in Contemporary Feminist Theory* (New York: Columbia University Press, 1994), 41.

5. " — Iré. Trataré de que no me maten. Observaré todas las reglas de la precaución. Entraré sin que nadie se percate que soy yo.
— Difícil. Eres gordo. Eres calvo. Tienes la cara redonda. Te delatará la voz. Hace muchos años que hablas por radio. La policía te la concoce bien. Nadie puede disimular la voz ni el paso. Y tu voz y tu paso son demasiado característicos, despacios, como los de un señor que no tiene apuro. Te reconocerán a la legua" (Volodia Teitelboim, *En el país prohibido: Sin el permiso de Pinochet* [Barcelona: Plaza y Janés, 1988], 13; all translations from this text are my own).

6. I am indebted to Anna Nordenstam for reminding me of the importance of gesture to speech and of the ways gesture can impede intercultural communication.

7. León Grinberg and Rebeca Grinberg, *Psychoanalytic Perspectives of Migration and Exile*, trans. Nancy Festinger (New Haven: Yale University Press, 1989); translation of *Psicoanálisis de la migración y del exilio* (Alianza, 1984), 110. They explain that the patient "is fleeing from language and primitive objects which he experiences as persecutory, since his native language is closely linked to more primitive fantasies" (110). This physical piece of language is connected to the primitive, to childhood, to the psychosomatic.

8. María Lugones, "Purity, Impurity, and Separation," *Signs* (winter 1994): 461. I will return to this essay in chapter 8.

9. Román Soto, personal communication.

10. In later years, Inti Illmani began to meld native and the popular instrumentation of Italy, where the group lived its exile. Exile, as we have seen, is not a static condition. To stay alive as musicians the group incorporated into its music what was in its environment; an album from this period is called, tellingly,

Palimpsesto. Yet there was always a demand for the old songs. Inti Illmani in Chile and Mercedes Sosa in Argentina returned to their homelands as heroes.

11. "Como el canto atraviesa el espacio, la Junta no puede impedir que lleguen desde lejos mensajes disolventes" (Teitelboim, *En el país prohibido*, 72).

12. *Esdrújula* is both noun and adjective. It refers to a word whose spoken stress is on the antepenultimate syllable. (Most Spanish words are stressed on the penultimate or last syllable.) Viglietti's song entitled "Esdrújula" strings a long series of these words together, creating a rhythmic pattern that is at once familiar and unfamiliar. The song's meaning is created by juxtaposition, as grammar and syntax dissolve.

13. This story was published in *Simetrías*. It also appears at the end of Valenzuela's published MLA talk, "Five Days That Changed My Paper," concerning the attempted coup discussed in chapter 5. The connection between the desire for linguistic transparency and military desire for order and control is implicit.

14. The Grinbergs, like other exiled psychoanalysts, treated many of their compatriots. It was common for psychotherapists from the Southern Cone, whose very work made them suspect at home, to wind up as exiles themselves and to make treatment available at little or no cost to other exiles. Donoso creates such a character in *El jardín de al lado*.

15. "[Y]o tengo dos lenguas, mi trabajo científico lo escribo directamente en francés y lo literario directamente en castellano; son dos mundos, porque son dos lenguajes, o sea, yo soy bilingüe, pero no puedo jugar con el idioma francés como puedo jugar con el castellano. En castellano yo puedo hacer un diálogo con errores gramaticales, pero suenan bien, porque son los hablados en castellano; en francés queda mal, queda un error de lengua" (Ana Vásquez, interviewed by Erna Pfeiffer, in *Exiliadas, emigrantes, viajeras: Encuentros con diez escritoras latinoamericanas* [Frankfurt am Main: Verveut; Madrid: Iberoamericana, 1995], 183; all translations from this text are my own).

16. "Después de varios años de aprendizaje y práctica, maneja más o menos bien la nueva lengua, sin que llegue a sentirla como un instrumento ductil y preciso" (Leonardo Rossiello, "La literatura del exilio latinoamericano en Suecia [1976–1990]," *Revista iberoamericana* 164–65 [July–December 1993]: 560; all translations from this text are my own).

17. "Por razones fáciles de comprender, el escritor en el exilio en países de lenguas no románicas, se plantea, más acusiosamente que otros (por ejemplo los exiliados en los países latinoamericanos o en España y Francia), el problema de para quién escribir. Ha llegado adulto al nuevo país. El 'fondo sentimental' del escritor del que hablara Pío Baroja, ya está formado por las experiencias de la niñez y la adolescencia. Su paisaje, el paisaje real con el que se identifica, y con el que vibra su paisaje interior, está lejos. Después de varios años de aprendizaje y práctica, maneja más o menos bien la nueva lengua, sin que llegue a sentirla como un instrumento ductil y preciso. Durante los primeros años, su referente natural y 'fuente de inspiración' no es, por lo general, la realidad cotidiana. Debe ir a buscarlos en la memoria o en la propia literatura. Escribe, mayoritariamente, en su lengua materna, que, sin embargo, no ejercita como debiera o quisiera. Y sus lectores inmediatos son sus amigos, su compañero o compañera. El camino a los

lectores latinoamericanos o españoles, aunque no imposible, es largo y complicado" (ibid., 561).

18. "¿Qué me retiene? Tal vez sólo una suerte de adherencia animal: el olor de estas calles, sonidos familiares, el barrio donde vivo ahora, una manera de alimentarme, un árbol, una cara amiga, las conversaciones contigo, el café del sur. Aunque tal vez haya una promesa en mi trabajo, una malsana curiosidad por saber adónde marcha el mundo que conozco, qué será del Teatro, cómo daremos la nueva versión (en inglés y con pieles) de *Hamlet,* cuándo me invitará a salir el atractivo pintor y escenógrafo llamado Claude, etcétera. Ya ves, qué miseria de argumento.... Porque me atrae más el curso del río que su origen, yo nunca encontraré esas fuentes. Pero te juro, Emilio, que cuando me despedí de Marga, cuando empecé a caminar hacia mi casa y vi la hermosa luz del otoño en las calles, y oí la lengua de esta ciudad, burlona, descalabrada, pícara, enredando las voces desconocidas de gente que pasaba a mi lado, uniéndolas en un fuerte nudo, en un tácito, involuntario abrazo, supe que había tomado el mejor decisión. No me retes, amigo, si estás en desacuerdo. Espero ansiosamente tu vuelta para explicarte mi sentimentalismo, estupidez o cobardía" (Vlady Kociancich, *Últimos días de William Shakespeare* [Buenos Aires: Emecé, 1984], 117–18, translated by Margaret Jull Costa as *The Last Days of William Shakespeare* [London: Heinemann, 1990], 97).

19. Luisa Valenzuela, *Como en la guerra* (Buenos Aires: Sudamericana, 1977), translated by Helen Lane as *He Who Searches* (Elmwood Park, Ill.: Dalkey Archive, n.d.).

20. "A la pregunta sobre cuál sería, a su juicio, el lector ideal de su obra, Viñas respondía en 1982: 'Yo no sé. Cuando vivía en Buenos Aires — allá — creía tener alguna idea aproximada. Hoy, ahora, qué sé yo. Ni en Dinamarca ni en Méjico. Escribo al boleo. ¿Francamente? Ni lector ideal ni obra ni juicio. Ni "sería..."'" (cited by Aníbal Jarkowski, "Sobreviviente en una guerra, enviando tarjetas postales," *Hispamérica* 21, no. 63 [December 1992]: 16–17; all translations from this text are my own).

21. Joseph Brodsky, "The Condition We Call Exile," *Renaissance and Modern Studies* 34 (1991): 3.

22. José Donoso, *El jardín de al lado* (Barcelona: Seix Barral, 1981), discussed further in chapter 5.

23. Brodsky, "Condition," 7.

24. "Su acento lo delata: arrastra un poco las eses y pronuncia de igual manera las b y las v. Entonces, se produce cierto silencio a su alrededor. No es un gran silencio, pero él percibe alguna curiosidad en las miradas y un pequeño reajuste en los gestos, que se vuelven más enfáticos. (Cambios imperceptibles para un observador común, pero el exilio es una lente de aumento)" (Cristina Peri Rossi, "El exiliado," in *Las mujeres del Cono Sur escriben,* ed. Ana Vásquez, Ana Luisa Valdés, and Ana María Araujo [Stockholm: Nordan, 1984]; all translations from this text are my own).

25. Fernando Aínsa, *Con acento extranjero* (Stockholm: Nordan, 1984).

26. "Sin embargo, estos españoles tienen un aire difícil de definir, un 'algo' que los delata como forasteros. Son detalles, son gestos que se les notan, sobre todo al

hablar. Palabras, dichos, giros de frases, modos de entender y de conjugar verbos, cosas que no pueden disimular con una indumentaria o una tarjeta de identidad.

"Digámoslo claro desde el principio: estos españoles hablan con un cierto acento extranjero" (ibid., 12; all translations from this text are my own).

27. "[C]omo si 'hubiera nacido aquí, igualico,' según le dicen con simpatía" (ibid., 12).

28. Nadine Gordimer, *None to Accompany Me* (London: Bloomsbury, 1994).

29. Isabel Álvarez-Borland, "Displacements and Autobiography in Cuban-American Fiction," *World Literature Today* (winter 1994): 43–48, and Eliana Rivero, "From Immigrants to Ethnics: Cuban Writers in the U.S.," in *Breaking Boundaries,* ed. Asunción Delgado et al. (Amherst: University of Massachusetts Press, 1989), 189–200, have suggested that, in the case of Cuban writers in the United States, a distinction can be made between exile writers, who write in Spanish, and ethnic, Cuban-American writers who write in English. While this discussion is beyond the scope of the present chapter, it suggests the extent to which identity is a function of language. As I was completing revisions of this manuscript, Tessa Bridal's novel *The Tree of Red Stars* (Minneapolis: Milkweed Editions, 1997) came to my attention. As far as I know, it is the first novel published in English by a Southern Cone writer (Bridal was born in Uruguay) concerning the effects of her natal country's military dictatorship, and it may signal a shift from exile to ethnic writing in Borland's and Rivero's formulation.

30. Sergio Badilla, *Terrenalis* (Stockholm: Bikupa, 1988), n.p.

31. Sharon Magnarelli, *Reflections/Refractions: Reading Luisa Valenzuela* (New York: Peter Lang, 1988).

32. Marta Traba, *En cualquier lugar* (Bogotá: Siglo XXI, 1984). See chapter 3 for a fuller discussion of this novel.

33. José Leandro Urbina, *Cobro revertido* (Santiago: Planeta Biblioteca del Sur, 1992). See chapter 3 for a fuller discussion of this novel.

34. Ana María Araujo, "Mercedes," in *Las mujeres del Cono Sur escriben,* 89–92; all translations from this text are my own.

35. "Mercedes, desapareció Mercedes.

"Je sais...Mais écoute, Isabelle, calme toi. Nous sommes ici; allez, de toutes façon tu peux rien faire....On va appeller sa soeur; et aprés....

"En ese preciso instante, Isabel comprendió que las distancias invaden inexorablemente, para siempre, los cuerpos" (ibid., 92).

36. Mario Benedetti, *Primavera con una esquina rota* (Madrid: Ediciones Alfaguara, 1982), 9; all translations from this text are my own.

37. Cristina Peri Rossi, "La índole del lenguaje," in *Cosmoagonías* (Barcelona: Laia, 1988), 83–92.

38. I am grateful to Nathan Stormer for suggesting the term "language labor" to me.

39. "Este país no es el mío pero me gusta bastante. No sé si me gusta más o menos que mi país. Vine muy chiquita y no me acuerdo de cómo era. Una de las diferencias es que en mi país hay cabayos y aquí en cambio hay cabaios. Pero todos relinchan" (Benedetti, *Primavera,* 84). Still, we only get to know that the country of exile is Mexico late in the novel, and in a fleeting reference. Details,

including Beatriz's linguistic observations, are not sufficient to localize the place, only to corroborate, in a number of cases retroactively, the fact once stated.

40. "¿Qué era su tierra? ¿No daba casi igual Marruecos, Portugal o Colombia? Lo único que la ataba a ese país donde la imaginación de sus padres florecía, era una forma del español que seguramente ya estaba anticuada; un dialecto fósil rellenado con sueco, con inglés a lo mejor, con quién sabe qué, mezclado con los chilenismos y uruguayismos de sus amigos, con una melodía de frase indefinida ya para siempre. Llegó 'allá' y alguien comentó:

" — Habla como centroamericana.

"Ella no supo qué decir.

"A lo mejor era cierto" (José da Cruz, "Noticias de papá," in *La soledad de la guerra y otros cuentos* [Montevideo: Editorial Graffiti, 1994], 18; all translations from this text are my own).

41. "El lenguaje se me hispanizó, se borraron los perfiles típicamente chilenos. He pasado mucho tiempo en España y ahí, no se dice 'la plata,' se dice 'el dinero,' la plata es andar con un lingote de plata" (Vásquez, in Pfeiffer, *Exiliadas*, 183).

42. "Amnistía es una palabra difícil, o como dice mi abuelo Rafael muy peliaguda, porque tiene una M y una N que siempre van juntas. Amnistía es cuando a una le perdonan una penitencia" (Benedetti, *Primavera*, 173).

43. "Teresita no seas burra yo te amnistío quiere decir yo te perdono" (ibid., 174). More tears follow, but tears too have multiple meanings. Language must be renegotiated constantly.

44. "Los implacables, los que ganaron sus galones en la crueldad militante, esos que empezaron siendo puritanos y acabaron corruptos, ésos abrieron un enorme paréntesis en aquella sociedad, paréntesis que seguramente se cerrará algún día, cuando ya nadie será capaz de retomar el hilo de la antigua oración" (ibid., 96).

45. "Habrá que empezar a tejer otra, a compaginar otra en que las palabras no serán las mismas (porque también hubo lindas palabras que ellos torturaron o ajusticiaron o incluyeron en las nóminas de desaparecidos) en la que los sujetos y las preposiciones y los verbos transitivos y los complementos directos, ya no serán los mismos. Habrá cambiado la sintaxis en esa sociedad todavía nonata que en ese entonces aparecerá como debilucha, anémica, vacilante, excesivamente cautelosa, pero con el tiempo irá recomponiéndose, inventando nuevas reglas y nuevas excepciones, palabras flamantes desde las cenizas de las prematuramente calcinadas, conjunciones copulativas más adecuadas para servir de puente entre los que se quedaron y aquellos que se fueron y entonces volverán. Pero nada podrá ser igual a la prehistoria del setenta y tres" (ibid., 96).

46. Raquel Ángel, *Rebeldes y domesticados: Los intelectuales frente al poder* (Buenos Aires: Ediciones El Cielo por Asalto, 1992). Mario Benedetti, *El desexilio y otras conjeturas* (Madrid: Ediciones El País, 1984), tells an almost identical story. He recounts being told by a group of young Uruguayans that he does not sound Uruguayan — he is too direct, too assertive. Their timidity, fostered by the climate of fear in which they grew up, seems utterly foreign to Benedetti. Eduardo Galeano, "Sobre la importancia de tener ojos en la nuca" (*Araucaria de Chile* 41 [1988]: 75–83), gives an example of the fear still palpable in the language of postdictatorship Uruguay: "Fear, which never confesses its name, says its name is realism and it disguises itself as prudence. Anyone with eyes in his head can rec-

ognize it, however. Language, for example, is a giveaway. How can the language of Uruguayans not be sick with fear, after a dictatorship forced them to lie or be silent for twelve years? But in the middle of democracy, official language perpetuates fear. It is not the same to say: 'The military dictatorship tortured one Uruguayan out of eighty' as to say: 'During the Proceso, some citizens suffered illegal pressure.' " ("El miedo, que jamás confiesa su nombre, dice llamarse realismo y se disfraza de prudencia. Puede reconocerlo sin embargo, cualquiera que tenga ojos en la cara. El lenguaje, por ejemplo, es delator. ¿Cómo no va a estar enfermo de miedo el lenguaje de los uruguayos, después de una dictadura que durante doce años los obligó a mentir o callar? Pero en plena democracia, el lenguaje oficial perpetúa el miedo. No es lo mismo decir: 'La dictadura militar torturó a un uruguayo de cada ochenta', que decir: 'Durante el Proceso, algunos ciudadanos sufrieron apremios ilegales' " [76–77].)

47. "Quizá los oficiantes, los hacedores de esa patria pendular y peculiar sean los que hoy son niños pero siguen en el país. No los muchachitos y muchachitas que traerán en la retina nieves de Oslo o atardeceres del Mediterráneo o pirámides de Teotihuacán o montonetas de la Via Appia o cielos negros del invierno sueco" (Benedetti, *Primavera*, 97).

48. "A diferencia de los exiliados territoriales, que encontraron refugio en las inefables certezas del imaginario de la República Modelo, los dionisíacos, cortados del mismo, sufrió una doble orfandad que les obligó a poner en funcionamiento la productividad del exilio.... [E]n vez de desexiliarse radicalizaron su alteridad radical, para romper con la uruguayidad y desconstruir la nostalgiosa restauración de la homogeizante memoria histórica-pedagógica del imaginario de la República Modelo, amenazada por la proliferación de múltiples y antagónicas memorias cultural-performativas" (Abril Trigo, "Rockeros y grafiteros: la construcción al sesgo de una antimemoria," *Hispamérica* 24, no. 70 [1995]: 35–36).

49. "Si algo hemos de agradecer a las dictaduras neofascistas y las atolondradas restauraciones democráticas que las sucedieron, es precisamente el haber colocado la cuestión de la memoria en el centro de la problemática nacional" (ibid., 30).

50. For a compelling reading of gender and nation in *La ciudad ausente*, see Eva-Lynn Alicia Jagoe, "The Disembodied Machine: Matter, Femininity, and Nation in Piglia's *La ciudad ausente*," *Latin American Literary Review* 23, no. 45 (January–June 1995): 5–17.

51. Cristina Peri Rossi, *El museo de los esfuerzos inútiles* (Barcelona: Seix Barral, 1983); and Cristina Peri Rossi, *Los museos abandonados* (Montevideo: Arca, 1968).

52. I use this deliberately ambiguous abbreviation following Donna Haraway, *Primate Visions: Gender, Race, and Nature in the World of Modern Science* (New York: Routledge, 1989), 5 and 15, who in turn follows Judith Merril, eliding science fiction, science fantasy, speculative fiction, speculative futures, and even scientific fact.

53. Eduardo Galeano, "Estructura de la impotencia: Apuntes para un retrato," *Araucaria de Chile* 44 (1989): 125–36, writes: "Official language is delirious, and its delirium is the normality of the system" ("El lenguaje oficial delira, y su delirio es la normalidad del sistema" [127]).

54. To achieve this effect, the text requires a first-reading response. To lurk

about in the mechanics of it undoes the effect. Diamela Eltit's novels make the same sort of demand.

55. "Un relato no es otra cosa que la reproducción del orden del mundo en una escala puramente verbal. Una réplica de la vida, si la vida estuviera hecha sólo de palabras. Pero la vida no está hecha sólo de palabras, está también por desgracia hecha de cuerpos, es decir, como dijo Macedonio, de enfermedad, de dolor, de muerte. La física se desarrolla a tal velocidad, dijo de pronto, que en seis meses todo el conocimiento ha envejecido" (Piglia, *La ciudad ausente*, 147).

56. Compare this to José Donoso. Virginia Vidal, in "Algunos aspectos del lenguaje donosiano," *Araucaria de Chile* 39 (1987): 156–59, states that Donoso's collection of four novellas, *Cuatro para Delfina*, written when he moved back to Chile after decades of expatriate living in Spain, documents "the pleasure of his reencounter with the language" ("el goce del reencuentro con el idioma" [156; my translation]).

57. "Llevo un cuaderno por si se me ocurre anotar ideas sobre Carlos o frases de él, que borraré cuidadosamente para írmelo sacando de la cabeza. Llevo como cinco lápices de la oficina, de esos con goma en la otra punta. Llevo también una goma blanda, porque de eso se trata. Voy a anotar cosas de Carlos y las voy a ir borrando. Cuando vuelva éste va a ser de nuevo un cuaderno en blanco, pero todo borrado. Ya me gusta" (Valenzuela, "Viaje," in *Simetrías*, 53–54; all translations from this text are my own).

58. "A veces, en un arranque que podríamos calificar de valentía, [los hombres] levantan la cabeza y emiten en voz decidida el vocablo mozo como llamando.

"Cuando suena esa palabra creo notar la aceleración de las hormonas en la nuca de algunas de las mujeres. Esa palabra, mozo, dicha así en voz grave, tan cargada de óoos, creo que también a mí me eriza los pelitos.

"Reconozco que algunas de las mujeres, como la que está sentada justo delante de mí, no se inmutan por nada. Debe ser que llevan más tiempo — años/quizá — en este café tan quieto y saben, entre mil otras cosas, de la poca eficacia del llamado. El mozo vendrá cuando corresponda, sin ritmo fijo o previsible, o vendrá cuando se le antoje o cuando consiga más café" (Valenzuela, "El café quieto," in *Simetrías*, 37–38).

59. "El problema sobrevendrá cuando se me agote la tinta y se gaste hasta la última servilleta de papel y se acabe el café y se diluya el mundo" (ibid., 39).

60. See Alicia Partnoy, *The Little School* (Pittsburgh: Cleis Press, 1986), for one example among many.

61. "After all, my exile is my own. Not everyone has their own exile. They wanted to stick me with someone else's. Good try. I made it my own. How? It's not important. It's no secret, no revelation. I'd say that you have to begin by taking control of the streets. The street corners. The sky. The cafés. The sun, and what's more important, the shade. When you begin to perceive that a street isn't foreign to you, only then does the street stop looking at you as a foreigner. And it's like that with everything...." ("Después de todo, mi exilio es mío. No todos tienen un exilio propio. A mí quisieron encajarme uno ajeno. Vano intento. Lo convertí en mío. ¿Cómo fue? Eso no importa. No es un secreto ni una revelación. Yo diría que hay que empezar a apoderarse de las calles. De las esquinas. Del cielo. De los cafés. Del sol, y lo que es más importante, de la sombra. Cuando uno

llega a percebir que una calle no le es extranjera, sólo entonces la calle deja de mirarlo a uno como a un extraño. Y así con todo..." [Benedetti, *Primavera*, 21; my translation].)

62. "Y fue así como
      ahora
            estoy sola en el bosque y de mi boca
s a l e n s a p o s y c u l e b r a s.
No me arrepiento del todo: ahora soy escritora.

Las palabras son mías, soy su dueña, las digo sin tapujos, emito todas las que me estaban vedadas; las grito, las esparzo por el bosque porque se alejan de mí saltando o reptando como deben, todas con vida propia" (Valenzuela, "La densidad de las palabras," in *Simetrías*, 146).

63. "¿Por qué tengo que vivir mi vida entera ahogado por estas metáforas, en vez de metabolizarlas para reanimar mi obra?" (Donoso, *Jardín*). The oral metaphor itself shifts from production, in the case of the successful writer whose mouth emits language, to consumption, in the instance of the failed writer who cannot properly ingest it.

64. "Mi hermana se me acerca corriendo por el puente y cuando nos abrazamos y estallamos en voces de reconocimiento, percibo por encima de su hombro que a una víbora mía le brilla una diadema de diamantes, a mi cobra le aparece un rubí en la frente, cierta gran flor carnívora está deglutinando uno de mis pobres sapos, un escuerzo masca una diamela y empieza a ruborizarse, hay otra planta carnívora como trompeta untuosa digiriendo una culebra, una bromelia muy abierta y roja coge a un coquí y le brinda su corazón de nido. Y mientras con mi hermana nos decimos todo lo que no pudimos decirnos por los años de los años, nacen en la bromelia mil ranas enjoyadas que nos arrullan con su coro digamos polifónico" (Valenzuela, "La densidad," 151–52).

65. Robert Pogue Harrison, *Forests: The Shadow of Civilization* (Chicago: University of Chicago Press, 1992). I am grateful to Abby Peterson for bringing this study to my attention.

5. Between Exile and Return

1. "Y nosotros, escritores desterrados del Sur, quedamos, ya menos solos, enfrentados a una paradoja: para nosotros el exilio ha terminado; su literatura no" (Leonardo Rossiello, "La literatura del exilio latinoamericano en Suecia [1976–1990]," *Revista Iberoamericana* [July–December 1993]: 165).

2. Leonardo Rossiello, *Solos en la fuente y otros cuentos* (Montevideo: Vintén, 1990); Leonardo Rossiello, *La horrorosa historia de Reinaldo y otros cuentos* (Montevideo: ARCA, 1993); and Leonardo Rossiello, *La sombra y su guerrero* (Montevideo: Banda Oriental, 1994).

3. Carlos Liscano, "Retrato de pareja/Porträtt av ett par," script published with the support of ABF Stockholm, 1995. Rossiello's comments remain unpublished. I thank him for making them available to me.

4. "[T]ienden a reafirmar... el legado de una memoria histórica y a valorar, muchas veces a sobrevalorar, aquellas obras centradas en la experiencia del golpe o que comportan una visión crítica de la dictadura" (Juan Armando Epple,

"El estado actual de los estudios literarios en Chile: Acercamiento preliminar," *Hispamérica* 19, no. 56/57 [August–December 1990]: 39).

5. José Donoso, *El jardín de al lado* (Barcelona: Seix Barral, 1981), translated by Hardie St. Matin as *The Garden Next Door* (New York: Grove Press, 1981).

6. Ricardo Gutiérrez Mouat, "Aesthetics, Ethics, and Politics in Donoso's *El jardín de al lado*," *PMLA* 10, no. 1 (January 1991): 9.

7. Lucille Kerr, "Authority in Play: José Donoso's *El jardín de al lado*," *Criticism* 25, no. 1 (winter 1983): 41–65, writes that Donoso left Chile in 1964, well before the coup, and returned in 1981. Donoso's sojourn outside Chile overlapped, rather than coincided with, the dictatorship and permitted him the artistic luxury of distance from political writing. In his first major work written after going home to Chile, *La desesperanza* (*Curfew*), discussed in chapter 7, he feels constrained to write about the political situation to which he returned.

8. Donoso may be caught in a bind by writing Carlos, the authentic revolutionary, into this novel, thereby reinscribing the very political plot (albeit truncated and relegated to a secondary plane) he is condemning in others.

9. Donoso, *Jardín*, 43; *Garden*, 33.

10. Donoso, *Jardín*, 59; *Garden*, 48.

11. See, for example, Lucille Kerr, "Authority in Play," published shortly after *El jardín de al lado* appeared. M. I. Millington, "Out of Chile: Writing in Exile/Exile in Writing — José Donoso's *El jardín de al lado*," *Renaissance and Modern Studies* 34 (1991): 4–77, esp. 77, is an exception.

12. Rosemary Geisdorfer Feal, "Visions of a Painted Garden: José Donoso's Dialogue with Art," in Rosemary Geisdorfer Feal and Carlos Feal, *Painting on the Page: Interartistic Approaches to Modern Hispanic Texts* (Albany: State University of New York Press, 1995), 170.

13. According to María Luján Leiva, whose comments refer to the Argentine case, the return is made difficult by the scarcity of jobs, exacerbated among intellectuals by the reluctance of those who stayed at home to make space for the returning exiles. The first wave of Argentine returnees, mostly from Mexico and France, did return to jobs at the university. But later groups of returnees have found it virtually impossible to find jobs, restrained by the fear of those who remained that they would be made to *pagar la factura*, that is, be required to pay for the suffering undergone by the exiles. Resentment, fear, guilt for having accommodated, real political differences, and self-protection on the economic and psychic levels all enter into this sad situation. I am grateful to Inger Enqvist for informing me of the presentation where Luján Leiva made this point.

14. Donoso, *Garden*, 148. "Ahora que mi madre ha muerto podría volver sin miedo a quedar atrapado allá por mi emoción, y habitar el auténtico — no el reflejo en esta artificiosa agua de lujo — jardín de al lado. Patrick, entonces, volvería a ser Pato, y Gloria a beber sus pisco-sours charlando con sus amigas, entregada a una versión contemporánea y, si es posible, politizada, de la labor que desarrollaba mi madre con 'sus mujeres.' No, tendrá que trabajar en algo que nos dé dinero porque yo no tengo nada y la herencia de mi madre será insignificante.

"No puedo volver. ¿Cómo? ¿Sin un libro publicado en España, con la cola entre las piernas, sin trabajo, sin reintegrarme a la universidad de la cual me despidieron? En España por lo menos es posible rondar las editoriales mendicando trabajo..., escribir solapas..., traducir del inglés..., corregir estilo..., apenas suficiente para sobrevivir. ¿Pero allá? Nada" (Donoso, *Jardín*, 165–66).

Although the experiments in economic manipulation in Chile make the situation in that country quite different from Argentina, the basic fact of higher unemployment in the Southern Cone than in Europe remains.

15. "What are you talking about? Do you think we could drag Pato back to Chile now that he's already seventeen?" (Donoso, *Garden*, 160). "— ¿Qué hablas tú...? ¿Crees que a los diecisiete años que Pato tiene ahora podríamos arrastrarlo de vuelta a Chile?" (Donoso, *Jardín*, 177).

16. It appears only once (*Jardín*, 71; *Garden*, 58). Once again we encounter a character whose name calls up the homeland. Here, the figure of the male child, brought up outside and with new names that mask the original and its connection to *patria*, points to the impossibility of ever recovering the lost homeland.

17. Mauricio Rojas, *Sveriges oälskade barn: Att vara svensk men ändå inte* (Sweden's unloved children: To be Swedish but still not) (Stockholm, 1996). Rojas's pessimistic, if not alarmist, analysis does not tell the whole story, however. Marta Inostroza and Gustavo Ramírez, *Exilio y retorno* (Stockholm: ABF, 1986), demonstrate that the children and adolescents of exile, while facing unusual challenges, can create opportunities for themselves in their adoptive countries and in those of their origin.

18. The possibility that Núria not only commissioned but wrote this chapter, noted by Lucille Kerr ("Authority in Play"), is supported by its different, upbeat tone and by the very inverisimilitude I have been discussing. Julia withholds the diaries that were the source of her novel from Núria. This chapter is written as though it did not have access to that material, at least from the point of view of the tone.

19. Leonardo Rossiello, "Paparamborda a bordo," *La horrorosa tragedia de Reinaldo y otros cuentos* (Montevideo: ARCA, 1993), 35–48.

20. "[C]aga solemnemente en los turistas, en los viajes y en todos los archipélagos del mundo" (ibid., 48).

21. Mario Benedetti, *Primavera con una esquina rota* (Madrid: Ediciones Alfaguara, 1982).

22. See Amy K. Kaminsky, *Reading the Body Politic: Feminist Criticism and Latin American Women Writers* (Minneapolis: University of Minnesota Press, 1993), for a complete discussion of Partnoy's text.

23. "... [E]l 'Muñeco' se las ingenió para propagar en la cárcel de Libertad y por altoparlantes el triunfo del No en el plebiscito" (María Gianelli, "Aquí no pasó nada," in *Antología del cuento latinoamericano en Suecia*, ed. Víctor Montoya [Falköping: Författarna Invandrarförlaget, 1995], 87–88).

24. Ricardo Pérez Miranda, *En esa copia feliz del Edén* (Santiago: Editorial Aura Latina, 1990); all translations for this text are my own.

25. "Esa guerra la perdimos....La perdimos en el año ochenta y tres, según creo yo" (ibid., 24).

26. "Ironías del destino, mi ratita, los que formaron tu partido en una democracia les tocó actuar y defenderse en un escenario militar y a los cuadros que formaron en un escenario militar les tocará actuar y defenderse en uno público y civil" (ibid., 26).

27. "Y esta novela es un argumento para que no confinemos a la maldad y al miedo en los territorios del olvido, para que capaces de asumir nuestros defectos y recuerdos, luchemos por superarlos" (ibid., 7).

28. "estaré en mejor posición para luchar por un cambio en las relaciones de poder" (ibid., jacket copy).

29. Ana Pizarro, *La luna, el viento, el año, el día* (Mexico City and Santiago: Fondo de Cultura Económica, 1994). Sylvia Molloy's novel *En breve cárcel* (Barcelona: Seix Barral, 1981), which takes place in a claustrophobic room in Paris, ends with the protagonist risking her new and tender skin, gently sheathed in the pages of a text she has written, about to board a plane. The plane ride back to wholeness has no specific destination in this novel, a book that is not quite about exile and so will also not be quite about return. Ana Pizarro's narrative, in contrast, is very much about exile.

30. Silvia Larrañaga, *La fusión de la siluetas* (Montevideo: Signos, 1988). Although the novel was printed in Uruguay, it carries the name of a French distributor as well — Paris: Éditions Caribéenes.

31. "[H]ombres y mujeres que flotan en el aire, en un tiempo y espacio suspendidos" (Cristina Peri Rossi, "Los desarraigados," *Cosmoagonías* [Barcelona: Laia, 1988], 141); all translations from this text are my own. Weightlessness here should be understood as in Milan Kundera's *The Unbearable Lightness of Being.*

32. "Comen hamburguesas Mac Donald [sic] o emparedados de pollo Pokins, ya sea en Berlín, Barcelona, Montevideo. Y lo que es mucho peor todavía: encargan un menú estrafalario, compuesto por gazpacho, puchero y crema inglesa" (Peri Rossi, "Los desarraigados," 141).

33. Luisa Valenzuela, *Como en la guerra* (Buenos Aires: Sudamericana, 1977), translated by Helen Lane as *He Who Searches* (Elmwood Park, Ill.: Dalkey Archive, n.d.).

34. Vlady Kociancich, *Últimos días de William Shakespeare* (Buenos Aires: Emecé, 1984), translated by Margaret Jull Costa as *The Last Days of William Shakespeare* (London: Heinemann, 1990).

35. "Mario: Claro, es bueno...la verdad es que...uno...no sé, pero uno quiere volver, no...no por las empanadas, tampoco por el vino tinto, ni todas esas cuestiones,...ni siquiera por la tierra misma....Uno vuelve sobre todo por la gente, por su gente, por ustedes" (cited in Marta Inostroza and Gustavo Ramírez, *Exilio y retorno* [Stockholm: ABF, 1986], 88–89).

36. "Carecer de raíces ortoga a sus miradas un rasgo característico: una tonalidad celeste y acuosa, huidiza, la de alguien que en lugar de sustentarse firmemente en raices adheridas al pasado y al territorio, flota en un espacio vago e impreciso" (Peri Rossi, "Los desarraigados," 142).

37. "En medio de su discurso, sopla un viento fuerte y desaparecen, tragados por el aire" (ibid.).

6. Making Meaning

1. Vlady Kociancich, *Últimos días de William Shakespeare* (Buenos Aires: Emecé, 1984), translated by Margaret Jull Costa as *The Last Days of William Shakespeare* (London: Heinemann, 1990).

2. Mario Benedetti, *Primavera con una esquina rota* (Madrid: Ediciones Alfaguara, 1982).

3. "¿Qué me retiene? La imaginación tal vez, que me acobarda y me muestra otra cara posible de París: ser nadie salvo entre las paredes de una colonia de exiliados; convertirme en la caricatura de esa madeja de virtudes, defectos y costumbres que he sido y soy aquí sin verme; perder la lengua, tan duramente adquirida, e internarme en otra; abrazar la nostalgia de lo que nunca quise demasiado" (Kociancich, *Últimos días,* 117; *Last Days,* 97).

4. Luisa Valenzuela, *Como en la guerra* (Buenos Aires: Sudamericana, 1977), translated by Helen Lane as *He Who Searches* (Elmwood Park, Ill.: Dalkey Archive, n.d.).

5. Ricardo Piglia, *Respiración artificial* (Buenos Aires: Pomaire, 1980), translated by Daniel Balderston as *Artificial Respiration* (Durham, N.C.: Duke University Press, 1994).

6. Yossi Shain, *The Frontier of Loyalty: Political Exiles in the Age of the Nation State* (Middletown, Conn.: Wesleyan University Press, 1989), 92–93; see also *Araucaria de Chile* 38 (1987): 72–73.

7. Volodia Teitelboim, *En el país prohibido: Sin el permiso de Pinochet* (Barcelona: Plaza y Janés, 1988).

8. "Es la naturaleza la que me da la sensación más neta de que he vuelto a un país muy personal" (ibid., 69).

9. "La vista del paisaje en que había vivido hasta una edad madura iba haciendo reaparecer, asomar de nuevo, por encima del nivel del agua, la tierra sumergida, que afuera se me volvía más borrosa a medida que transcurrían los años. Ahora la recobraba como un territorio moral, afectivo. Rescataba la historia del sentimiento que posee cada persona por el solo hecho de vivir la mayor parte de su vida en un país determinado" (ibid., 27).

10. "Casi todo lo que veía me traía remembranzas, me devolvía pedazos de la vida" (ibid., 26).

11. "La naturaleza se me apareció desnuda, como una mujer concreta y hermosa. Le aspiré la fragancia. Me golpeó su belleza" (ibid.).

12. "A ratos el paisaje se pone hosco. Es una caverna en la cordillera. Y a trechos es de las tierras más cordiales del mundo, como una mujer flaca, huesuda, pero de carne cálida y sabrosa y de muchas curvas. Delgada, se ofrece como una vista panorámica, un cuerpo extendido donde se dan todos los climas. Es una hembra de barrancos profundos, los muslos; pechos de ricos pezones que dan todas las leches nutricias, los dulces frutos de su zona templada. Tiene las ancas de los buenos valles, remansos y regazos. Es una mujer frutal y mineral. Fría en el norte, hasta que se le descubren sus tesoros. Tibia en el centro, caliente si se penetran sus honduras. Fría en las nieves magallánicas; pero abrigadora con su lana de merino" (ibid., 69–70).

13. Mary Ellman, *Thinking about Women* (New York: Harcourt Brace and World, 1968), 7n. Like Virginia Woolf before her, Mary Ellman wrote feminist criticism at a time when humor was perhaps the only way to break the stranglehold of straight-faced sexism.

14. For a discussion of Littín's film in the context of Chilean documentary filmmaking, see Zuzana M. Pick, "Chilean Documentary: Continuity and Disjunc-

tion," in *The Social Documentary in Latin America*, ed. Julianne Burton (Pittsburgh: University of Pittsburgh Press, 1990), 109–30. The first-person story of Littín's clandestine return has been chronicled by Gabriel García Márquez in *La aventura de Miguel Littín, clandestino en Chile* (Madrid: Ediciones El País, 1986).

15. "La mujer chilena en 1987: Conversaciones con Carmen Rojas y Julia Monasterio," *Araucaria de Chile* 38 (1987): 57–71.

16. Volodia Teitelboim, "El retorno de dos mujeres," *Araucaria de Chile* 38 (1987). I take the notion of intelligibility and its lack from philosopher Naomi Scheman, "Queering the Center by Centering the Queer: Reflections on Transsexuals and Secular Jews," in *Feminists Rethink the Self*, ed. Diana Tietjens Meyers (Boulder, Colo.: Westview Press, forthcoming).

17. Jean Franco, "Beyond Ethnocentrism: Gender, Power, and the Third World Intelligentsia," in *Marxism and the Interpretation of Culture*, ed. Cary Nelson and Lawrence Grossberg (Urbana: University of Illinois Press, 1988), 514. See also Alejandro Diago, *Conversando con las Madres de la Plaza de Mayo: Hebe, memoria y esperanza* (Buenos Aires: Ediciones Dialéctica, 1988). The pitfalls and claims of language show even in the language used to name the dictatorship. The "Proceso de reconstrucción nacional" is the euphemistic term created by the dictatorship to refer to its own period in power; the process of national reconstruction was a process of state terror. The Mothers of the Plaza de Mayo, vindicated by a Nobel Peace Prize in their weekly silent marches around the square in front of the presidential palace, were referred to by the dictatorship not as the "mothers" but as the "madwomen" of the square.

18. Estela Grassi, "Redefinición del papel del estado en la reproducción y cambios en el discurso sobre familia y mujer en Argentina," in *Mujeres y relaciones de género en la antropología latinoamericana*, ed. Soledad González Montes (Mexico City: El Colegio de México, Programa Interdisciplinario de Estudios de Mujer, 1993), 231. Grassi uses the concept of familialist discourse "in the sense of paradigm; that is to say, as a general orientation predominant in the different instances referring to the family, directly or indirectly: techno-scientific disciplines, political and religious institutions, instances of communication, etc." ("en el sentido de paradigma; es decir, como orientación general predominante en las diferentes instancias referidas directa o indirectamente a la familia: disciplinas técnico-científicas, instituciones de orden político y religioso, instancias de divulgación, etc." [223–24n.; my translation]).

19. "Lo que estoy sugiriendo es que existe una línea argumental coherente entre los diversos niveles del discurso familiarista que fue tornándose hegemónico a partir de los setenta, y que recupera elementos de la ideología tradicionalista, básicamente católica, arraigada en los sectores conservadores de la sociedad argentina, de cuya ideología las fuerzas armadas se han considerado garantes. Es esta 'coherencia argumental' lo que hizo posible que el modelo de enfermedad mental, como emergente de una interacción familiar patógena, fuera utilizado desde la normatividad establecida por el Estado terrorista para equiparar valores de transformación social con patología y colocar de esa manera a la familia en un lugar de producción y culpabilidad respecto de la desaparición o muerte de sus miembros" (ibid., 239).

20. Marta Inostroza and Gustavo Ramírez, *Exilio y retorno* (Stockholm: ABF, 1986).

21. Aidan Rankin, "Reflections on the Non-revolution in Uruguay," *New Left Review* 211 (May–June 1995).

22. Rankin mentions gay issues on the same page, linking them by proximity to women's issues, and saying that homosexual relationships were "discreetly decriminalized" in 1934, and in a note comments that the gay movement emerging now is about lifestyle issues, not politics (ibid., 132n.).

23. "Los partidos de izquierda, creo yo, tienen un pecado muy grande, y es que no se han preocupado de elaborar una verdadera política con las mujeres, lo que es grave, porque la derecha sí lo ha hecho, ahí tienes la historia de las cacerolas y lo del 'voluntariado femenino' de Pinochet.... Las mujeres no han dejado de nunca de estar de algún modo presentes pero la historia la han escrito siempre los hombres. Ahora, lo que pasa es que en períodos de crisis las mujeres aparecemos de modo más visible" (ibid., 63).

24. "Yo asumo un rol diferente con respecto a la relación hombre/mujer cuando empiezo a militar en un partido político (a pesar de que los puestos de mayor responsabilidad dentro del partido siempre están ocupados por hombres). Pero Suecia me ha ayudado a modificar y ajustar mis ideas. Estos dos factores (militancia de un partido político y vivir en Suecia), han contribuido a que yo piense ahora que yo, como mujer, tengo valor, que una persona puede vivir parte de su vida aplastada, e inclusive ignorante, sin tener una educación formal, y sin embargo, de pronto descubrir que a pesar de eso, tienes valor, que posees una capacidad para hacer una serie de cosas que antes ni siquieras podías imaginarte" ("Teresa," interview by Jaime Vieyra-Poseck, in *Mujeres chilenas en Suecia: ¿Emancipación o sumisión?* [Spånga, Sweden: Ediciones ALAM-Mujer, 1990], 91–92).

25. "Los hombres, que son los que dirigen, dicen comprender estos problemas [ley de matrimonio, el aborto, la madre sola, et. cet.], pero argumentan que este cambio debe darse dentro del problema global de la sociedad chilena. Pero en esa globalidad, hasta ahora, no están incluidas las reivindicaciones de la mujer. Desde el momento en que nosotras militamos en un partido junto con los hombres, es porque nosotras aceptamos la acción política en su conjunto con ellos. Teniendo en cuenta que las mujeres son un grupo social claramente discriminado en la sociedad, se debe exigir reivindicaciones objetivas para la mujer, dentro de los programas y la oferta electoral de los partidos" (ibid., 92–93).

26. "El que sectores de mujeres latinoamericanas hayan encontrado formas de desarrollo individual y colectivo, diferentes a las existentes en América Latina, puede interpretarse como un beneficio del exilio" (Inostroza and Ramírez, *Exilio y retorno*, 56).

27. "Anteriormente dijimos que el exilio, a pesar de sus múltiples aspectos dolorosos, había permitido a la mujer latinoamericana ocupar un rol más equilibrado e igualitario en la familia y en la sociedad. Esta situación se ve y se siente amenazada ante la perspectiva del retorno. La evolución del rol social de la mujer en nuestros países no es comparable a la de Europa, más aún en estos años de dictadura donde se han fortalecido las tendencias conservadoras que postulan la defensa del estado discriminatorio de la mujer y perpetuación de los roles tradicionales" (ibid., 59–60).

28. Santiago Colás, *Postmodernity in Latin America: The Argentine Paradigm* (Durham, N.C.: Duke University Press, 1994), 148.

29. "Primero necesitan abordar la historia para volverla a contar desde el reducto privado y medido del género mujer; segundo, el discurso hegemónico impone desde las prácticas represivas una sintaxis, cuyas reglas, en sí, dificultan la lectura crítica de la Historia oficial" (Ester Gimbernat González, *Aventuras del desacuerdo: Novelistas argentinas de los 80* [Buenos Aires: Danilo Albergo Vergara, 1992], 24).

30. Colás, *Postmodernity in Latin America*, 148.

31. Ibid.

32. "Pienso que el volver la mirada hacia el siglo XIX en este fin de siglo no es un acto vacío de la Academia; pienso que la fractura de la memoria operada por las dictaduras del Cono Sur tiene mucho que ver con esta mirada hacia atrás" (Hugo Achugar, "El Parnaso es la nación o reflexiones a propósito de la violencia de la lectura y el simulacro," in *Las otras letras: Literatura uruguaya del Siglo XIX*, ed. Leonardo Rossiello [Montevideo: Editorial Graffiti, 1994], 35; all translations from this text are my own). See also Juan Armando Epple, "El estado actual de los estudios literarios en Chile: Acercamiento preliminar," *Hispamérica* 19, no. 56/57 (August–December 1990): 45, who discusses critics who have returned and those who have not, who nevertheless can do their work connected to what is now going on in Chile: "Comparten el mismo desafío histórico." In 1988 CENECA invited Chilean critics working inside and outside the country to participate in designing a project — never done before in the country — on literary theory and historiography. Ultimately, Epple argues, it is the local critics who will have to do the work (45n11).

33. "[A]lgunas preocupaciones/obsesiones: una vinculación a la problemática existencia de Uruguay en un tiempo postdictatorial que intenta refundar el proyecto de un país que vio en las décadas pasadas la agonía y la muerte violenta de otro proyecto, en el que Uruguay aspiraba a ser la 'Suiza de América.' Una segunda relacionada con la supuesta caducidad u obsolescencia de la categoría nación en los estudios culturales y literarios. Más aún, se relaciona con la afirmación originada en cierto sector de la Academia del primer mundo según la cual la variable nacional es un fenómeno propio del 'tercer mundo.' Y por último, una tercera preocupación u obsesión que está vinculada con el ejercicio de la crítica literaria" (Achugar, "El Parnaso," 27–28).

34. "[S]i la historia puede ofrecer metáforas que hagan tolerable la evocación de un terror todavía demasiado cercano, ella tiene muy poco que enseñar acerca del terror..." (Tulio Halperín Donghi, "El presente transforma el pasado: El impacto del reciente terror en la imagen de la historia argentina," in *Ficción y política: La narrativa argentina durante el proceso militar*, ed. Daniel Balderston et al. [Buenos Aires: Alianza, 1987], 94–95).

35. Blanca de Arancibia, "Identity and Narrative Fiction in Argentina: The Novels of Abel Posse," in *Latin American Identity and Constructions of Difference*, ed. Amaryll Chanady, Hispanic Issues, vol. 10 (Minneapolis: University of Minnesota Press, 1994), 67–68.

36. Gámbaro, living in exile since 1977, debuted her play in Buenos Aires when, as Tulio Halperín Donghi ("El presente," 74) writes, "the terror diminished sufficiently to come out from silence."

37. Halperín Donghi, "El presente," 75, discusses *Camila* and *La mala sangre*,

recognizing the domestic as a metaphor for the political, but missing the clear implication that domestic tyranny is itself of a political nature and of a piece with the public version.

38. Some of these poets, publishing in the journal *Piel de leopardo,* are discussed in María Esther Pezón, "Parricidio: En torno a la nueva poesía Chilena," paper presented at the Alumni Symposium on Hispanic and Luso-Brazilian Language and Literature, Pennsylvania State University, April 1994.

39. "[E]n vez de desexiliarse radicalizaron su alteridad radical para romper con la uruguayidad y desconstruir la nostalgiosa restauración de la homogeizante memoria histórica-pedagógica del imaginario de la República Modelo amenazada por la proliferación de múltiples y antagónicas memorias cultural-performativas" (Jorge Abril Trigo, "Rockeros y grafiteros: La construcción al sesgo de una antimemoria," *Hispamérica* 24, no. 70 [1995]: 35–36).

40. Among the many useful discussions of this novel are Santiago Colás, *Postmodernity in Latin America,* who discusses the rewriting of history in *Respiración artificial,* and several of the studies in *Ficción y política,* including Tulio Halperín Donghi, "El presente" (71–95, esp. 80–85), and Daniel Balderston, "El significado latente en *Respiración artificial* de Ricardo Piglia y en *El corazón de junio* de Luis Gusmán" (109–21, esp. 111–15).

41. This version of the lost exile is a view from home, contested by those exiled intellectuals and writers who enter a transnational discourse, but reminiscent of Cortázar's complaint.

42. "[E]so que llamamos amor a falta de mejor palabra" (Luisa Valenzuela, "Simetrías," in *Simetrías* [Buenos Aires: Sudamericana, 1993], 174).

43. The torturer who recruits one of his victims as his "lover," who becomes obsessed with her or who is sexually enthralled by his own power over her, is a figure who emerges in a number of texts dealing with the repression: *En esa copia feliz del Edén,* "Cambio de armas," *En cualquier lugar,* and here in "Simetrías."

7. Stories of Return

1. María Lugones, an Argentine philosopher living and working in the United States whose work will be discussed in chapter 8, also injects Spanish into U.S. academic discourse and into the writing she does for academic journals. Like Valenzuela, and probably more intentionally, Lugones deploys Spanish as a gesture of defiance against English hegemony.

2. Luisa Valenzuela, *Realidad nacional desde la cama* (Buenos Aires: Grupo Editor Latinoamericano, 1990), translated by Margaret Jull Costa as *Bedside Manners* (London: High Risk; New York: Serpent's Tail, 1995).

3. This story of a woman made mad by the rest cure that is prescribed for her is most famously treated in Charlotte Perkins Gilman, "The Yellow Wallpaper," *New England Magazine* (May 1892), but in her *Respuesta a Sor Filotea* (1691), Sor Juana Inés de la Cruz already writes of an illness made worse by the prescription of absolute rest.

4. Luisa Valenzuela, *Novela negra con argentinos* (Hanover, N.H.: Ediciones del Norte, 1990), translated by Tony Talbot as *Black Novel with Argentines* (New York: Simon and Schuster, 1992).

5. According to Sharon Magnarelli (personal communication, September 1997), Valenzuela first intended to write *Realidad nacional desde la cama* as a play.

6. In "Transparencia," the parable with which Valenzuela ended her MLA talk, and which appears in the volume *Simetrías* (Buenos Aires: Sudamericana, 1993), she again tropes the club to signify humanity. In that story the mind of God proposes a club that will consist of all people willing to comply with certain rules of language and representation.

7. Valenzuela, *Bedside Manners*, 52. "Moralmente es que no puedo moverme. No tengo voluntad" (Valenzuela, *Realidad nacional*, 48).

8. Valenzuela, *Bedside Manners*, 52–53. "—Usted sufre del conocido 'mal del sauce' tan típico de nuestras riberas. Ya no hay voluntad de moverse, sólo de contemplar, recordar, de atar cabos.

— No tanto, doctor. Soy una mujer prudente y sé que recordar puede no ser sano.

— Todo lo contrario.

Alguien le dijo a ella hace poco, sin embargo, le dijo que más vale no pensar ni recordar. Como una amenaza, casi, se lo dijo, y ya ni se acuerda quién fue. Se ve que es fácil de aprender, eso de olvidar.

— De momento siento como si quisieran borrarme la memoria, qué sé yo, tachármela con otras inscripciones. No entiendo nada.

— Eso sucede mucho, acá. ¿Qué más le preocupa?" (Valenzuela, *Realidad nacional*, 49).

9. Valenzuela, *Bedside Manners*, 78. " — Esa era mi ciudad, la del televisor. La de ahora no es más mi ciudad, me lo cambiaron todo. Ahora no sé quién es el enemigo, no sé contra quién pelear. Antes de irme sabía, ahora el enemigo no está más o dice no estar y está y yo ya no sé dónde estoy parada.... Volví para encontrarme con eso y no con esto. Volví para recuperar la memoria y me la roban, me la borran. Me la barren. ¿Y si esto de estar metida en una cama ajena sin poder moverse fuera de la forma de preservar la memoria, todo lo que tan rápido nos están quitando...?" (Valenzuela, *Realidad nacional*, 69).

10. Valenzuela, *Bedside Manners*, 95. "'Conocemos tu misión. Vos querés la memoria, te vamos a bajar. La historia empieza con nosotros'" (Valenzuela, *Realidad nacional*, 82).

11. Valenzuela, *Bedside Manners*, 96. "[Y] sabe que de esa situación sólo puede salir recuperando el habla como quien recupera un recuerdo perdido" (Valenzuela, *Realidad nacional*, 82–83).

12. Valenzuela, *Bedside Manners*, 114. "[S]e siente como computadora recargada" (Valenzuela, *Realidad nacional*, 98).

13. Valenzuela, *Bedside Manners*, 119. " — A bailar, insiste el muy versátil. La señora toma la mano, no más, pero intenta tirarlo hacia la cama.

—No. De pie, propone él.

—No. Vertical todavía no, le suplica ella.

—Sí, vertical. Con la frente bien alta.

—Necesito un poco más de tiempo.

—El tiempo es ahora.

—Esperá. Quiero entender. Tengo miedo.

—Levántate. Sólo la muerte puede paliar el miedo a la muerte. No vale la pena. Mejor es estar vivos y moverse, mientras se pueda. Tenemos que celebrar" (Valenzuela, *Realidad nacional,* 103–4).

14. Valenzuela, *Bedside Manners,* 121. " — ¡El club ya es nuestro! se oye la voz de él, zapateando sobre las armas.

— ¿Y el país? pregunta ella, la muy realista" (Valenzuela, *Realidad nacional,* 106).

15. Valenzuela, *Bedside Manners,* 119–20. " — Basta de taxista, de coronel, de médico, de loco, puedo por fin volver a ser yo mismo.

— ¿Y quién sos, vos? le pregunta la señora medio alarmada" (Valenzuela, *Realidad nacional,* 104).

16. Valenzuela, *Bedside Manners,* 120. " — ¿Yo? ¿Yo? Y bueno, digamos que soy el que vino a acabar con esta farsa. O al menos con los farsantes, con todos los farsantes. En lo posible" (Valenzuela, *Realidad nacional,* 104).

17. José Donoso, *La desesperanza* (Barcelona: Seix Barral, 1986), translated by Alfred MacAdam as *Curfew* (New York: Weidenfeld and Nicolson, 1988). Sharon Magnarelli also juxtaposes texts by Donoso and Valenzuela in her illuminating study, "Images of Exile/Exile(d) Images: The Cases of Luisa Valenzuela and José Donoso," *Revista de Estudios Hispánicos* 31 (1977): 61–75, where she reads *El jardín de al lado* together with *Novela negra con argentinos.*

18. "Se me multiplica la admiración por muchos periodistas opositores. Desfilan por las calles, encabezados por sus dirigentes, con una mordaz en la boca" ("My admiration for many oppositional journalists is multiplied. They parade through the streets, led by their editors, with gags in their mouths") (Volodia Teitelboim, "El valor de Ellas," in *En el país prohibido: Sin el permiso de Pinochet* [Barcelona: Plaza y Janés, 1988], 141). In this article, Teitelboim names Patricia Politzer (author of *Miedo en Chile*), María Oliva Monckeberg, María Eugenia Camus, and Pamela Jiles (*Crimen bajo estado de sitio*), and María José Luque and Patricia Collyer (*José Carrasco, asesinato de un periodista*), and he dedicates an essay to Mónica González, jailed by the regime for printing an interview she conducted in which the interviewee, a Christian Democrat politician, discussed his views of Pinochet. She merely asked the question, "What do you think of General Pinochet?" (see Teitelboim, "El delito de preguntar," in *En el país prohibido,* 140).

19. Lars Palmgren, "Chile påminns om terrorn" (Chile remembers the terror), *Göteborgs Posten,* sec. 2, April 16, 1996, 24.

20. The temporary returnee is also a feature of Carlos Cerda's *Una casa vacía* (An empty house), discussed in chapter 3.

21. Doris Sommer, *Foundational Fictions: The National Romances of Latin America* (Berkeley: University of California Press, 1991).

22. Volodia Teitelboim, *En el país prohibido: Sin el permiso de Pinochet* (Barcelona: Plaza y Janés, 1988).

23. "[E]sas montañas parecen masas petrificadas, dinosaurios que se extinguieron, según dicen, hace 65 millones de años y se volvieron roca" (67).

24. "No sé por qué tengo la sensación, seguramente imaginaria, que en mi ausencia, el tiempo, la erupción de cenizas ha seguido modelando la topografía" (ibid., 69).

25. "Nada es más ajeno a este paisaje que la monotonía. Su ley es el contraste. Su principio, la ruptura" (ibid.).

26. "Tal vez Chile sea un ejemplo drástico de la traumática evolución del universo, lo que explicaría su naturaleza desgarrada. Como parte de un sistema único, creo que tanto ella como el hombre nuestro, víctima por su lado de la violencia de la Historia, obedecen, sin embargo, al imperativo de la vida" (ibid., 67).

27. Amalia Pereira, "Interview with José Donoso," *Latin American Literary Review* 15, no. 30 (July–December 1987): 62.

28. Donoso, *Curfew*, 303–4. " — ¿A qué volvió a Chile en estos momentos? — interrogaron a Mañungo los reporteros.

— A quedarme.

— ¿Por cuánto tiempo?

— Para siempre.

— ¿No declaró en la casa de Neruda, anoche, que su visita sería corta porque no entendía la situación de su país?

— Ahora la entiendo.

Lo pensó un instante y luego continuó:

— He cambiado mis planes. En todo caso, después de veinte horas en mi país puedo asegurarles que nunca he tenido nada tan claro como que me vengo a quedar.

— ¿Para definir su acción política?

— Puede ser.

— ¿Lucha armada?

— No, si no es para defender mi vida, o la de alguien....

— ¿Canciones?

— Eso quisiera. Aunque quién sabe si las bombas no van a ser la única alternativa. Ellos tienen la culpa. ¿Por qué se pude [*sic*] hacer, si nos fuerzan a la violencia quitándonos toda esperanza? No justifico las bombas. Pero las comprendo" (Donoso, *La desesperanza*, 323).

29. Luisa Valenzuela, *Simetrías* (Buenos Aires: Sudamericana, 1993).

30. Marina Warner, *From the Beast to the Blonde: On Fairy Tales and Their Tellers* (London: Chatto and Windus, 1994), points out that Perrault is ambiguous in his telling of the tale. The moralizing language says that the wife should not disobey, but ultimately she is rewarded for doing so. She is rescued by her sister and brothers and inherits the monster's fortune.

31. With the end of compulsory exile, trips back home, rather than absolute return, have also become possible for some. In Juan Rivano's *Época de descubrimientos* (Furulund, Sweden: Alhambra de Lund, 1991), one couple decides to leave exile in Sweden, but not to return to the precarious economic situation in Chile. Their plan is to set themselves up in the tourist business in what they perceive as a kind of compromise place — Spain, not as forbiddingly foreign as Sweden, but not home either. Chile will be where they go for vacations. These two would not expect a particularly happy welcome back. A sequence late in the novel depicting interviews of Chileans who remained at home on their attitudes toward returning exiles expresses feelings ranging from indifference to anger (because they were left in the lurch, because returnees just add to the competition for jobs). The loving mothers longing for the exiles' return have, predictably, died.

8. Beyond Exile

1. Isabel Álvarez-Borland, "Displacements and Autobiography in Cuban-American Fiction," *World Literature Today* (winter 1994): 43–48; and Eliana Rivero, "From Immigrants to Ethnics: Cuban Writers in the U.S.," in *Breaking Boundaries*, ed. Asunción Delgado et al. (Amherst: University of Massachusetts Press, 1989), 189–200.

2. Saldívar-Hull, cited in María Lugones, "Purity, Impurity, and Separation," *Signs: Journal of Women in Culture and Society* (winter 1994): 458–79. Gustavo Pérez Firmat, *Life on the Hyphen: The Cuban American Way* (Austin: University of Texas Press, 1994).

3. See Amy K. Kaminsky, "Gender, Essay, and Mestizaje," in *The Politics of the Essay: Feminist Perspectives*, ed. Ruth Ellen Joeres and Elizabeth Mittman (Bloomington: Indiana University Press, 1993), 113–30, for a fuller discussion of the hybrid nature of the essay as genre.

4. One exception is Lugones's use of this practice, in an early, coauthored piece with Elizabeth V. Spelman, "Have We Got a Theory for You! Feminist Theory, Cultural Imperialism, and the Demand for 'the Woman's Voice,' " *Women's Studies International Forum* 6, no. 6 (1983): 573–81. There, Lugones writes a long introduction in Spanish that remains untranslated, after which she writes exclusively in English. This is not, however, an example of typical code-switching, in which linguistic items from the two languages form part of the same utterance. Similarly, in her 1990 essay "Hablando cara a cara/Speaking Face to Face: An Exploration of Ethnocentric Racism," in *Making Face/Making Soul: Haciendo Caras*, ed. Gloria Anzaldúa (San Francisco: Aunt Lute, 1990), 46–54, Lugones uses a strategy that draws an overt distinction between the truly bilingual reader and those who understand only one of her languages.

5. Ana Martínez, "Nyckfull Älskare" (first broadcast summer 1983, repeated August 1996), in *På Blommigt Alvar* (Uddevalla, Sweden: Sveriges Radio Förlag, 1987). This and further citations from Martínez are from the radio broadcast; all translations are my own.

6. María Lugones, "Playfulness, 'World'-Travelling, and Loving Perception," *Hypatia* 2, no. 2 (summer 1987): 397.

7. I refer here to the end of "Hablando cara a cara."

8. Lugones is primarily interested in bridging differences among women. She does not extend her desire for loving perception toward white, heterosexual males, for example.

9. Lugones, "Purity," 460.

10. Ibid., 478.

11. Lugones, "Playfulness, 'World'-Travelling, and Loving Perception," 4.

12. Ibid., 6–7; emphasis added.

13. I am grateful to Debra Castillo for reminding me of Perón's love of mayonnaise.

14. It is no surprise, then, that for many women writers there is a close relationship between writing and the rituals of food preparation. Marta Mercader's *Juanamanuela Muchamujer* (Barcelona: Planeta, 1983, translated by Carol and Thomas Christensen [New York: Doubleday, 1992]), a historical novel based on the life of patriot and writer Juana Manuela Gorriti, a nineteenth-century woman

who spent much of her life in exile from Argentina, is sprinkled with recipes. Laura Esquivel's immensely popular *Like Water for Chocolate* contains so many recipes that it has been sold in the cookbook section of bookstores as well as among the novels. Rosario Ferré's autobiographical essay on her initiation as a writer is called "The Writing Kitchen" (*Feminist Studies* 2 [summer 1986]: 227–42, translation of "La cocina de la escritura," in *La sartén por el mango*, ed. P. E. González and E. Ortega [Puerto Rico: Huracán, 1984], 137–54), and Debra Castillo begins her brilliant study of Latin American women writers, *Talking Back: Toward a Latin American Feminist Literary Criticism* (Ithaca, N.Y.: Cornell University Press, 1992), in the kitchen, in conversation with her mother-in-law. In these texts, the kitchen is the place where women interact with each other. It is the place of instruction and love, where women hand down the magic arts of transformation. Kitchens bereft of interaction produce disasters, like the violently bloody, and later burned, roast that Rosario Castellanos's newly married but utterly isolated protagonist produces in "Cooking Lesson" ("Lección de cocina," in *Álbum de familia* [Mexico City: J. Moritz, 1975]). Kitchen dialogues are not necessarily a matter of unadulterated good feelings. In Mercader's novel the protagonist and her maid-cum-amanuensis battle over menus and recipes, enacting the struggle over pressing questions of race, class, and nation in the space of the kitchen. Inucha, Juana Manuela's Indian servant, modifies the recipes her mistress collects from her Europeanized friends and correspondents to make them more American. The cookbook the two women collaborate on is a text of an America independent from but still dependent upon Europe. It is a political statement in which culinary decisions distinguish Europe from the New World and champion pan-Americanism, but whose internal differences remain unresolved. In Ana Vásquez's *Mi amiga Chantal* (Barcelona: Lumen, 1991), Chantal's kitchen, however fraught a place it is for Ana, is also the place where women go to talk to each other: "Acompañé a Chantal a la cocina, preguntándome por qué las mujeres tendríamos que hablar entre nosotras justamente en la cocina. Lavábamos lechuga. — Edgardo está espantoso, me dijo" (178) ("I went into the kitchen with Chantal, asking myself why we women had to talk together just there in the kitchen. We washed lettuce. 'Edgardo is being horrible,' she said to me").

15. Lugones explicitly rejects Marilyn Frye's insistence on independence as a condition of freedom in "Playfulness, 'World'-Travelling, and Loving Perception," and Sara Lucia Hoagland's call to lesbians to reject their home cultures, in "Hispaneando y lesbiando: On Sarah Hoagland's Lesbian Ethics," *Hypatia* 5, no. 3 (fall 1990): 138–46.

16. Ana Vásquez and Ana María Araujo, *Exils Latino-Americains: La malédiction d'Ulysse* (Paris: CIEMI and Editions L'Harmattan, 1988).

INDEX

Created by Eileen Quam

AMY K. KAMINSKY is professor of women's studies and a member of the graduate faculty in Spanish and Portuguese at the University of Minnesota. She is the author of *Reading the Body Politic: Feminist Criticism and Latin American Women Writers* (Minnesota, 1993) and editor of *Water Lilies/Flores del agua: An Anthology of Spanish Women Writers from the Fifteenth through the Nineteenth Century* (Minnesota, 1996).